*The Scott and Laurie Oki Series in Asian American Studies*

D0052105

*The Scott and Laurie Oki Series in Asian American Studies*

# GROWING UP BROWN

MEMOIRS

*of a*

FILIPINO

AMERICAN

## PETER JAMERO

*University of Washington Press* ❧ *Seattle & London*

*This book is published with the assistance of a grant from the Scott and Laurie Oki Endowed Fund for publications in Asian American Studies, established through the generosity of Scott and Laurie Oki.*

© 2006 by the University of Washington Press
Designed by Ashley Saleeba
Typefaces: Aldus and Sistina
Printed in the United States of America
12  11  10  09  08  07  06    5  4  3  2  1

All rights reserved. No part of this publication may be reproduced or transmitted in any form or by any means, electronic or mechanical, including photocopy, recording, or any information storage or retrieval system, without permission in writing from the publisher.

University of Washington Press
P.O. Box 50096, Seattle, WA 98145
www.washington.edu/uwpress

This book is printed on New Leaf Ecobook 50, which is 100% recycled, containing 50% post-consumer waste, and is processed chlorine free. Ecobook 50 is acid free and meets the minimum requirements of ANSI/NISO Z39-48-1992 (R 1997) (Permanence of Paper). ♾ⓡ

Library of Congress Cataloging-in-Publication Data can be found at the back of this book.

# Contents

# Foreword

FOR ALL OF US THERE COMES A TIME WHEN A chance encounter changes our lives. In 1969, one Peter Madelo Jamero Sr.—who had just arrived from Washington, D.C., to work in the Region X office of the Department of Health, Education, and Welfare—called to make my acquaintance. This began a friendship and collaborative community endeavors with the Jamero family that have spanned more than thirty-five years.

Peter, whom we fondly call "Pete," and his wife, Terri, have six children whose ages almost mirror the ages of our own eight children. The initial reason for the phone call was to put their older children in Filipino Youth Activities (FYA), especially the renowned Princesa Drill Team, Cumbanchero Percussioneers, and Mandayan Marchers. We were privileged to work with the Jamero family for almost twenty years in many FYA activities.

Pete was the first federal bureaucrat we knew, and we were in awe of his sophistication and ability to navigate the ins-and-outs of government red tape. In 1971, FYA had the opportunity to tap local Model City monies to expand our youth programs and create a small office to meet the increasing needs of a fast-growing Filipino American population in the state of Washington. An enthusiastic group met in our home, and Pete guided us in writing the required "proposal"—a bureaucratic term none of us knew at that time.

The late 1960s and 1970s were heady times. Society was changing, and long-silent Asian Americans had joined the civil rights battles begun by courageous African Americans and were challenging entrenched racism in the forms of prejudices and biases. Qualified

American-born minorities who first broke into fields once denied an early generation of immigrants found they had a special role. They were expected to be superachievers but were often restricted by the glass ceiling, which prevented them from being fully rewarded for their hard work. Pete was one of these pioneers who broke ground but often endured personal disappointments.

He has held more prestigious and diverse positions than any other Filipino American: assistant secretary of the Washington State Department of Social and Health Services and director of the Division of Vocational Rehabilitation, assistant professor at the University of Washington, director of the King County Department of Human Resources, vice president of United Way of King County, executive director of the San Francisco City and County Civil Rights Commission, and finally executive director of Asian American Recovery Services. Through all these positions, he has been a good role model for countless young people.

On a more personal note, Pete and Terri were among the first to respond to my call for help in 1982. I hoped to form an historical society that would continue to collect Filipino American history and share materials already accumulated through a two-year National Endowment for the Humanities project titled "Forgotten Asian Americans: Filipinos and Koreans." After two years of meetings, we were ready to incorporate the society but needed a name that would proclaim the group's intent and at the same time be catchy enough so that people would remember us. Pete won the contest with Filipino American National Historical Society (FANHS).

Thanks, Pete, for giving us a name that continues to grow in national recognition. Thanks also for many years of pleasant memories.

DR. DOROTHY LAIGO CORDOVA
*Executive Director, Filipino American National Historical Society*
*Seattle, August 2005*

# Introduction

THE TWENTIETH-CENTURY HISTORY OF FILIPINOS
in America is still an unfinished story. Academics in Asian American Studies programs, which began flourishing on American college
campuses in the 1970s, have done admirable work in recapturing
the histories of the early Chinese and Japanese communities. But
more than three decades later, comparatively little is known about
the *manong* generation, those intrepid pioneers who immigrated to
the United States when the Philippines was still an American colony.

Peter Jamero's autobiography, *Growing Up Brown in America:
Memoirs of a Filipino American*, fills an important historic niche.
Carlos Bulosan's classic work *America Is in the Heart* describes
pre–World War II anti-Filipino racism on the West Coast and the
Filipino response to the poverty and hostility of that era. However, Bulosan's autobiography, which deftly combines elements of
history and literature, should not be read literally. Fred Cordova's
*Filipinos: Forgotten Asian Americans* fills in many of the gaps.
Cordova succeeds in creating a sweeping vista of Filipino American life from the eighteenth century to modern times. Then there
is *Philip Vera Cruz: A Personal History of Filipino Immigrants and
the Farmworkers Movement*, by Craig Scharlin and Lilia Villanueva. Their focus on the life and times of Vera Cruz, a former
United Farm Workers vice president, is a valuable contribution to
the history of Filipino efforts to organize strong agricultural
unions. Finally, there is Chris Friday's authoritative history, *Organizing Asian American Labor: The Pacific Coast Canned-Salmon*

*Industry, 1870–1942.* The chapters devoted to Filipino-dominated cannery workers' unions complement the work of Scharlin and Villanueva.

These works are undoubtedly important contributions to Filipino American history. However, they do not focus on the lives of those whom Jamero terms the "Bridge Generation"; born in America before the end of World War II, the Bridge Generation comprises the sons and daughters of the *manangs* and *manongs*, the first generation of Filipinos to reside in the United States. Their story remains untold. Hence, the value of Jamero's engaging memoir. It begins with a description of his life in his parents' farm-labor camp in Livingston, California. It was there that he learned the value of discipline, a trait reinforced by his parents' lives and the lives of the other *manongs* who worked on the farm. This experience—of earning a living from the land—has all but disappeared among today's urbanized and suburbanized Filipino communities. Young Jamero was successful in school and quickly came to grasp, with his parents' strong encouragement, the value of education. He understood that further schooling would be a ticket to success in the larger postwar America that was slow to become less hostile to the aspirations of his people. Jamero's engaging, informative narrative allows readers to follow the path of his life, which takes him far beyond Livingston—to the U.S. Navy, college, graduate school, and a series of professional positions of increasing responsibility (Jamero was the first Filipino to hold a number of these jobs). He eventually returned to the Livingston area, where he and his wife, Terri, live today.

The narrative dovetails with a number of major historical events—the civil rights movement and the Vietnam War, among them—that helped shape this nation. Jamero, no stranger to racism, describes the growing sense of political power among Filipino Americans, many of whom became skilled and influential political players. Jamero's memoir was originally intended for his family. However, it is much more than a personal record. It is an important firsthand account of a person who was part of several pages of the still unfinished story of Filipinos in America.

PETER BACHO
*Tacoma, Washington*
*April 2005*

# Preface

I WAS INSPIRED TO WRITE THESE MEMOIRS BECAUSE of my children. Most kids, including mine, know little of what their parents have experienced in life. As youngsters, their interests naturally gravitate toward school, their peers, and what is in vogue. It is not until adulthood that people begin to be curious about their parents' experiences. It also must be acknowledged that parents are often so busy raising their children and making a living that they have little time to spend on imparting their experiences. I know, because this happened to me, first as a child, with my parents, and later as a parent, with my own children.

These memoirs are dedicated to my family. First, to the love of my life, my devoted wife, Terri, who has been constantly by my side, and then to our six wonderful children, Karen Noreen Armada, Cheryl Louise Organo, Peter Madelo Jamero Jr., Julie Anne Hada, Jacqueline Teresa Berganio, and Jeanine Elizabeth Silverio, and their spouses, Ronald Armada, Philip Organo, Ted Hada, Richard Berganio, and Michael Silverio. And, finally, to our pride and joy, our thirteen beautiful grandchildren: Zachary Armada; Janel, Marisa, and Cecily Organo; Lauren Jamero Hoolboom and her husband, Patrick; Jeremy and Jordan Jamero; Erika, Alexander, and Lindsey Hada; and Michael Jr., Matthew, Bonifacio Silverio. I hope that these remembrances will fill in some of the gaps and answer some of their questions.

I also dedicate these memoirs to Filipino American history, particularly the growing-up experiences of my Bridge Generation contemporaries. The formal study of Filipino American history began only in 1984, with the founding of the Filipino American National Historical Society (FANHS) in Seattle. Terri and I are proud to be among the founders of FANHS. With FANHS, Americans of Filipino descent have a national organization that works to document and legitimize their presence in America, dating back to 1763, as a significant part of their country's diversity. Before FANHS, virtually all the published literature was related to the Manong Generation, those intrepid souls who left the Philippines during the 1920s to work in the pineapple fields of Hawaii, the croplands of California, and the fish canneries of Alaska.

However, very little has been written about members of the Bridge Generation, the children of these pioneer *manongs* and *manangs*. I coined the term "Bridge Generation" for the 1994 FANHS conference, to describe children born before 1946 with at least one parent who was a Filipino pioneer. Members of the Bridge Generation are now in their sixties, and seventies, and eighties. It is my sincere hope that my memoirs of growing up brown in America will become a small part of the larger and more important process of documenting the history of the Bridge Generation.

Readers may wonder why I chose to use the phrase "growing up brown" as the title of this book. From the beginning of European settlement in America, color has been a pejorative used to describe supposedly inferior non-Caucasians. Those of African ancestry were derided as "blacks," Asians from the Far East were "the yellow peril," Native Americans were called "red savages," and Filipinos were "brown monkeys." By the time of the civil rights movement of the 1960s, these descriptions had taken on a more positive connotation. "Growing up brown" was coined by Seattle activists Fred and Dorothy Cordova in an effort to differentiate Filipinos from their Chinese, Korean, and Japanese brothers and sisters. The phrase received wide acceptance at the first national conference of what later became the Filipino American National Historical Society in 1987 and has been a workshop fixture at every FANHS conference since.

Having lived through its various iterations, I believe that

"brown" is a perfect description of my life experiences as a Filipino in America. It captures the hurt of being likened to an ape, of being considered inferior to whites, of being excluded from social activities, of being ashamed of my color, and of being discriminated against in employment and housing. "Brown" also encompasses my subsequent pride in my ethnicity and, finally, in who I am as a Filipino American.

Interspersed throughout these memoirs are comments on national and world events, civil rights issues, the New York Yankees, jazz, and Filipino American history. Their significance to me? Next to my family, they are all topics of great personal interest.

With undying love for my family and deep respect for all Filipinos who have called America home.

PETER JAMERO

# I

## CAMPO LIFE

### 1930–1944

THE FIRST FEW YEARS OF MY LIFE WERE YEARS of splendid isolation—so isolated that until I entered public school, I believed the nation consisted largely of Filipinos. As a country boy, growing up in central California at a time when there was no TV or radio, I thought that the strange white people I saw from time to time were foreigners. I was like most boys in the predominantly rural America of the time, aware that there was something called the "Great Depression" but oblivious to the social and economic devastation it was causing in other parts of the United States. I was oblivious in the sense that I did not feel deprived. Living in the country, we were able to raise or grow all our basic necessities for food. We had a roof over our heads.

Later, like most boys, I was aware of World War II but was interested mainly in the ultra-patriotic aspects as depicted in Hollywood movies. Perhaps the most significant impact of the war for me was the change in attitude toward Filipinos. We no longer were regarded as "brown monkeys" but virtually overnight became America's "brave brown brothers." The euphoria did not last long. Shortly after the end of the war, the "brave brown brothers" disappeared from the conscious mind of America.

I may have been like other boys but there was a major difference—my family included eighty to one hundred single young men residing in a Filipino farm-labor camp. It was as a "campo" boy that I first learned of my ancestral roots and the adventuresome and sometimes tortuous path that Filipinos took in sailing halfway around the world to the promise that was America. It was as a campo boy that I first learned of the values of family, community, hard work, and education. As a campo boy, I also began to see the two faces of America, a place where Filipinos were at once welcomed and excluded, were considered equal and were discriminated against. It was a place where the values of fairness and freedom often fell short when Filipinos put them to the test. ❦

# 1 The Adventure Begins

SEVERAL FILIPINO CAMPS AND SMALL FILIPINO businesses operated in Oakdale, the place of my birth. Oakdale, a small rural town in central California, was a magnet for Filipinos who worked in the agricultural fields and in the nearby lumber mills of Sonora. Oakdale benefited from its close proximity to Stockton, the home base of Filipino farmworkers, who were the major source of labor at the time. Area farmers valued Filipinos for their industriousness and willingness to work for lower wages. Farmers also believed that the Filipinos' generally short stature made them better suited to the backbreaking stoop labor of harvesting crops such as asparagus, onions, and sugar beets. This was a fiction—work was scarce, and Filipinos were just glad to have the jobs. They would never have admitted it to the white farmers, but their backs hurt as much as those of taller farmworkers from other ethnic groups.

Sonora was where Papa and Mama married in 1929 and is the place they first called home. They spent their honeymoon in the picturesque gold-mining town of Twain Harte, named after Mark Twain and Bret Harte, the legendary authors and former residents. Papa was twenty-nine, light of skin, and handsome in his pinstriped navy blue suit. Mama was pretty, petite, and a picture-perfect *pinay* (Filipina) bride of twenty-four. Mama and Papa had known each other from childhood, when they lived in the town of Garcia-Hernandez, on the Visayan island of Bohol. They were also third cousins. Given the relative isolation of the seven thousand Philippine islands, it was commonplace for residents of these *barrios* (villages) to have such close biological ties.

Papa, Ceferino Ladesma Jamero, was born on August 26, 1900, in the Lungsod Daan (Old Town) area of Garcia-Hernandez. He was the elder child and only son of a politically prominent family in Garcia-Hernandez. A sister, Erberta, was his only sibling. Papa was athletic and achieved some renown as a long-distance runner at his school. Although he was stocky in build, like other family members, Papa was decidedly different from the rest of the Jamero men. The extended Jamero family was quiet, serious, and civic minded. But Papa was not interested in school, often cut class, played the guitar in a *rondella* (a musical group featuring the *banduria*, a Filipino adaptation of the mandolin) that toured Bohol, and dropped out of school after the sixth grade. He was also *pilyu* (mischievous) and engaged in numerous pranks. Once, he led a group of boys underneath a nipa hut, elevated on stilts, where girls often gathered. In those days, girls did not always wear undergarments. In their hiding place, Papa and the other boys often played a game that involved guessing the girls' identities by peering up their dresses. According to often-told stories, Papa usually won.

Papa was also adventurous. When he was twenty-one, he became a *sakada* (one who climbs up, or rises), one of the thousands of Filipinos recruited as field workers for the Hawaiian sugar and pineapple industries. The Philippines was a convenient source of cheap labor. The country had an agrarian economy, and its people were used to hard work. Moreover, Filipinos were nationals rather than aliens and thus could avoid lengthy immigration procedures. This legal distinction came in the aftermath of the 1898 Spanish-American War, which initiated more than forty years of American colonialism. Papa was part of the first wave of Filipino immigration to Hawaii and the U.S. mainland, when Filipinos, like the Chinese and the Japanese before them, were recruited by the thousands to perform difficult agricultural work. Filipino recruitment, however, unlike that of Chinese and Japanese, was focused on young single men. Recruiters targeted Filipino men from the Visayas and the Ilocos, regions with a tradition of working long hours in the fields. In examining potential workers, recruiters looked for strong young men with hands that were rough from hard work. Papa was a muscular five foot six, but he had relatively smooth hands, presumably because of his family's independent economic situation and his pampered lifestyle. Papa rubbed his hands for days against rocks, sand, and other rough materials so that recruiters would accept him. He was finally selected and set sail on the steamer *Hawkeye* on October 19, 1921. He worked in the sugarcane and pineapple fields on the big island of Hawaii and then on Oahu.

Papa and other Filipino workers toiled long hours for low wages. Without the protection of labor unions or the civil rights granted to U.S. citizens, they often were at the mercy of the agricultural barons and their supervisors. Wages frequently ended up to be much less than had been agreed upon earlier. Most of the laborers lived in squalid quarters without running water. Subsequently, Filipinos joined Japanese workers in protesting their working conditions. Under the leadership of labor leader Pablo Manlapit, Filipinos participated in a major strike in 1924 that crippled Hawaiian plantations. However, the strike eventually led to the blacklisting of Filipinos in Hawaii and forced many, including Papa, to move to the U.S. mainland.

On September 23, 1925, Papa sailed to California aboard the SS *President Wilson* to seek his fortune in the fields and orchards of the Central Valley. The pidgin English he had learned in multicultural Hawaii was not helpful in mostly white, monolingual California. He found it difficult to communicate even the most basic of needs. For example, the only item he knew how to order in a restaurant was "hom eg" (ham and eggs), so he even had ham and eggs for lunch and dinner. Necessity may have forced Papa to learn rudimentary English, but pidgin expressions such as "bumbye" (by and by) were still sprinkled throughout his vocabulary. Moreover, he was never able to shed his distinctive Filipino accent when speaking English: F was pronounced as P, V as B, and T often became D. Papa did go along, albeit reluctantly, with an anglicized pronunciation of his Spanish last name. The Spanish surnames date back to the 1700s, when Catholic priests authorized the names as part of the process of converting to Christianity. In Spanish, the J is spoken as an H sound, but Papa decided he had more important things to do in America than repeatedly correct the pronunciation of his name.

Mama was born Apolonia Lacre Madelo on February 9, 1905. She came from a relatively poor but fun-loving family in the Barrio Canayaon area of Garcia-Hernandez. The last of thirteen children, Mama was nearest in age to her nieces and nephews, who were her childhood playmates. One of her nieces, Genoveva (Bebay), was her best friend. Mama chose a career as a schoolteacher, and Bebay followed suit.

While Papa was seeking a new life in America, Mama became a schoolteacher in Garcia-Hernandez. She was outgoing, well liked, an excellent teacher, ambitious, and active in the civic and social life of the town. Her dream was to go to the States, as she often said in the accent she denied having, "tu pinis my eskulling" (to finish my schooling). In 1928, her brother Silverio asked her to emigrate with him to the United States. Two other brothers, Calixto in Washington, D.C., and Emiliano in Montana, had written in glowing terms about the opportunities in employment and education available there. Mama believed that an advanced college degree would give a boost to her promising career as a grade-school teacher in Garcia-Hernandez. Without hesitation, she agreed to accompany Silverio.

By 1929, she had saved enough money and, together with Silverio, boarded the SS *Madison* on June 22, bound for the United States. On July 15, they disembarked at the Port of Seattle, after a three-week voyage across the Pacific Ocean. They picked strawberries in the rural community of Bellevue, across Lake Washington, for a few days to pay for their train fare and then traveled to Stockton, California, where Papa and other Garcia-Hernandez *kababayans* (townmates) greeted them. At the time, Papa was working at a Sonora lumber mill and lived in a camp consisting largely of Visayan workers. Their visit was joyous but brief. Mama and Uncle Silverio were strongly motivated to move on as soon as possible and join their brother Calixto, who was living in an apartment at 609 Longfellow Street in Washington, D.C.

Mama was eager to get to Washington, D.C., to fulfill her dream of furthering her education. However, she received a severe jolt soon after her arrival in the nation's capital. From the outset, Calixto's Caucasian wife, Colleen, was hostile, rude, and inhospitable and asked Mama to leave within a few months. To her dying day, Mama never knew the reason for Colleen's hostility. Mama wanted to go back to California, where she felt more comfortable, but she had spent most of her savings. Silverio did not have the $25 required for the cross-country train fare. With her brothers unable to offer either financial or emotional support, Mama felt so alone. She soon ran out of money and seemingly had no one to turn to in this strange, new country. Suddenly, she remembered Papa in California. In Garcia-Hernandez, she had known him to be someone she could count on. While theirs may not have been a romantic relationship, there apparently was a feeling of closeness between them. Now, Mama turned to him in her time of need. She wired him about her predicament and asked for $25 for train fare; he sent her the money to join him in Sonora.

As to the events leading up to their marriage, I can only surmise that it was a combination of several factors. First, the moral standards of the time would never have allowed Mama, an unmarried woman, to live in a camp of single men. Second, Mama's religious and family upbringing had a similar influence. (Years later, she said in a taped interview that she felt *ulaw* [shame] at having to accept money from a man to whom she was not married.) Third, Papa reportedly had a crush on Mama when they lived in the Philippines. Fourth, Mama's situation offered her little in the way of realistic alternatives. On her first day in Sonora, Papa asked Mama to marry him. She readily accepted, and they were wed the next day, November 9, 1929, in a civil ceremony in the Sonora town hall.

Shortly after their wedding, Papa and Mama moved forty miles down the road to Oakdale, since there no longer was work at the lumber mill in Sonora. I was born soon after. I first saw the light of day on Wednesday, August 27, 1930, at 3:00 P.M. My parents named me Peter, the anglicized version of my paternal grandfather's name, Pedro. In keeping with Filipino tradition, I received my mother's maiden name, Madelo, for my middle name. I was the first child in what would eventually be a family of eight children, six boys and two girls. The delivery at home went without incident, which was remarkable, considering that Mama was only four foot nine and weighed less than a hundred pounds and I was eight and a half pounds at birth. My infancy would be the only time in my life when I was taller and larger than my contemporaries.

When I was only two days old, the attending physician decided to perform a circumcision, not a standard medical procedure at the time. Papa and his *kababayans* took the unexpected surgery as a good omen because, according to Filipino custom, males approaching their teens underwent circumcision as a coming-of-age ritual and a sign of virility. You could say that undergoing circumcision at only a few days of age brought me instant virility. What I now know, however, is that it spared me the more painful Filipino-style circumcision I would otherwise have had to endure during adolescence.

I was born in the farm-labor camp where my father served as labor contractor and cook. His primary function was to secure work for Filipino men with local farmers. Typically, men from the same part of the Philippines lived and worked together, an understandable phenomenon since their homeland is not a homogenous country. Rather, the Philippines is an archipelago of more than seven thousand islands with diverse peoples, customs, and languages resulting from centuries of isolation. In our camp, the men were largely from the town of Garcia-Hernandez. I called them "Manong," a title of respect in the culture. Many of these *manongs* were actually blood relatives, uncles of varying degrees, as well. This extended family structure would form my home life for my first seventeen years.

Mama was primarily responsible for taking care of us children and also acted as camp bookkeeper, keeping track of the *manongs'* wages and expenses. Together, Papa and Mama maintained housing and fed the men. The *manongs* paid *kacera* (room and board) for these services. Operating a farm-labor camp would become the main source of income for Papa and Mama. This division of labor would remain unchanged for the rest of their lives.

We did not stay in Oakdale very long. When I was about eighteen months old, we began a migrant existence that would take us to farm-labor camps in the agricultural communities of Fowler, Atwater, Stockton, and Livingston. Fowler is located in a peaceful, grape-growing region just south of Fresno. A converted chicken coop served as our camp and home while the men worked in the nearby grape fields. However, our experience in Fowler was far from peaceful. One night, we awoke to gunshots. Our camp was then set ablaze by hostile *puti* (white people). We fled through the smoke and fire and scrambled into our car, which took us to safety.

During this period, it was not unusual for Filipinos in California to be treated violently by white men, many of whom resented Filipinos for taking the farmworker jobs they felt were rightfully theirs. During the preceding decade, agribusiness had eagerly recruited great numbers of Filipinos to work in the critical farm-labor jobs generally shunned by white Americans. By 1930, however, the country was deep in the Great Depression, and the state's predominantly white workforce had come to regard Filipinos as unwelcome competitors for jobs that were once again desirable as other work became scarce. In 1930, in the lettuce-growing community of Watsonville, a Filipino farmworker, Fermin Tobera, died at the hands of a white mob. Filipinos were subjected to discrimination and became targets of blatant racist hatred. They were often insultingly referred to as "monkeys," and as bizarre as it may seem today, some ignorant *puti* actually believed Filipinos had tails. (Once, in grade school, some boys cruelly asked me to show them my tail.) In Stockton, hotels and restaurants posted signs that read "No Filipinos Allowed." Filipinos were restricted to a four-block area around El Dorado Street and were not allowed to see first-run movies on Main Street. Neighborhoods pulled up their welcome mats, permitting Filipinos to live only on the south side of town.

According to the 1930 census, Filipinos were a significant population in America, numbering 45,208—up from a minuscule 160 in the 1910 census—not counting the more than 60,000 in Hawaii. Predominantly white communities conveniently forgot that the *manongs* had been brought to the United States as agricultural laborers at a time when Americans did not consider such work desirable. Several bills, patterned after earlier Chinese and Japanese exclusion acts, were introduced in 1928 and 1930 by Congressman Richard Joseph Welch, to rid the state of the latest Asian "peril."

Not only did whites resent Filipinos for competing for "their" jobs, many perceived Filipinos to be arrogant and despised the men's flashy style of dress and attraction to white women. The reality, however, was that Filipinos constituted a bachelor society, since there were very few available Filipino women in America for these mostly young, single men. The ratio of Filipino men to women during the early 1930s was fifteen to one. Consequently, these men sought the company of other, non-Filipino women. Whites considered relationships between Filipinos and women of color—such as Mexican, Indian, Asian, or black—acceptable, but relationships with white women were viewed as strictly taboo.

If Filipinos behaved as if they belonged in America, their attitude had its roots in the American approach to colonialism in the Philippines. Ceded to the United States by the Treaty of Paris of 1898, which concluded the Spanish-American War, the islands were an American colony until attaining independence in 1946. American teachers taught American democratic ideals in schools that mandated English, effectively de-emphasizing Filipino culture. "All people in America are equal," said the teachers. Moreover, the Filipinos' status as nationals rather than aliens gave them an additional reason to believe they had a special relationship to America. They were told they would be welcome in America—the land of freedom and opportunity. Once they arrived, however, Filipinos found that the reality was quite different. An amendment to California's anti-miscegenation law, extending its provisions to Filipinos, halted marriages between Filipinos and white women. Anti-Filipino sentiment reached its high point in 1934 with the passage of the Tydings-McDuffie Act, also known as the Philippine Independence Act. One of its provisions reclassified Filipinos residing in the United States as aliens, no longer U.S. nationals, and restricted immigration to fifty persons per year. The law marked a victory for isolationists and racists who considered Filipinos the latest Asian "peril" to threaten their vision of a white America.

Ironically, the act also granted the Philippines independence in ten years, a concession to those Filipinos who had sought independence ever since Emiliano Aguinaldo began an insurrectionist movement against Spain in 1896. The insurrection was aided by the Spanish-American War, which led to the defeat of Spanish forces by the United States in the battle of Manila Bay. The Aguinaldo-led insurrectionists believed they had finally attained independence for the Philippines only to find that America had no intention of leaving. The Treaty of Paris ceded the Philippines to the United States, thus ending its brief independence. Once again, Aguinaldo found himself in the role of a rebel leader. The ensuing Philippine-American War ended in 1902, only after Americans and Filipinos both endured heavy casualties.

In retrospect, the Treaty of Paris should have alerted Filipinos that America's word was not necessarily to be trusted. Curiously, most Filipinos immigrants during the next several decades appear to have believed otherwise. They believed the American teachers who told them they would be welcomed with open arms in America. They believed they would be treated as equals. They believed that America was a land of milk and honey. Sadly, subsequent events would prove them wrong.

In 1935, Congress passed the Filipino Repatriation Act, which provided Filipinos with free transportation to the Philippines on the condition that they never return to the United States. However, because of pride and feelings of *walay ulaw* (avoiding shame), only a few Filipinos took advantage of this provision. One of my favorite uncles, Mama's cousin Fructuso Madelo, was the only relative to do so. (In 1971, Uncle Tuso and I had a joyous reunion on my first visit to the Philippines. With his hard-earned money from America, he had purchased beach property and rice fields to provide for his family. Uncle Tuso was well off and highly respected in Garcia-Hernandez. However, he was reluctant to talk about his decision to return to the Philippines; he apparently still felt *ulaw*, even after thirty-six years.)

While Filipinos faced blatant discrimination from white America, some were also mistreated by their own people. Papa and Mama learned this bitter lesson firsthand. A Filipino labor contractor named Sotero recruited Papa and Mama to cook for a camp of Filipino grape pickers in Fowler. By verbal agreement, Papa and Mama were to share equally in the profits. The only problem was that Sotero fled with all the money, cheating not only Papa and Mama but the farmworkers, who had not yet been paid.

We were all forced to move north about eighty miles, to Atwater, where we rented two houses on Main Street. We would be in Atwater for only a very short time. After a week, two police officers knocked on our door with orders to evict us. A sympathetic woman had rented the houses to us while her husband was out of town, and when he returned, he became furious with her, declaring that he did not want Filipinos living in the middle of his town. We had no choice but to leave—again.

Fortunately, Mama knew a woman in nearby Livingston who found a two-story place that would accommodate our extended family. Our first stay in Livingston was significant for several reasons. First, my brother Herbert—named after Papa's sister, Erberta—was born there on August 10, 1933. Second, Livingston was where Papa began to establish himself with area farmers and growers as a contractor who delivered what he promised. His good reputation was to sustain us well during our early years.

Our first stay in Livingston was brief as we again migrated to follow the crops, but for the last time. The third child in the family, Ceferino Jr., was born on New Year's Day 1935, when we were living on Union Island, on the delta near Stockton. We had just moved to a camp in preparation for the upcoming asparagus season; Filipino laborers were to predominate in harvesting this crop for fifty years. We lived in a typical asparagus camp. The bunkhouse, with its peeling green paint, was long and starkly furnished. Junior was born in the midst of a severe rainstorm, and Mama's ride to the hospital was doubly dangerous because the dirt road was almost impassable due to the mud. Mama's trip started on December 31, 1934. By the time she got to the hospital, it was January 1—a brand-new baby for a brand-new year.

When I was younger, I often expressed relief that Junior was the one with Papa's first name, and not I, as it is often the custom in Filipino families to give the first son the father's name. "Ceferino" sounded foreign to me and contradicted my burgeoning efforts to assimilate into the American mainstream. Today, I know better. Some of my proudest moments were when several of my own children chose to name their boys Ceferino.

## 2  Maeda's Place

OUR MIGRATORY LIFE ENDED WHEN WE MOVED back to Livingston in 1935. Papa found a place owned by a Japanese farmer named Yoshitaro Maeda. The property was part of the Yamato Colony; established in 1906, it is the only planned Japanese settlement in U.S. history. The Yamato Colony comprised a series of farms on three thousand acres located on the northeastern boundary of Livingston. There, early Japanese settlers built canals that converted arid desert land into productive agricultural property. Maeda was in the first group of these Japanese farmer-colonists, and his property, one of the largest, was in the middle of the colony. Today, descendants of these Japanese pioneers continue to tend their neat rectangular plots of grape, almond, and peach orchards.

We lived on the original Maeda homestead, which consisted of a two-bedroom house, a tank house, several outbuildings, and a forbidding grove of tall eucalyptus trees. The property was located about two miles from Livingston and was connected to the main road by about five hundred feet of dirt road. It was ideal for our family and the ever growing extended family of Filipino farm laborers. A long room in the main house became the new mess hall. The tank house was a three-level structure topped by a windmill that provided the power to pump our drinking water. Two of its levels served as living space for the men, and the third level contained a large water tank. (Herb and I occasionally swam in the tank, too young to realize the dangers of swimming alone or of contaminating the drinking water.) The outbuildings were readily adapted for a bunkhouse and a community bath. Perhaps just as important, there was plenty of room for the gamecocks, a standard part of our entourage.

The location was also perfect for Papa's labor-contracting business. During our previous stay in the area, Papa made a good impression on area farmers and growers with the quality of workers he was able to supply for their harvests. Maeda's place offered an ideal base from which to build his contracting business. Papa negotiated an agreement with Maeda: instead of paying rent, he would be responsible for meeting Maeda's farm-labor needs and maintaining the immediate living area. We would stay at Maeda's place for eight eventful years.

These early years of my life were during the Great Depression, a time when 25 percent of the country was unemployed, banks closed, homes were lost, and food was in scarce supply. To make matters worse, after years of drought, thousands left the Dust Bowl states of Arkansas, Kansas, Louisiana, Oklahoma, and Texas to find a better life in California. Disparagingly called "Okies" regardless of their state of origin, these new migrants sought work in the agricultural fields of the Central Valley. Once they arrived, however, they were met by a hostile community that was already competing with Filipinos for scarce jobs. The new migrants faced discriminatory treatment similar to that encountered by Filipinos. They were relegated to the balconies in movie houses, could not eat or sleep in reputable places, and were often chased out of town by local residents. After the passage of the Tydings-McDuffie Act in 1934, which effectively reduced Filipino immigration in ensuing years, the Dust Bowl migrants became the major source of farm labor in the Central Valley. This continued until the Great Depression ended with the onset of World War II. Farm labor in California's agricultural belt has long been the domain of ethnic minorities; the Okies have the distinction of being the only exception to the rule.

Today, these erstwhile Dust Bowl migrants are established as respected citizens in Central Valley communities, while Filipinos, their counterparts during the Great Depression, continue to struggle to assimilate into mainstream America. When I was growing up, I thought, like many Americans, that the Okies' plight was of their own making. I believed that if people worked hard, as my parents and the *manongs* did, they would pull themselves up by their own bootstraps. I now know that it is not that simple. Conditions such as those caused by the Dust Bowl and the stock market crash are outside an individual's control. Perhaps more important, I now know that racism has been a major barrier that continues to block ethnic minorities from participating fully in American life.

My experiences during the Great Depression were quite different from those of many other Americans. It was not until much later, during my college years, that I learned about the widespread unemployment, food lines, and bank closures that characterized the Depression. My personal reality at the time was frolicking around the countryside of Livingston and enjoying life—like any other kid. There were many things to keep me occupied. I learned how to make paper airplanes. I took old newspapers and fashioned hats as well as boats that I would sail in the numerous pools that appeared after it rained. I created a fleet of tractors from discarded thread spools, rubber bands, and matchsticks. The *manongs* often made colorful kites for me out of bamboo and paper pasted together with day-old steamed rice. They also made tops and yo-yos that were far better than store-bought ones. I learned later that these toys originated in the Philippines. No wonder the *manongs* made theirs so well.

I did not consider us poor. As far as I was concerned, we were like most other people we knew. We always had a roof over our heads, and, being in the country, we did not need money in order to eat. We hunted cottontail rabbits and game birds, fished in nearby streams and rivers, and picked wild mustard and watercress for salad. We raised and slaughtered our own pigs and chickens. We grew our own vegetables, such as tomatoes (*kamatis*), eggplant (*talong*), Chinese squash (*tambaliong*), bitter melon (*paliya*), and string beans (*batong*). When times were tough, there was always rice and soy sauce and the ever present mung beans (*mungus*), the source of bean sprouts.

During the winter spawning season, Papa and the men often went to spawning areas in nearby rivers and streams under cover of night. When I was about six, I was able to accompany them. Catching spawning salmon was fun, but illegal. Everywhere I looked, salmon glittered beautifully in the moonlight. Lookouts, strategically posted, made sure we weren't caught by the authorities. The salmon spawned in shallow streams and riverbeds, which made it easy for the men to snatch them and put them into gunnysacks. Since sophisticated freezing methods were not yet a reality, the fish had to be consumed or dried during the next few days; otherwise, they would spoil. Strips of salmon were marinated in a sauce of garlic and vinegar and hung in a small lean-to. The cured salmon was a real delicacy. Most of the time, it was the snack of choice, which the men washed down with claret or burgundy wine.

One night, our illegal salmon raids came to an abrupt end when the police stopped Papa on his way home with a carload of salmon. Immediately jailed in the closest town of Gustine, he awaited sentencing before the local judge. Mama came to the rescue. Knowing that we had no money for a fine and that the welfare of the camp and her children were in jeopardy, Mama shrewdly brought all of us kids to the court. She then went on to let the judge know that Papa was the major source of family support. She pleaded that the children would suffer the most from any sentence or heavy fine that he might impose. Mama was at her eloquent best as she said, "Ip yu put my hasban in gel, mi an my sildren gu tu" (If you put my husband in jail, me and my children go too). The judge released Papa without a fine or a sentence.

During these years, we did not have most of the conveniences we now take for granted. Papa cooked on a wood-burning stove Mama did the laundry on a washboard, and the children who were tall enough to reach the clotheslines hung the wash out to dry. We did our homework by kerosene lamp. As for toilets, the reliable old outhouse (*casillias*) served our purpose. Our outhouse had three seats to accommodate our extended family of farmworkers. The multiseat outhouse served us well, but hens and chicks that freely roamed the camp occasionally entered the outhouse, fell through the seats, and had to be rescued and cleaned up by the *manongs*.

We did have a nice car. It was a green 1926 Dodge Brothers sedan with a running board and fenders. Actually, we did not own it by ourselves but shared ownership with several of my uncles. Whatever the arrangement may have been among the car's owners, Papa seemed to have it most of the time and drove it whenever he wanted.

Although the Great Depression had little impact on me in that I did not feel deprived, this is not to say that it did not affect me at all. I now realize why I learned to eat all the food served at the table and to finish everything on my plate. Old habits are slow to change. I continue to eat whatever is served; I finish the food on my plate. However, I no longer go barefoot as I did most of the time during the Depression. Then, I was limited to one pair of good shoes a year—for school. If the shoes wore out, Mama simply inserted a piece of cardboard inside them to cover the holes. If I outgrew the shoes, I squeezed my feet into them for school and took them off as soon as I got home.

Mama shopped for us through the Montgomery Ward catalog. I remember looking at the latest fashions for boys in the catalog even though I knew that the clothing I saw would not be for me. Mama was much more practical and frugal in what she ordered. The clothes had to serve our needs for both school and home, which meant I usually wore overalls made of durable denim. These were the days before consumer protections, and the goods we received were not necessarily as advertised. Shoes could wear out quickly, and clothes might be the wrong size. The Montgomery Ward catalog was also one of the few pieces of reading material available to us and offered us much information about the outside world. And since these were the days before affordable toilet paper, the catalog later served us well in the outhouse.

In looking back at those years, I realize I had only limited contact with the outside world. Most of the people I knew were like me—Filipino. On those rare occasions when I went to a town, I looked in wonder at the strange people who were white, much taller, had long noses, and spoke a strange language. Before I went to school, my world consisted of Filipinos. Everyone else was a foreigner.

My first language was the Visayan dialect of Cebuano, which was spoken by people from the central Philippine islands of Bohol, Cebu, Siquijor, and the southern parts of Leyte and Negros. By this time, our extended family had grown to include unrelated "uncles" from these islands. Since Cebuano was my only language, I was quite fluent and spoke with the *manongs* like a native. The *manongs* spent a lot of their time telling stories about the Philippines, and these stories were a rich source of learning about my heritage and culture. The stories they told while gathered around the fire on starlit nights were particularly vivid. They spoke not only of their memories of the Philippines but also of their dreams, their loneliness, and their hard work here in America. They also spoke about their sexual adventures. I listened, and I learned.

Under these circumstances, I inevitably became an imaginative storyteller. I took liberties with events I heard about from the *manongs* and inserted myself into most of my made-up stories. It did not matter that I mixed up real events, or confused happenings in the Philippines with happenings in America, or vice versa. I found them to be a willing audience. Since most Filipinos in America at that time were single men, the *manongs* didn't have much opportunity to interact with young children. It was as if listening to this little boy talk to them in their native tongue was the next best thing to being back home.

I was a boy with a very large imagination and did not always understand that my stories were inappropriate in mixed company, especially in front of Mama. There were times when Mama gently told me that it was not nice to talk about the sexual exploits of the mostly single men in their twenties and thirties. She said it was not good to talk about my imagined social adventures with pretty *dalagas* (single young women), although my stories may have been entertaining to the *manongs*. She scolded the men for exposing me to such mature realities. This did not influence their behavior for very long. Once, when I was about six years old, one of my "uncles" took me to a burlesque show in Stockton. I was fascinated by the bumping, grinding, and writhing of the blond strippers as they danced to syncopated swing music. It was also my first glimpse of unclothed women. The first thing I did when I got home was to show everyone how the strippers took off their clothes. Mama was not pleased. "Bata pa sia" (He is just a baby), she said, as she again scolded the giggling men.

My idyllic lifestyle ended abruptly in September 1936, when I started school. Suddenly, I was surrounded by people who spoke only English. Mama tried to prepare me by having me memorize three things in English—my name, my date of birth, and my parents' names. I did not have a problem memorizing them, although I did not fully understand what I was saying. This was all I said for almost the whole of first grade. No one understood my Cebuano dialect. There were three other Filipino boys in the class, Vincent Andam, Frank Hipolito, and Richard Supat; another boy, Joe Cabrillas, was two years ahead of me. While they understood me, they spoke only English. I was frustrated and felt so alone. This first year of school was the only time in my life that I have been so quiet.

My inability to speak English also led to my getting lost on the first day of school. Papa and Mama drove me to school and pointed out the bus I was to take home at the end of the day. They did not know, however, that the bus did not go down our road. When school was over, I boarded the bus, and it did not take me long to realize that I was lost. One by one, the children got off the bus. Finally, there was only the driver, an elderly man named Mr. Lehfeldt, whom everyone called "Gramps," and me. I tried to explain to him that he had to go to the other side of town, but of course, Gramps had no idea what I was trying to tell him. Suddenly, I spied the familiar house of Hildo Pomicpic, a good friend of Papa's, and signaled Gramps to let me off. By this time, I was in tears. Manong Hildo drove me home. As we approached the house, I could see Papa waiting for us. I was so happy to see him and to finally be home. Papa greeted me by taking off his belt and whacking me across the bottom, admonishing me for worrying everyone by getting lost.

After my traumatic first day of school, Mama became seriously concerned about my inability to speak English. When I was younger, Papa and Mama had disagreed about what language to teach me. Papa insisted that I learn Cebuano, but Mama felt that I should learn the language of our new country. Reluctantly, Mama gave in. Speaking only in the Cebuano dialect did not pose much of a problem in my preschool years. However, my experience on the first day of school convinced her that I must learn English. For the remainder of the year, I underwent a rigorous home course in English, taught by that former Garcia-Hernandez schoolteacher, Mama.

Mama's teaching methods were innovative. We started with the names of animals and familiar nouns, which she would describe to me in Cebuano. She then pointed to drawings of these same animals and nouns, which she had drawn on cardboard obtained from the wrappings of the men's laundered dress shirts. Next, she said the English equivalent for me to memorize. After I learned everyday nouns, we advanced to verbs, adjectives, adverbs, and conjunctions. I was a quick learner. I began to understand better what my first-grade teacher Mrs. Sheesley was trying to teach us. I began to figure out what my classmates were saying. But I still was not confident enough to speak much in class. I was more comfortable trying out my faltering English during recess with Japanese, Mexican, or Portuguese kids whose first languages also were not English and who were encountering similar language difficulties. My infrequent verbal contributions in class did not hurt me. At the end of the year, Mrs. Sheesley gave me my report card with the notation "Promoted to the 2nd Grade." I was so proud and happy, and so was Mama.

I was the only one of the Jamero children whose first language was not English. Papa and Mama learned their lesson, and my brothers and sisters grew up speaking English. Mama talked to us in English, while Papa usually spoke to us in Cebuano, and we answered in English. As a result, Papa became much more proficient with English and was increasingly comfortable talking to *puti*.

English was not my only new acculturation experience. I had to learn to eat *puti* food. On my first day of school, Mama fixed my favorite lunch of fried mackerel and rice, which she packed in my brand-new metal lunch box. After my classmates held their noses at the unaccustomed fish aroma, however, I began bringing sandwiches to school.

Our family grew by two more children while we lived at Maeda's place. Apola, the first girl in the family, was born in 1936, and George was born in 1939, between two stillborn baby girls. Apola's name is derived from Mama's first name, Apolonia. Most of the time, we called her "Pula." According to George's official birth certificate, his name is Claziruam. No one seems to know how Mama and Papa came up with that name. When asked, Mama would not respond. No wonder he always went by George! George was a preemie and weighed less than five pounds at birth, but he grew up to be the tallest member of the family. Meanwhile, I, the largest at birth, ended up being the shortest member of my family.

With two more children, we clearly had outgrown the two-bedroom house. Herb, Junior, and I occupied one bedroom. We slept in a double bed with Junior in the middle—an arrangement that was to last until I was about eleven. I have many fond memories of the countless nights when the three of us talked, played, shared jokes, and told ghost stories. The arrangement was also practical during the cold winter months, when we kept ourselves warm with our combined body heat. My sister Pula slept in Papa and Mama's room.

George's low birth weight and the two stillbirths were the result of Mama working so hard tending to her young family as well as a rapidly growing camp. The labor-contracting business had increased to such an extent that both Papa and Mama needed to work long hours to sustain it. During the peak harvests for peaches and grapes, the camp population swelled to more than eighty. Some of the men set up their cots on the front porch, while others slept in tents. Neither Papa nor Mama had enough time to spend with us children. This was all right with me, because there was always something in my young life to keep me occupied. I took care of my own personal needs and ate alongside the men in the mess hall. The outdoors was a playground for Herb, Junior, and me. It must have been more difficult for Pula and George, since they were both so young.

However, a few of our uncles were always around to help. One such uncle was Opong. His given name was Crispo Paguican, and he was also from Garcia-Hernandez. He was Papa's second cousin and had been part of the family camp entourage for as long as I could remember. He was muscular and well proportioned but stood only four feet seven inches tall. Because of his diminutive size, Opong was the butt of unkind jokes and comments. Children regularly used his height to gauge their growth. Because his small size did not inspire respect, most children called him by his first name. Even we Jamero children, brought up to call elders either "Manong" or "Uncle," called him simply "Opong." Opong was the main alternative childcare-giver among the men. He was obedient to a fault and carried out many of the unpopular tasks, such as changing diapers, without complaint. He had a good voice and often sang catchy little ditties to the little ones in the family. When he was in a particularly good mood, he would entertain the whole camp around the evening fire. His favorite tune was a beautiful love song he sang in three languages—English, Spanish, and Cebuano.

The Jamero camp always seemed to be the center of celebrations. Every new baby was given a baptism party complete with *lechon* (barbecued whole pig), adobo (a spiced chicken or pork stew), and all the trimmings. Mama was godmother to many Filipino kids in the area. The Jamero camp was often the place where the Filipino community held baptismal celebrations because it had the necessary cooking and eating facilities. We also celebrated the end of various harvests with a big party at the camp. The *manongs* did not need much of a reason to celebrate. After all, they were young and single.

Music was an integral part of our celebrations. Many of the men had learned to play instruments in the Philippines. They played the guitar, mandolin, *banduria*, a stand-up bass fashioned out of an old washtub, and sometimes the tenor saxophone or the trumpet. The musicians seemed to know all the latest tunes, such as "Who's Sorry Now?" and "Because of You." Someone usually had a song sheet or songbook so that everyone could join in. When one of the children sang, the men showed their appreciation by tossing money onto the floor. This could amount to a goodly sum. In 1938, I made so much money singing that I was able to buy Mama a new dress. Music was also a way for the *manongs* to remember loved ones back in the Philippines. When nostalgic Filipino love songs like "Ikaw" (You) were sung, conversations suddenly stopped, and eyes became misty.

Yet, despite all the camp celebrations, we did not celebrate birthdays with cake and presents. Celebrating birthdays was not a Filipino tradition. I do not remember resenting this, since other Filipino kids did not celebrate birthdays either. I had my first ever birthday party when I was in my thirties.

One evening, while I was eating dinner with the *manongs*, we smelled the distinctive odor of burning feathers. We rushed outside to find the chicken coops and rooster pens burning out of control. Cockfighting has long been a passion for Filipinos, and losing the gamecocks was a major blow. A few hours later, we learned that Junior and Pula had purposely set the fire. Why? They felt the men paid more attention to the roosters than to them. What was their punishment? They got several whacks from Papa's belt.

On December 7, 1941, we heard a bulletin on the radio announcing that Pearl Harbor had been bombed. Of more significance to the camp, Manila was also under heavy bombardment.

The beginning of World War II transformed the image of Filipinos; we went from being the despised "brown monkeys" to being "brave brown brothers." Almost overnight, Filipinos became desirable neighbors for Americans. The Filipino response was mixed. Most took an outwardly patriotic but guarded view of the sudden change in attitude. After all, it could not completely erase the years of discriminatory treatment they had experienced in America. Some men enlisted in the armed forces and went on to serve in the First and Second Filipino Army Regiments. A few *manongs* did everything they could to avoid the draft, such as falsely claiming they could not speak or understand English. The war years were also an unparalleled time of full employment. Anyone who wanted to work was able to find a job. Women became a major part of the workforce. It was not unusual to find disabled people in the workplace. Filipino men not only were needed in agriculture but were able to find new, better-paying jobs in airplane plants and shipyards.

I, too, had mixed feelings about World War II. At first, I embraced the patriotic fervor of the times and the ethnic pride of being a young "brown brother." I was in the sixth grade when the war started. A few months later, authorities descended without warning upon the school grounds and classrooms. They separated the children of Japanese ancestry, rounded them up, and took them to their homes in preparation for their imminent relocation. Teachers and other classmates could only watch in disbelief and fear. I had always had classmates of Japanese background. Thanks to the early Japanese settlers of the Yamato Colony, the Livingston area was home to a significant number of Japanese residents. By September 1942, all of them were gone—part of nearly 120,000 West Coast Japanese and Japanese Americans evacuated to so-called relocation camps. In actuality, these were concentration camps for people of Japanese ancestry, most of whom were American citizens. Surrounded by barbed wire fencing and guarded by armed soldiers, the camps would be their home for the duration of the war. Some men left the camps when they volunteered for the army's 442nd Regimental Combat Team. The Japanese American regiment gained fame on the battlefields of Europe and became the most decorated unit in the army. Sadly, it also suffered the most casualties. The Livingston area sent a disproportionate number of Japanese American soldiers to the 442nd and also lost a disproportionate number of soldiers killed in action. Today, pictures of these brave soldiers, who gave up their lives while their loved ones were confined in concentration camps, hang in silent memorial in the Livingston Museum.

As agriculture became critical to the war effort, the Jamero camp underwent unprecedented growth. By this time, Papa's reputation as a farm-labor contractor was at an all-time high. Not only did the farmers turn to him to fill their labor needs, but Filipino farmworkers knew that they could count on Papa to get top wages for them. The increased demand for workers meant that Papa had to make many more recruiting trips to Stockton and other nearby communities. He took me on some of his trips, which were always exciting adventures for me. I watched as he persuaded Filipino men to come to work for him, seeming to know instinctively how best to appeal to different men.

During the war, the country had to ration gasoline. The government distributed stickers, labeled A, B, and C, that determined the amount of gas one could buy. As a farm-labor contractor, Papa was deemed valuable for the war effort and was awarded the highest-rated C sticker, which entitled him to purchase almost any amount of gasoline. The C sticker was definitely prestigious. Riding in a car with a C sticker made this eleven-year-old kid feel special.

We also had special privileges when it came to the rationing of food and staples. Farm labor was vital to the war effort, so Papa and Mama were authorized to buy in bulk and had priority when it came to scarce items such as soap, sugar, and prime cuts of meat. Since these were the days before shopping carts, I usually went along to help carry the grocery bags. As we left the market, I always felt self-conscious and somewhat guilty seeing the stares of other shoppers, who were not allowed to buy the same quality of goods and in such quantities.

Our economic situation improved considerably during World War II. Papa bought a blue 1938 Chevrolet sedan to go along with his 1931 Model A Ford. Mama bought a battery-powered radio from Montgomery Ward. The radio proved to be a most valuable source of information and entertainment for all of us. I listened faithfully to Fred Allen, Jack Benny, and Red Skelton and kept up with *Your Hit Parade*. Radio made me into a baseball fan. I remember listening to my first World Series, between the New York Yankees and the Brooklyn Dodgers in 1941. Since the technology for airing programs live across the country was still in the developmental stage,

I listened to re-creations of the games rather than actual play. The radio re-creations demanded much from the imagination; broadcasters had to be entertaining and dramatic in their descriptions. I soon became a regular listener, much to my parents' consternation. They would have liked me to use the time being more helpful around the house.

## 3  Amid the Almond Trees

PAPA'S FARM-LABOR CONTRACTING BUSINESS
continued to prosper during World War II. We clearly had outgrown
the facilities at Maeda's place. George Horine, a gold medal winner
in the high jump in the 1916 Olympics, ran one of the largest peach
farms in the area. He offered a house and outbuildings on one of
his properties for a new Jamero campsite, rent-free. In return, Papa
would supply workers for Horine's vast peach orchards. The business arrangement was similar to the one Papa had negotiated with
Maeda. We moved in 1943.

The new site was about three miles away, in the unincorporated
area known as Fruitland. Hidden away in the middle of a large
almond orchard, it could be reached only by a mile-long, meandering
dirt road While the new Jamero camp may have been isolated, I never
felt lonely. The growing Jamero family and *manong* camp population provided plenty of company and excitement.

We made a number of modifications to the property. Some of
the outbuildings, formerly chicken coops, had to be disinfected and
structurally modified before serving as bunkhouses, and we built
another *baño* (bathhouse). The *manongs* brought the chickens and
roosters that had survived the fire and made new coops and pens
for them. Most of the labor was donated in the spirit of cooperation, or *bayanihan* (literally, "moving a house") style. The family
house was larger than the one we'd live in at Maeda's place. It had
two bedrooms, and we added on a mess hall and kitchen. Mama,
Papa, Pula, and our new baby sister, Luna Mary, born on October
15, 1943, slept in one of the bedrooms, while Herb and Junior occu-

pied the other. George and I slept in what had been a kitchen area, next to the new mess hall and kitchen. The house was white, a nice change from Maeda's unpainted, weather-beaten facade. The best thing was that this house had electricity and indoor plumbing. Turning the lights on and off fascinated us, and it was a wonder we did not wear out the light switches. Mama bought a toaster, which usually burned the bread, but that did not matter to us; we just had to learn to take the slices out faster. The indoor plumbing was yet another adventure. We kept flushing the toilet and turning the faucets on and off. No more cold night journeys to the outhouse.

But the wonders of electricity did not extend to the *baño* or the kitchen. We still had to carry firewood for the community bath and the kitchen stove. This could be an almost full-time chore during the cold winter months, since we also needed wood to keep warm. Getting firewood involved the whole camp. The *manongs* chopped down the trees that grew by the riverside, and Herb, Junior, and I helped haul the wood to the many vehicles that transported the wood back to the camp. These trips to the riverside were fun for us kids. They also may have been illegal. I do not remember Papa ever getting a permit or permission to chop down the trees from the owner of the river property.

The new mess hall and kitchen were by far the best equipped and roomiest I had ever seen. The mess hall was furnished with two newly built long tables and matching benches. Mama sewed curtains to give it a homier feeling. Three large *kawas* (woks) served Papa well in the kitchen—one was big enough to cook thirty cups of rice, the second held the main course, and the third was used for boiling water. There was also a wood-burning stove, a large double sink in which the Jamero kids washed the never-ending pile of dishes, and a storeroom for foodstuffs.

From the time we could reach the sink by standing on a chair, we Jamero kids washed dishes. After that, we graduated to other chores, such as cutting up meat and vegetables, sweeping the floors, and throwing out the *basura* (garbage). Mostly, we followed Papa's directions. The kitchen, or *kusina*, was his domain, and he ruled it accordingly. Enamel or tin plates and tablespoons, rather than forks, were used in the mess hall, which made dishwashing simpler. Still, washing and putting away dishes for more than eighty hungry farmworkers was a long and laborious process.

George and I, who shared the room next to the mess hall and kitchen, did not sleep well because of an army of ugly rats. Whenever the lights clicked on, the rats would scurry around. I don't know who was more frightened—the rats or us. We never could figure out where they came from. Papa bought rat poison, and although many died, they kept up their nightly forays into the kitchen. Traps weren't of much use because the rats were so large that they usually managed to break through the springs. Because of the rats, Papa and Mama took extra precautions with the handling and storage of food, and it must have worked, since no one got ill or died.

Adjacent to the camp was a concrete-lined irrigation canal. Irrigation had transformed the desert wasteland of the Central Valley into a rich agricultural center. Canals of various sizes crisscrossed the valley. Our canal was small compared to some of the giant waterways. It was so shallow that we could stand up in it—except for George, who was a toddler at the time. One day, George fell into the canal, and no one noticed, until we heard our family dog, Bugoy, barking. Miraculously, Bugoy pulled George from the water before any harm came to him.

Bugoy's heroics should not have surprised us. He literally was George's guardian. Mama and Papa had such a heavy workload that George was usually unattended in his crib. Bugoy took it upon himself to be George's bodyguard. If a stranger approached, Bugoy uttered a low warning growl. He was of mixed breed, and as I look back on it now, I believe he must have been mostly pit bull. I remember his ferocity when he fought with other dogs. His jaws were so strong that his foes rarely got loose. He never lost a fight, and most dogs backed off before there even was a fight. However, Bugoy was gentle with George. He tolerated Filipinos but could be dangerous with *puti*, and when white farmers came to talk to Papa, Bugoy had to be chained. In the Cebuano dialect, *bugoy* means "ruffian," big in a bullish way. Our dog may not have been big, but he certainly had some bullish traits.

After overcoming the language barrier, I continued to do well in school. I became a class officer a number of times and played in the Livingston Elementary School Band. At first, I played the drums. But after struggling with the snare drum on a hot summer day during a Fourth of July parade in Merced, I decided I should switch to an instrument that was much easier to carry. I looked over at my clarinet-playing friend Johnny Nunes. He and I had hit it off in the first grade, probably because we both did not speak English, his language being the Portuguese spoken by his immigrant parents. We were now in the sixth grade, and Johnny, who was almost six feet tall, carried a small clarinet. I was less than a hundred pounds, already had reached what would be my full height of five feet two inches, and was lugging around a heavy drum. I decided to play the clarinet.

I was one of several students to speak at my eighth-grade graduation in 1944, selected for my good grades and participation in school activities. Mama and Papa were understandably proud of their eldest son's achievements. I had long ago lost virtually all traces of a Filipino accent and become articulate in my new language. The theme of my talk, befitting the patriotic climate of the war years, was the opportunities America offered to children of immigrants, like me. I ended my remarks with the statement "Even I can become President." Former classmates still tease me about that phrase today.

During the summer of 1943, when I was almost thirteen, Papa decided I was old enough to work in the fields alongside the *manongs*. Was I old enough? Maybe—rural teenagers typically did physical labor. Was I strong enough? Hardly. I was rail thin and did not even weigh a hundred pounds. My first job was as part of a crew picking peaches. Papa assigned me to Henry Koehn, a Mennonite farmer known for his tolerance of slow pickers. His peach orchard required only eight-foot ladders rather than the ten-foot ones used on other farms. Nevertheless, the eight-footer was so heavy for me that after the first few days my muscles ached unbearably. I could not understand how the *manongs* were able to do this kind of work day after day and year after year. We worked ten hours a day with a half hour for lunch and only Saturdays off when picking for the canneries. Sunday was a workday because the markets and canneries needed to have the peaches on hand when they opened on Monday. I was paid $0.75 an hour, the same as the men, which made the work more tolerable.

The best part of the workday for me was when it was time to go home. When I was a teenager, this was especially true on Saturday if we were picking for the market and not for the canneries because I could look forward to a night of socializing and dancing in Stockton. When I was older, Papa promoted me to straw boss—the worker authorized to call time for breaks, lunch, and the end of the workday—in the hope that the extra responsibility would inspire me to be a better worker. It didn't. After feeling a few raindrops one hot and humid late Saturday afternoon, and eager to get a head start for Stockton, I ordered the work crew to go home early. When asked why, I simply replied, "Because it's raining." Of course, it wasn't rain, just a few sprinkles that soon stopped. Papa was so furious with me that it was the last time I served as straw boss.

In addition to peaches, I also picked apricots, grapes, and pears. The most distasteful of jobs was topping onions. This was piecework, which means my pay was based on the number of sacks I filled. It was backbreaking work. I sat all day in the hot sun, topping the onions, placing them in baskets, and finally emptying the baskets into sacks. Sitting on the hard ground took its toll on my rear end, using a knife to top the onions left calluses on my hands, and holding the sacks gave me bruised and bleeding fingers. Topping onions was by far the hardest farm-labor job for me. It also paid the worst. I was so slow that I was lucky if I made $3 a day.

The Jamero boys worked in the fields only during the summer and on school holidays. Mama always insisted that school came first. Until I left home at seventeen, I spent every summer working in the fields. I wish I could say that I was a fast, conscientious farmworker, but I was not. That may have been disappointing for Papa, although he never told me in so many words.

Soon after I began working in the fields, I learned a painful truth about the American approach to labor: the more menial the work, the more people of color performed it. Here in the Central Valley, white people owned most of the farms and ranches, while brown people, Filipinos or Mexicans, did almost all the labor. I did not yet fully understand the socioeconomic dynamics behind my observations, but suddenly, I began to question whether my goal of assimilating into American life was realistic. Was I destined to be a farmworker? Was it realistic for a brown person or any person of color to aspire to anything beyond menial work? It also dawned on me that prevailing role models such as the all-American boy or girl, movie and sports stars, and the country's political leaders were all white. Was this yet another message that brown people need not apply? My distaste for farm labor was not necessarily due to carrying a heavy ladder or working long hours in the hot sun. It came from my fear that I was predestined to be a second-class citizen.

There was another Filipino farm-labor camp in nearby Winton, and a friendly volleyball competition soon developed between the two camps. Filipinos were skilled at the game, having played it extensively in the Philippines and in Hawaii. Residents of both camps followed the volleyball matches with a great deal of enthusiasm. They played for camp pride, a gallon of red wine, and a small pot of money.

The competition between the camps extended to a boxing match after I got a pair of boxing gloves for Christmas. Almost immediately, I received instruction and training in throwing jabs and punches and in proper footwork from the *manongs*. Boxing was a national passion in the Philippines. The men were eager to share their knowledge and skills with me. At the same time, the *manongs* at the other camp began training their own potential pugilist, a boy of about my age. Finally, our respective handlers agreed to a match at the Jamero camp. Boxing fans from each camp backed their fighter with friendly boasts and bets. Scheduled for three rounds, the fight lasted less than one round after I landed a punch squarely on my opponent's face and drew blood. The punch elicited loud cheers from the partisan Jamero camp crowd, and the cheers continued with every punch I threw. Intimidated by the noise and the sight of his own blood, my opponent decided he'd had enough. After my victory, I grew cocky. In bouts sponsored by the 4-H Club and a local boys' club, I dazzled my opponents with my footwork. My fourth foe would be my last. He landed a punch flush against my nose. When I saw my own blood flowing, I, too, decided that was it and hung up my gloves for good.

Operating the farm-labor camp took all the hours Papa and Mama were able to give. It was hard for both of them, particularly Mama. Luna had been a breech birth, like the two stillborn babies before her, which meant that Mama had experienced three difficult births in the space of a few years. She also had to look after five kids while carrying out her bookkeeping duties. But Mama rarely complained. "Agwanta lang" (Learn to suffer and bear it), was all she would say after a particularly hard day. Mama also made extra money by taking in the men's laundry and doing their ironing. Sometimes she sewed shirts and undershorts and sold them to the *manongs* for a small profit. The men were generous in their support of Mama's various enterprises, knowing that the money went to support her growing family. Mama gave back by being active in the Filipino community. True to the Filipino value of *utang ng loob* (internal debt of gratitude), Mama always had time for her community. She took the lead in starting collections for needy families and was instrumental in organizing the Garcia-Hernandez Association, a mutual aid society devoted to covering the medical and funeral expenses of *manongs* from her Philippine hometown.

There is a superstitious belief among Filipinos that people who undergo breech delivery have unusual healing powers. Luna's breech birth was something of a miracle, as the doctor was able to reposition her and avoid further difficulties. Junior tested Luna's "power" on his sore and swollen wrist. He asked her to spit on it and rub it, and the aching in his wrist soon subsided.

I must admit I am skeptical about Luna's supposed power. I do know, however, that Filipinos are superstitious and believe in the supernatural. They rely on *anting-anting* (amulets) to ward off evil. Filipinos believe in a variety of spiritual beings, including the *wakwak* (witch) and the *kapri*, an apparition that lives in trees and steals the souls of unsuspecting people who happen to walk by. The tiny Visayan island of Siquijor, just southwest of Bohol, the ancestral home of many of the *manongs* at the Jamero camp, is supposedly the home base of ghostly spirits. It is also the home island of *mananambal*, Filipino medicine men or sorcerers, who possess magical powers that can drive away evil spirits. They are called "Dr. Laway" (Dr. Spit) because they use saliva in their treatment. Some *mananambal* have *tambal* (healing powers) and are white sorcerers, while those who seek to do harm are black sorcerers. A *mananambal* lived only a few miles from the Jamero camp. According to the *manongs*, he once correctly predicted the coming of a comet. I noticed that no one talked to him unless he spoke first. Having heard many frightening stories of the *mananambal*'s powers, I always ran to Mama whenever he approached. He later was thought to have died in a mysterious fire but his remains were never found.

The prominent role of superstitions in Filipino culture contributed to the Filipinos' rapid conversion to Catholicism during Spanish colonial times. Pagan idolatry resembled such Roman Catholic practices as belief in the Holy Ghost and prayers to religious statues. To this day, many devout Filipino Catholics continue to hold onto their old superstitious beliefs.

The strong Catholic faith Mama brought from the Philippines helped her through some difficult times. Since Sunday was a busy day at the camp, Mama could not go to Mass. She turned to God in her own way, through prayer and by decorating her room with religious objects and pictures. She also made sure that her children respected religion, although it might not have been in the Roman Catholic tradition. Once, an evangelical preacher offered to take us children to Sunday school, and Mama readily consented. We found ourselves in a Holy Roller church. Another time, we went to a Mennonite service after one of the peach farmers who did business with Papa convinced Mama that we would be welcomed. Later, when we moved to Livingston, my brothers and sisters were able to go to Catechism and receive the sacraments of the Church. I was in my teens and felt embarrassingly out of place with six-year-olds, so I refused to go. Not until I was twenty years old did I receive my First Holy Communion, aboard a navy ship on patrol during the Korean War. At age thirty-one, I would receive the Sacrament of Confirmation, with my brother Junior as my sponsor.

Papa was a master negotiator. His success in recruiting farmworkers was in large part due to the competitive wages he negotiated with farmers and growers. This was all the more remarkable since there were no legal protections at the time, and Filipinos did not always earn competitive wages. In Salinas during the late 1930s, for example, whites were paid $.75 an hour, Japanese $.50, and Filipinos $.35, all for doing the same work. Such practices led to a number of labor disputes involving Filipinos in the Imperial Valley, Salinas, Santa Maria, and Stockton. There were no labor disputes in our area. In 1943, the hourly wage Papa negotiated with George Horine was a competitive $1 an hour.

Papa's negotiations were sealed with a handshake. He did not need a written contract. The trust he had built working with the same farmers and growers over the years was sufficient. However, there was one unfortunate exception—George Horine's son, Bill. When the elder Horine's health began to fail, he looked to his son to run the ranch. Bill Horine proceeded to ignore the basic agreements negotiated between his father and Papa. First, he demanded an exorbitant rent. Second, he arbitrarily reduced the hourly wage to $.95 an hour. The younger Horine mistakenly thought he had Papa in a corner. But Papa held his ground and stuck to his principles. I will never forget how he stood up to the more educated rancher and skillfully argued his position. I was so proud of Papa. For a man who did not make it past the sixth grade in the Philippines, he was a hard negotiator who was not about to cave in on the important issues. He told Bill Horine that $.95 an hour was an insult to his "boys." (Papa always referred to his farmworkers as "boys" and continued to do so even when they reached their sixties and seventies.) After discussing the matter with Mama, he told the men about the bargaining impasse and recommended that we reject the wage cut. Furthermore, he proposed that we immediately vacate the premises. The *manongs* unanimously agreed to do both.

We did not know at the time that Papa had an ace in the hole. He had $5,000. Mama had secretly put away money, penny by penny, over the years, hoping to someday have her own piece of land. Anti-alien land laws prevented Filipinos from owning property, but with the wartime shift in American attitudes toward Filipinos, these laws would later be repealed. When Bill Horine reneged on his father's agreement, Mama saw it as the perfect opportunity to make her dream come true, by acquiring property in my name, since I was a U.S. citizen. She shared the secret of her hidden cache with Papa, who used the information to outfox Bill Horine.

This was a win-win situation for all of us. Mama got her property, Papa outmaneuvered a greedy grower, and the *manongs'* wages were not cut. It was now the spring of 1944. We would soon embark on yet another adventure.

# 4 *Livingston*

IN THE SPRING OF 1944, THE TWO THOUSAND RESI-
dents of the small town of Livingston did not know it, but their
population was about to increase by one hundred—all Filipino. If
the move back to Livingston was an adventure for the Jamero kids,
then it was an unforgettable scene for Livingston's townspeople.
Never before had they seen so many Filipinos with all their worldly
belongings, riding in every conceivable type of vehicle, and accompanied by almost as many fighting roosters. It was like a parade. I
rode in an uncomfortable truck amid assorted furniture and outbuildings such as the mess hall and kitchen, sheds, and several outhouses. After the shabby manner in which Bill Horine had treated
us, Papa was adamant about taking away every capital improvement
we had made at the Fruitland property. Besides, it made good economic sense to do so.

The new property consisted of the main house and a large barn
on forty acres of open agricultural land located about three miles
outside of town, not far from Livingston High School. A lawn of
lush Bermuda grass and a small goldfish pond were located between
the house and the barn. The lawn quickly became the favorite place
for the *manongs* to tether their gamecocks. In no time at all, the
green grass turned brown and then was gone forever, victim of the
roosters' daily pecking and the constant pounding of a hundred pairs
of Filipino feet. The small pond, also pecked at and trampled, soon
dried up and disappeared as well.

For the next few months, the camp was a beehive of activity. The
men transported the combination mess hall and kitchen using two-

by-fours so that it could be attached to the main house. I watched in fascination as the *manongs*, placed strategically on every side, slowly moved the structure. Our neighbor across the road, a dairy farmer named John Cordes, couldn't see the *manongs* and thought the building was actually self-propelled. Later, he jokingly said to Papa, "When I saw the building move, I thought Filipinos had magic powers."

A brand-new pool hall, equipped with two pool tables and a billiard table, rose up on the property. The tables were from Uncle Nick Jamero's pool hall in Stockton, which had just gone out of business. The next few years would see several expansions to the pool hall. The first accommodated several gaming tables for *pinoy* rummy and *pi-que*, a Chinese gambling game played with domino-like tiles. The second expansion housed a *sari sari* store (the Filipino version of a mom-and-pop store) that sold wine, beer, soda, cigarettes, and candy. This was Mama's domain, where she spent most of her days and evenings. Her entrepreneurial skills, with help from the Jamero kids and sometimes Uncle Opong, made the little business into yet another source of income for the family.

The barn received a major upgrade and became three levels of living space for the men. An unofficial pecking order determined who resided on each level. The most desirable space was in the midsection of the ground floor containing about twelve individual rooms. A core group of loyal uncles and *manongs* who had worked with Papa from the beginning lived in these rooms. With the promise of improved privacy, they gladly paid for the modest cost of construction. Other longtime workers occupied the dormitory rooms on each side of the ground floor. The second and third levels were barracks-style accommodations, available on a first-come first-served basis to mostly itinerant workers. The barn expansion increased the camp's farmworker capacity to more than one hundred men for the peak harvests of peaches and grapes.

Another community *baño* took shape. (The *baño* was a males-only facility; the three female members of the Jamero family used the bath inside the family house.) Like the one at Fruitland, it featured a large, rectangular, galvanized metal tub heated from the outside with firewood. The function of the tub was not to hold bathers but to hold enough hot water for their baths. We used small enamel pots to dip hot water out of the tub and then pour it over our bodies. After a few years, the *baño* underwent several upgrades, converting to butane fuel and adding six showerheads along two walls.

The gamecocks, as befitted their exalted place in the hearts of Filipino men, enjoyed luxury accommodations. Roosters had individual coops just beyond the barn in several rows of raised wooden pens. The slat doors were fitted with feeding bins fashioned out of old tin cans. The men planted a row of fast-growing cottonwood trees to shade the roosters during the hot summers and to act as a windbreak in stormy weather.

The amenities at the camp greatly contributed to strengthening the traditional *bayanihan* spirit among the *manongs*. Some of them had always been helpful around the camp—assisting in food preparation, cleaning up the grounds, and maintaining their spaces—but now they seemed to be doing even more to keep up the appearance of the camp, particularly the core group of *manongs*.

Conditions at the Jamero camp as well as other camps in the Livingston area were markedly different from conditions at Filipino camps I saw in other parts of the state. In those camps, the facilities and any amenities were the exclusive domain of the farmer or rancher. Year after year, these farmers provided the same inadequate plumbing and flimsy housing, with little regard to the workers' basic needs. Rarely were there recreational amenities. At the Jamero camp, Papa held the reins of power. He made sure that plumbing and housing were maintained. He provided amenities such as a pool hall, television, and gaming room. Papa never overcharged for *kacera*. He took the lead in negotiating fair wages and decent working conditions with area farmers and growers—instead of leaving these decisions to them.

Farming conditions in the Livingston area were also different. Unlike the giant, corporate agribusiness holdings around Stockton and Delano, for example, family-run farms were the norm in the

Livingston area. These farmers were not rich, in contrast to wealthy growers in other areas of the state. Consequently, Livingston-area farmers readily related to the hardworking Filipinos, were more approachable, and were inclined to negotiate fairly with Papa. This empathetic relationship was to serve both the farmer and the laborer well for the next several decades.

The Jamero family lived in a rustic two-bedroom house with a large dining room and a tiny kitchen. The house had a small library area with a fireplace and a back porch. There were only two bedrooms, making it somewhat crowded for our family. The space needs of the Jamero family, however, unlike other needs of the new Jamero camp, were not a high priority. Improvements to the family house were not to come for a few more years and only after two more additions to the family.

The camp grew larger, as did the Jamero kids and their list of chores. We all helped in washing the dishes, throwing out the *basura*, feeding the pigs, and assisting in food preparation. In addition, we Jamero boys took on a major role in the slaughter of the pigs (*baboy*) and chickens (*manok*) when we were older.

A pig was slaughtered almost every month to meet the needs of the growing camp population. The Jamero boys were only interested bystanders as small youngsters. However, when we became teenagers, we inherited the job of catching the elusive pigs. The increased responsibility was supposedly in recognition of our approaching manhood, but we knew otherwise. This was one of the dirtiest jobs at the camp. No one wanted to slosh through the mud of the pigsty. Catching the slippery pigs was a two-person operation. After donning our "pigpen" clothes, we separated the targeted pig from the others and chased it into a small holding pen. One Jamero brother held a short rope with a noose at one end on the ground and pulled it tight as soon as the pig placed a foot in the noose. At the same time, the other brother, reaching from the other side, pulled both of the pig's legs toward him. The pig fell with a dull thud, was quickly bound, and then was carted off in a wheelbarrow for slaughter.

The *ihaw baboy* (slaughter of the pig) took place on a wooden platform about two feet high, just behind the *baño*. As the pig lay on its side with its head hanging over one end, its legs were tied together and then bound to the platform. Several people sat on the pig to help hold it down. Once, I was careless and sat too close to the animal's snout. In the final moments of its death throes, the pig grabbed my rear end in his jaws. I still have the scars to remind me of the incident.

Papa usually was the executioner; he used a long, sharp knife to slit the pig's throat. In order to control the animal's thrashing, he inserted a blunt wooden stick into its mouth. Another person, often me, held a pot containing a small amount of vinegar, which prevents coagulation, to catch the pig's blood; it would be used later to make *dinuguan* (blood stew). We then waited to see if the pig squealed loudly. (Filipinos believe that the louder the squeal, the greater the flow of blood.) After the pig expired, boiling water was used to loosen the thick hair. Scraping away the hair with sharp knives and razors completed the cleaning phase.

Butchering the pig was yet another *bayanihan* activity for the men at the camp, with Papa as general overseer. There were enough knives and cutting boards for everyone who wanted to help. The men made separate piles of meat, bones, ribs, fat, internal organs, and entrails. There was no waste. The fat became cooking lard. The pork rind, or *chicharon*, made a delicious snack as well as a garnish for Filipino dishes. The internal organs and entrails, cleaned and chopped, went into the *dinuguan*. The head was roasted in the oven and became the source of a great snack.

We always kept a few slices of lean meat for *sinugba* (barbecue), which we cooked outdoors on a grill made from a hollowed-out washtub. We ate the bite-sized meat community style, with our hands, dipping it into a delicious concoction of soy sauce, vinegar, and very hot red chili peppers and accompanying it with steamed white rice. The men washed down the *sinugba* with claret or burgundy wine. The *sinugba* was Papa's way of thanking everyone for their *bayanihan* spirit, not only for pitching in with the slaughter but also for their countless contributions to the smooth operation of the camp during the year. It was a great way to end the day of *ihaw baboy*.

We purchased chickens for slaughter from the numerous poultry farms in the Livingston area. On Sundays during the harvest season, we slaughtered, plucked, and cut up at least four dozen white leghorn hens. The slaughter of the chickens was often a two-person operation, with one Jamero boy holding the hen by its legs and wings while the other did the killing. It could just as easily be a solo activity, however. Herb and Junior developed the knack of holding the chicken's neck with one hand while wielding the killing knife with the other, an art I was never able to master. Next, we threw the carcasses into a large washtub, where they thrashed about in their last dying gasps or flew out of the washtub, as many were apt to do. After the chickens stopped thrashing, George and I dipped them into a *kawa* of boiling water to soften their feathers. The *manongs* usually joined us in plucking the chicken feathers. Lastly, we cut up the chickens for food preparation.

Just as with the pigs, we used the chicken blood to make *dinuguan*. While I liked both, my personal preference was the chicken *dinuguan*. Sometimes, Papa and Mama invited *puti* to dine with us. (This seemed to carry over from the colonial mentality in the Philippines, since invitations were never reciprocated.) The *puti* invariably asked what was in the *dinuguan*. If they asked in a polite way, I simply said it was "chocolate meat." However, if they were patronizing or arrogant, as some *puti* were inclined to be, my answer was "blood and guts."

Fish (*isda*) was a regular feature of the camp diet. From time to time, the men would fish in nearby rivers for striped bass or catfish (*pantat*), casting off their lines without the use of rods. However, we got most of our fish from San Pedro via the Southern Pacific Railroad, which stopped in Livingston. Papa usually ordered Spanish mackerel along with sea bass or kingfish. He deep-fried the mackerel in the same cooking fat, which over time developed a distinctive delicious flavor that I have not tasted since. Deep-fried fish was often the main dish in the hot lunches Papa delivered to the fields during harvest season. The fish was placed on a plate inside a pan of rice, which in turn lay atop unbreakable enamel or tin plates. The pan and plates were then neatly bundled inside an old rice sack tied at the corners for easy carrying. To this day, I still remember the wonderful taste of the fried mackerel in the middle of the hot, dusty summer days in the orchards.

Digging was another one of our chores as teenagers. It seems there was always a need to dig a hole for a *basura* dump, an outhouse, a cesspool, or an irrigation pump. Herb, Junior, George, and I were the designated diggers. Papa, of course, was the supervisor. Livingston lies right in the middle of the Central Valley, which had been a desert before irrigation transformed it into a rich agricultural area. Much of the upper soil was sandy, but we did not shore up the sides of the holes as we dug. Thus, there was always the danger of a cave-in as we went deeper. Once, a massive cave-in covered Herb and me up to our shoulders. Fortunately, Junior and George were there to pull us out. What was Papa's response to the cave-in? He saw to it that we started digging again.

The Jamero kids enjoyed relatively good health. We did not have a regular doctor, and health insurance was a generation away, so Papa and Mama turned to an assortment of folk remedies to treat our ailments. If we got a rash, the nicotine residue from Papa's pipe stem took care of it. For aches and pains, we were given a massage (*hilot*). For the flu, Papa and Mama prescribed *tuub*. This consisted of a steamy pot of hot water into which they placed a jar or two of Vick's Vapo-Rub. I can still remember sitting naked on a chair, covered with a blanket, with a pot of steaming water under the chair. I breathed in the vapors, perspired, and away went the flu. It may have been unbearably hot under the blanket, but the treatment worked every time. This was the Filipino version of a vaporizer, which was yet to be invented.

The major rite of passage for Filipino boys was *tuli* (circumcision), performed before they were thirteen. (In those days, circumcision was not a routine hospital procedure performed on infants. I was one of the few exceptions, having been circumcised when I was only a few days old.) Filipino boys accepted the eventuality of circumcision after undergoing years of teasing from their elders for being unclean. Boys in my generation often had *tuli* at home, without benefit of a hospital procedure or medical practitioner. A Filipino man named Kamandag usually performed the circumcisions in Livingston, employing a slit of smooth bamboo, placed between the penis and the foreskin, and a very sharp knife. The procedure was quick and, from all accounts, safe. However, Mama did not have confidence in the local *tuli* specialist. Herb, Junior, and George were circumcised at the hospital in nearby Turlock.

By this time, Papa's reputation as a labor contractor was well established. *Manongs* were charged $1.60 a day for *kacera*. Farmworkers' wages were $1.10 an hour, higher than in most Filipino camps in the state, with a ten-hour workday, thanks to Papa's skillful negotiations with farmers and growers. Papa had no trouble attracting good workers. He no longer had to make as many recruiting trips to Stockton, except in the late spring, when he moved some of his steady boys back to Livingston.

"Steady boys" was Papa's term for the longtime members of our extended family. Many had been with us from the early days in Oakdale. Most of the men were relatives from Garcia-Hernandez: Anastacio "Tayo" Abucijo, Rustico "Ticoy" Cadiz, Canuto Galindez, Teodulo "Doloy" Pagaran, and Crispo "Opong" Paguican. Also from Garcia-Hernandez was Ponciano "Oncing" Alaan, whom we Jamero kids called "Uncle Sniffer," because of his resemblance to a comic-strip character of the time. Other steady boys included Lucio Asotique, Pascual Beltran, Rufino "Chief" Delima, Margarito "Jerry" Lomoljo, Juan "Johnny Topdown" Pelligrino, and Arcadio "Cadio" Simangca, who had emigrated from other parts of Bohol and the Visayas. All spoke Cebuano. Among the steady boys, there was only one Ilocano, Rosendo Navarro; one Tagalog, Tom Torralba; and one non-Filipino, Isias Mata (an illegal immigrant from Peru who learned to speak the Cebuano dialect fluently).

Virtually all the Filipino pioneer old-timers had nicknames. Consistent with Filipino custom, few were ever called by their given first names. Nicknames were often derived from first names or were related to physical characteristics and personal idiosyncrasies. Opong was also known as "Putot" (Shorty) because of his stature. The nickname "Johnny Topdown" came from Pelligrino's refusal to put up the top of his convertible, even when it was raining. He was also an original Filipino hippie, with long curly hair that became even curlier when he was driving with the top down in the rain. As if he needed another nickname, Johnny Topdown was also known as Johnny "Pagow" (Hoarse Voice). Rufino Delima's resemblance to the stereotypical cigar store Indian inspired the nickname "Chief." However, he preferred to be called "Blue Eyes," thinking that his light eye color made him more attractive to *dalagas*. It did not. He tried to be attractive to *dalagas* in other ways. Once, at a riverside picnic, he decided to show off his physique by climbing to the top of a tree and diving into the river below. He took his time preening atop the tree before he dived into the water. Unfortunately, the river was only a few feet deep, and he got stuck face down in the mud. Only his legs were visible. But the mishap did not deter him. Wiping the mud off his face amid laughter from his audience, he asked, "How du yu like my dibe?"

Although no one seemed to take his nickname personally, some of the names could be cruel by American standards. For example, a man with a harelip was known as "Bungi" (Harelip). A pock-marked man was called "Buluton" (Pock Face). A person who could not speak because of a hearing disability was known as "Amang" (Deaf). An uncircumcised man was invariably called "Pesut" (Not Circumcised), and an amputee would be known by the nickname "Putol" (Cut Off). If a man happened to be effeminate, he was called "Bayut" (Homosexual). A man of mixed Filipino and other ethnic background was always "Mestizo." Some, like Navarro, were called by their last names. One *manong* answered to the name "Hagu," because he responded to nearly everything with the word *hagu* (tired). Perhaps the most unusual nickname was "TuHee TuHee." Curious, I asked a *manong* if he knew the origin of the name. He said, "Yu pollo heem, yu will see." It did not take me long to find out. When he spat, the resulting sound was *tuhee, tuhee.*

Some chroniclers of the Filipino experience in America during the 1920s through the 1940s have described the Manong Generation as made up of uneducated men, without ambition, eager to squander their hard-earned money on women and gambling. Having lived among them for most of my young life, I strongly disagree with such sweeping generalizations. Most of the *manongs* I knew were literate and had learned English from American teachers under the system of American education mandated in the Philippines. They came to the United States to further their education or to improve their family situations. Many men faithfully sent money home, not only to their immediate families but also to distant relatives. When they went into town on their days off during harvest season, they always dressed fashionably, as if to tell the world that they were as good as anyone else. However, only a few recreational outlets were open to them and only in certain parts of town. Some Filipino men went to fleapit movie theaters. Others went to gambling houses. Most caught up with old friends at pool halls or simply hung out on El Dorado Street in Stockton.

Despite the lack of available women, only a few *manongs* regularly frequented Stockton's notorious "ten cents a dance" establishments. Occasionally, a fight would erupt over a woman, and these incidents always received wide coverage in the newspapers. I am convinced the media attention contributed significantly to the stereotypical view of woman-crazy Filipinos, which certainly was not my perception of the Manong Generation. They may not have found the pot of gold in America, and they may have felt *ulaw* over their lack of success. However, the *manongs'* failure to meet personal goals was due to the anti-Filipino sentiment of the times and the discrimination they experienced in employment, housing, and education—not because they were woman-crazy or inherently weak.

As to gambling, I must acknowledge that most of these Filipino pioneers indulged in *sabong* (cockfights). *Sabong,* brought over from the Philippines, was their most popular pastime. Although only a small number of *manongs* owned gamecocks, those who did averaged from four to six roosters so that poultry could easily outnumber people at the camp, particularly during harvest seasons. Each *sabongero* (gamecock owner) dreamed that his rooster would be a champion and make him rich. The most desirable cocks were *talisayons*, those with green-white or yellow-white plumage, which were thought to be unbeatable. Most gamecocks were purchased through mail-order catalogs and came from Arizona, North and South Carolina, or Texas. In these states, unlike California, cockfighting was legal, and their game farms did a flourishing catalog business with Filipinos. Caring for fighting roosters was an important part of campo life. The birds were fed the best corn. They received health care from the *sabongeros*, who seemed to have a remarkable body of knowledge on the birds' medical needs. Tethered outside their individual cages by homemade macramé-like leashes tied to one leg, the roosters had a regimen of regular exercise and massages similar to that of prizefighters.

As soon as a rooster arrived from the game farm, the *sabongero* began a training program calculated to make the bird mean and lean. First, the rooster was fed raw meat in a darkened pen. Some *sabongeros* blew cigar smoke at the cocks as part of the toughening-up process. After a few days, the rooster had a sparring session with another rooster. The sparring began with the cocks alternately pecking each other on the neck while the handlers held them firmly. When the birds were flush with anger, they were placed face to face on the ground while their handlers held their tail feathers. The roosters glared fiercely at each other but were not allowed to touch. By this time, the fighting cocks were so angry that they dug deep lines in the ground with their claws as they lunged at each other in frustration. These sparring sessions lasted for about five minutes and took place several times a week until the rooster was so mean that he was constantly in a fighting mood. According to Uncle Onsing, "Wance dey get min, dey stay min" (Once they get mean, they stay mean). Subsequently, the roosters engaged in brief, controlled

matches. After successfully undergoing a number of such skir-
mishes, the cock was ready for the "big fight."

This big fight took place on Sunday afternoons at the *sabong*.
The *sabong* was more than a cockfight; it was like a county fair, Filipino market day, and community celebration all rolled into one.
All Filipinos, not just the *manongs*, looked forward to *sabong*.
Women could supplement family incomes by selling homemade
treats such as Filipino sweet rice (*biko*), sweet potato fritters (*bitsu
bitsu*), and pork or chicken adobo. Mama usually sold *binangkal*, a
deep-fried pastry covered with sesame seeds. *Sabong* Sundays
were also a time for kids to play and young people to check one
another out.

The Jamero camp, the largest and most private Filipino settlement in the area, usually hosted *sabongs*. Privacy was important,
since cockfighting was and still is illegal in California. Papa used
his influence (and monetary incentives) to persuade the local
authorities that activities in the privacy of the Jamero camp should
be outside the purview of the law.

The really big *sabong* took place once a year at riverside property two miles from the camp. It was sponsored by the local Mactan Lodge of the Legionarios del Trabajo, a Filipino Masonic
organization. *Sabongs* at the Jameros' drew a few out-of-towners,
but the annual Mactan event attracted people from throughout
northern and central California, including more food vendors. For
this teenager, it was a time to meet many other young people, particularly girls. Filipinos referred to all *sabongs* as "picnics," a code
word used to provide cover for the event. The word "picnic," not
"cockfight," was prominently displayed on promotional fliers.
Lodge members, strategically placed on Livingston street corners,
gave directions to the isolated river location. Additionally, a guard
at the gate scrutinized all approaching cars while collecting an
entrance fee of $.50 per car. The only identification required for
admission was to be Filipino. Others were turned away, unless they
were accompanied by Filipinos. The lodge also turned to Papa to
help ensure there would be no raids by the authorities. One year,

however, a raid did take place. Most of the *sabongeros* were able to flee with their roosters and avoid arrest—thanks to the time it took the police to get from the gate to the *sabong* site and the confusion of the crowd. Rumor had it that a sore-loser *sabongero* tipped off the authorities. No one ever remembers seeing this person at the *sabong* again.

At the Mactan Lodge *sabong*, the fights were held in a fenced, circular lath structure surrounded by four rows of seats. (Cockfights at the Jamero camp took place in the open.) Entrance to the arena cost an additional $2. The preliminary activities were a show in themselves, also reminiscent of what typically occurs at prizefights. Weigh-ins to assign the cocks to competitive weight divisions were a time for crowing—literally speaking, for the roosters, and figuratively speaking, for their handlers. Such preliminaries often influenced the amount of money wagered by the principals as well as side bets among the crowd. Spectators held their own animated assessments of the combatants' strengths and weaknesses. Total bets often were as high as $2,000 per contest. Several *manongs* took side bets, acknowledging each bet with a simple nod of the head. Their speed and proficiency reminded me of auctioneers, although, unlike auctioneers, they did not speak and had no help from others. They never seemed to make an error when it came time for payoffs, and their decisions were rarely contested. Once, a man publicly questioned a payoff determination, but like the resentful *sabongero* mentioned above, he was never seen again.

The cockfight was literally a fight to the finish. It took place in an inner ring with a referee and two handlers. Each combatant rooster was fitted with a razor-sharp blade tied securely to the spur on its right leg with thread. If the gamecocks' weights were unequal, a small weight attached to the leg of the heavier chicken reduced the advantage. As in earlier practice fights, the handlers prepared their birds by allowing them to peck each other on the head and then to lunge at each other while their handlers kept them apart by holding their tail feathers. Finally, the handlers removed the protective sheaths, exposing the deadly sharp blades, and carefully placed the combatants on the ground. The roosters leaped, simultaneously thrusting their lethal legs at each other. The fight was usually over in a few minutes, with one rooster lying dead in its own blood and the wounded survivor literally crowing in triumph. As long as each cock attempted to peck the other, the fight continued, regardless of the seriousness of the injuries. If a rooster failed to peck its opponent, the referee declared the opponent the winner. If neither rooster pecked, the fight was a draw. It was also ruled a draw if the combatants were still fighting after an hour.

Clearly, the *manongs* retained their strong passion for the Philippine national pastime of *sabong*. They also brought their love of boxing from their homeland. The *manongs* closely watched the careers of Filipino fighters featured in bouts on the U.S. mainland and in Hawaii. In the 1930s, a Filipino, Ceferino Garcia, reigned as world middleweight champion. Later, other boxers from the Philippines such as Speedy Dado, Little Dado, Small Montana, and Clever Censio won recognition as world-ranked lightweights, bantamweights, and featherweights. Crowd-pleasing fighters like Seattle's Sammy Santos had a faithful West Coast following. In the fifties, Filipino champions such as Bernard and Max Docusen from New Orleans, Dado Marino and Johnny Efhan from Hawaii, and Flash Elorde from the Philippines would continue the boxing legacy. For the *manongs*, boxing was another welcome respite from the drudgery of farm labor and the loneliness of single life.

The boxing arena closest to Livingston was the Stockton Civic Auditorium, fifty miles north up Highway 99. Bouts involving Filipino fighters drew big crowds, especially when the opponent happened to be Mexican. These fights were sure sellouts. Boxing promoters booked innumerable fights between Filipinos and Mexicans to take advantage of the nationalistic fervor that such bouts engendered. Filipinos from the Jamero camp piled into their cars and headed to all the Stockton matches featuring their compatriots. When I became a teenager, I was included in these excursions. The trip to Stockton was always a celebration. We ate Chinese food and visited with other *pinoys* in El Dorado Street's Little Manila before going to the Civic Auditorium just a few blocks away. The boxing card featured three or four preliminary fights that usually included lesser-known Filipino fighters. Vocal support for the fighters was loud, boisterous, and, despite the nationalistic partisanship exhibited by both sides, usually good-natured.

Boxing matchmakers scheduled bouts involving Filipinos in Stockton during the asparagus harvest in order to attract as many Filipinos as possible. El Dorado Street was the closest thing to the Philippines I could imagine. It was crowded mostly with Filipino farmworkers eager to meet up with longtime *kababayans* and admire the *dalagas*, who were invariably chaperoned by their parents. Fourth of July in Stockton was the busiest day of the year for Filipinos. In addition to celebrating the end of asparagus season, Filipino workers were also attracted to the town's annual Independence Day parade, which included a number of Filipino floats and marching bands.

The Jamero boys usually accompanied Papa to Stockton on the Fourth of July since he also recruited workers on this day. Stockton was an exciting place in the 1930s and 1940s. Our uncles were generous with their recently earned asparagus money and eager to treat us to Chinese food at the Gan Chy restaurant or take us to a movie at the Star or Lincoln Theater, both fleapits. We never ventured to theaters on Main Street, since Filipinos were not allowed in that part of town at the time. The Fourth of July was also a time when I met other young *pinoys* and *pinays*, mostly from the Stockton area. They seemed so much more sophisticated in dress and in their knowledge of music and cultural fads. This awkward farm boy with the dusty shoes often felt intimidated.

Filipinos adopted American professional wrestling with almost the same passion. They followed Filipino champion Pantaleon Manlapig, who was then in his prime. His matches drew almost as many people as those of more widely known Filipino boxers. Professional wrestling even then was more of an exhibition than a contest. Filipinos knew the outcome of the matches was predetermined but did not let reality dampen their enthusiasm. *Manongs* from the

Jamero camp went to weekly wrestling matches at the Merced County Fairground Pavilion, only fifteen miles away from Livingston. Since Merced was close, it was not necessary for us to stop along the way for dinner as we did on our trips to Stockton. However, the *manongs* often made a mysterious stop on the way home. The Jamero boys were instructed to stay in the car while the men entered a darkened house. We would later learn that the mysterious stop was in Merced's red-light district on Thirteenth Street.

When I was younger, Mama counseled me on the dangers of prostitution and gambling. Regardless, I knew that she looked the other way when it came to gambling, a regular pastime among the *manongs* at the camp, as well as visits to prostitutes. I had already reached my own conclusions about the twin sins but did not share them with Mama. Undoubtedly influenced by the men, I considered prostitution and gambling to be necessary outlets for the *manongs*. I knew that some men lost their life savings at the gambling tables or were fleeced by the women, particularly in cities such as Stockton and San Francisco. Most *manongs* from the Jamero camp, however, exercised moderation. Rarely were there arguments over money or women. By the time I was a teenager, Mama was more accepting of gambling and prostitution and no longer railed about the twin sins to her children. I never knew what changed her mind, but I suspect it was because she learned what Papa already knew—these activities were a source of additional income for the family. It also probably helped that Mama had recently experienced the pleasures of gambling in Reno and Lake Tahoe, Nevada.

Growing up in a Filipino farm-labor camp was a mixed blessing for me. On the one hand, I could not have had a better orientation to Filipino culture and life in the Philippines. I had a better appreciation of the harsh realities that my parents and the *manongs* faced in a sometimes unfriendly America. On the other hand, as I became older, I grew increasingly conflicted by my unusual family lifestyle. None of my classmates lived with as many single men or had as many uncles. Moreover, growing up in a camp setting was far different from the all-American nuclear family experience of my contemporaries. It helped that some of my closest friends came from immigrant families in which English was also not the language of choice. However, it would be many years before I felt secure in my ethnic identity and my years as a campo boy.

The Jamero clan grew by two shortly after our move to Livingston, with the births of Silverio (Titi) in 1945 and Joseph in 1946. We were now a family of eight children. Considering the large span of years between them and their older siblings, Luna, Titi, and Joe were like a second family. Rarely did their misbehavior result in a spanking. This may have been because Papa and Mama were in their forties and had mellowed with age, or it may have been because of Papa's newly enlightened view of the value of spanking. In our early years, Papa did not hesitate to spank his five older children, particularly me. At the time, I resented being singled out for spanking, especially when I was not always responsible for the alleged transgressions. Years later, I learned that Papa was simply following traditional practice in his hometown in the Philippines, where the eldest son was automatically sought out for punishment. The eldest son was supposed to be a model for his siblings and was punished when he was not; the other children were considered too young to know better.

Spanking had always been a sore point with my parents. Mama preferred to pinch and/or preach to get her point across to us. Their differences over the appropriate punishment continued until one day when George was about eight years old. Papa started to take out his belt to punish George, and Herb, Junior, and I got between them. It was an emotional confrontation and the first time we openly challenged Papa's authority. That day marked the end of corporal punishment in the Jamero family.

Silverio is named after Uncle Silverio, Mama's older brother. I do not recall how he got the nickname of Titi, but I believe it was a term of endearment Mama used when he was an infant. Papa and Mama thought that Titi would be their last child. Consistent with the Filipino kinship tradition, they previously had chosen some of their closest friends as *compadres* (godfathers) and *comadres* (godmothers), or *ninong* and *ninang*, for their children. In Filipino culture, the family is not limited to those who are directly descended from parents and their siblings. Rather, the extended family complex also includes godparents. Godparents are responsible for ensuring a better life for their godchildren by assisting with such necessities as education and jobs and often strengthen the family's circle of influence. A long list remained when it came time to choose Titi's godparents. Consequently, he ended up with twelve godparents, compared to the lone pair of godparents for each of the other Jamero children.

The godparent system is deeply ingrained in Filipino culture and dates back to before Spanish colonial days. When I was growing up, it was not unusual for parents of large families to give one of their children to childless relatives or close friends who would bring up that child as their own. The parents' contemporaries generally knew about the arrangement, but the child was never told and grew up believing that these guardians were his or her biological parents. Consequently, children inevitably heard the real story from outside sources, often with emotionally traumatic results. If this practice is still followed today, I hope the parents are more honest with the children so that there is less chance of emotional damage.

I was responsible for naming Joe. When Mama was expecting, I suggested that she give the baby an "American" name. What I thought but did not verbalize was that there were enough unusual-sounding names among the Jamero children. Mama was noncommittal. However, when she came home from the hospital with Joseph Jamero, I knew she had listened, although she insisted that she simply wanted to give the baby a biblical name.

The years in Livingston were kind to the Jamero family. Papa's farm-labor business prospered, he supervised the planting of twenty acres of Thompson seedless grapes, the children all did well in school, and Mama's *sari sari* store seemed to reenergize her. Mama became more involved in her community. She joined the Livingston Chamber of Commerce, organized a Cub Scout troop, was an active member of the Parent Teachers Association, and founded the Livingston-based Leonora Rivera Women's Lodge of the Legionarios del Trabajo. She also began a Filipino community Christmas celebration.

In honor of her many years of civic contributions, Mama was chosen Grand Marshal of the annual Livingston Day Parade in 1969. Among the parade watchers were her children, grandchildren, Papa, and a proud Filipino community. She may have appeared small as she waved to the crowd from the large convertible, but to us, no one in the world was taller.

*Papa with Mama and Uncle Silverio, newly arrived in the United States, September 1929.*

*Mama and Papa's wedding picture, November 29, 1929.*

*Papa, Hawaii, circa 1925.*

*Peter Jamero, three years old, 1933.*

Meeting of the Sons of Garcia-Hernandez of the U.S.A., a mutual assistance organization. Papa is in the third row, wearing the jaunty cap. In the second row (left to right) are Jean and Helen Galanida, sitting on the laps of their parents, Uncle Usting and Aunt Emma; and Jimmy Galanida, who is next to Uncle Canuto Galindez. Uncle Doloy Pagaran is at the left end of the front row; Uncle Onsing Alaan is kneeling at the right. Peter Jamero is kneeling in front. Salinas, California, December 25, 1939.

*The Jameros at Maeda's place. (Left to right) Herb, Pula, Peter holding George, and Junior. Livingston, California, 1939.*

*The Jameros. (Left to right) Junior, Herb, Pula, Mama, George, and Peter. Livingston, California, circa early 1940s.*

The "campo" that housed the eight-person Jamero family and more than one hundred Filipino farmworkers. The family house is at the bottom left corner, and workers were housed in the three-level converted barn and the buildings flanking it. Livingston, California, circa 1940s.

The sabong (cockfight), the Manong Generation's favorite weekend pastime, is legal in the Philippines but illegal in the United States. Courtesy of Herb Jamero.

*Filipino workers pose in the peat dirt of an asparagus field, in Stockton, California, circa 1930s. Uncle Onsing Alaan (front row, far left) holds an asparagus bunch. In a few weeks, many in this crew would return to the Jamero camp in Livingston to harvest peach, grape, and almond orchards. From* Filipinos: Forgotten Asian Americans; *courtesy of Fred Cordova.*

High school pals Bob O'Dell (far left) and Clyde
Collard (third from left), tennis coach and favorite
teacher George Smith, with Bert Stinson, April 1948.

Graduation day, June 10, 1948,
just ten days before Jamero
enlisted in the U.S. Navy

*On a weekend pass after boot camp, with (left to right) Bob O'Dell,
Joe Lema, Bob Bettencourt, Peter Jamero, and Tony Amarant.
Livingston, California, September 1948.*

*Among the rubble of war-torn Inchon, Korea, 1951.*

*Peter Jamero, Yeoman, Second Class. San Diego,*
*California, 1951.*

First Jamero family portrait. Back row (left to right): George, Herb, Pula, Junior, and Peter; front row: Luna, Joe, and Titi, with Papa and Mama. Livingston, California, December 1951.

*Terri and Peter Jamero. Livingston, California,*
*January 2, 1954.*

*Peter Jamero receiving his BA degree from San Jose State College, with Mama, Karen, and Pula. San Jose, California, September 2, 1955.*

*Peter and Terri Jamero with Peter Jr., Cheryl, and Karen in front of Veterans Housing unit. Los Angeles, June 5, 1957.*

*Peter Jamero on the job as an adoption worker, with assigned Sacramento County car, September 1957.*

*Peter Jamero, chief of the Division of Special
Services, with staff member Sara Cory.
Courtesy of* Sacramento Union,
*August 19, 1962.*

*Jamero family at the San Francisco International Airport en route to Washington, D.C., August 1966. Left to right: Cheryl, Jeanine, Julie, Jackie, Terri, Peter, and Karen.*

*High school classmate Pat Suzuki (second from right, top row), who starred on Broadway in* Flower Drum Song, *visiting the Jamero family in Falls Church, Virginia, 1967.*

# II

## LEARNING ABOUT
## THE REAL WORLD

### 1944–1957

IT WAS MY GOOD FORTUNE TO HAVE GROWN UP in the small town of Livingston (pop. 2,000), located virtually at the geographic center of California, along busy Highway 99 and the route of the Southern Pacific Railroad. Not only did its small size accommodate my ever increasing curiosity about the outside world, but its ethnic diversity provided the opportunity to learn about other cultures. Many of its original inhabitants were descendants of immigrants from the British Isles, France, Germany, Italy, Mexico, and Spain, who arrived in the wake of the California Gold Rush of 1849. Livingston subsequently attracted Armenians, Assyrians, and Greeks, who found that the familiar crops of their native lands, such as grapes and figs, thrived in the area's rich soil. Portuguese brought their considerable skills as dairymen to the area. Japanese immigrants established the Yamato Colony southeast of town. East Indian, Filipino, and Mexican farmworkers were recruited to work the vast orchards and fields. About the time that our family settled in Livingston, large numbers of refugees from Dust Bowl states came to the area seeking work.

Livingston valued diversity. It was more welcoming to persons of color than were other communities. In the early 1970s, historian Anne Loftis interviewed a number of Livingston residents to get material for her book *California: Where the Twain Did Meet*, primarily because of the town's reputation as a community that was open to many different peoples.

I found that I could relate well to the children of these settlers, particularly those whose parents were recent immigrants. Some would become my closest friends, particularly during my high school years. My friends also became a deep source of inspiration for my interest in other cultures—an interest that profoundly influenced the choices I would make in my professional, community, and political life.

These years of becoming educated about the real world, attending high school and college and serving in the military, were not limited to the formal instruction I received in these institutions. I learned about other aspects of life, some of which were disquieting. As a high school student, I was a victim of stereotyping and racial bias. I first experienced overt racism as practiced in the segregated Deep South and in the U.S. Navy, and housing and employment were unfairly denied me during my college years. I learned of the futility of war and found that the real victims of the Korean War were the thousands of orphaned children. At the same time, I began to develop more maturity in handling the ups and downs of life. The fun-loving youngster of high school was replaced by the serious college and graduate-school student. Events on the national and international stage began to attract my interest.

In high school, I socialized less and less with my old Filipino friends, largely because most had dropped out to help support their families. By my navy years, however, I found myself increasingly drawn back to the interests and issues of my Bridge Generation contemporaries. As I met other Bridge Generation Filipino Americans during my travels, whether in the Central Valley or in cities like San Francisco or in the far reaches of Seattle, I learned that we have much in common. We have the same attitudes toward our experiences as Filipino Americans; our dreams and aspirations are remarkably similar. The camaraderie I felt for other Bridge Generation Filipinos would turn out to be a consistent motivating force for the rest of my life. ❦

## 5 High School Years

I LOOKED FORWARD TO THE BEGINNING OF EACH school year with much anticipation since it meant I no longer had to labor in the hot fields picking peaches, apricots, and grapes. As in most Central Valley school districts at the time, Livingston schools opened their doors in late September, so that youngsters could spend more time helping with the crops. Despite this accommodation, some of my classmates still missed the start of the school year because their parents needed them to work in the fields. Their late start inevitably interfered with their educational growth. The Jamero boys were more fortunate. Although we worked alongside the men every summer from the time we were thirteen, Mama insisted that nothing get in the way of school. So every September, even if it was peak harvest time, we took off our work clothes, put on our "good" clothes, and went off to school.

I will never forget my first day of high school, September 27, 1944. After three months of farm labor, I looked forward to getting together again with my old classmates. In past years, I spent the first day of school listening to some of my more economically fortunate classmates talk about what they had done for summer vacation. They spoke of traveling to faraway places like San Francisco or to the beach in Santa Cruz. Travel was not part of my summer vacation, and I was not particularly eager to talk about my farmworker jobs. When asked what I had done, I usually told a white lie, such as saying I'd visited relatives in Stockton. Now, I expected that my classmates would bore us again with stories of their travels. However, my very first day of high school had nothing to do with vacation show-and-tell; instead, we faced the school's traditional Freshmen Initiation Day. On this day, freshmen had to put up with the indignity of being painted with lipstick by upperclassmen and keeping the lipstick on for the full day. We also had to run impromptu student gauntlets in the narrow hallways. One of my new classmates was "pantsed" (had his trousers removed) because he refused to participate. But most of the rituals were conducted in the spirit of fun, and freshmen accepted the hazing accordingly. Freshmen Initiation Day may have caused me some anxiety on my first day of high school, but at least I did not have to tell another white lie about summer vacation.

Our freshman class numbered 124 students, a new record for Livingston High School. Consistent with the times, most of my classmates lived in the country rather than in town. The class was 83 percent white, with 11 students of Mexican background, 2 blacks, and 3 Filipino Americans. The other Filipinos were family friends Dick Supat and Vincent Andam. This would be their only year of high school, since their family situations demanded that they go to work as early as possible. There should have been a sizable number of children of Japanese ancestry in the class, which would have made Japanese Americans the largest ethnic minority, but these American-born U.S. citizens were still being held at relocation camps (America's euphemism for "concentration camps") in the deserts of Arizona, Colorado, and Utah and in the isolated wetlands of northern California. Most of my new classmates were unsophisticated about my Filipino ancestry. After trying without success to answer their inevitable questions about the location of the Philippines, I finally said, "The Philippines is where my ancestors killed Magellan. He didn't sail around the world; his crew did."

The freshman class also included twelve students of the Mennonite faith. Similar in ethnic background and religion to the better-known Amish, Mennonites had migrated to Livingston and Winton from Pennsylvania. Girls wore braids and dressed in traditional, plain frocks. Mennonite boys grew beards. They were well-mannered and friendly but generally socialized only with other Mennonites. Their faith did not permit them to participate in extracurricular school or community activities or go to movies. Since school attendance was mandatory only up to the age of sixteen, almost all our Mennonite classmates dropped out of school by the end of our sophomore year to assume greater responsibilities in their families, farms, and church.

Everything appeared big to me in high school. The boys all seemed like giants. I had already reached what would be my full growth of just under five feet two inches and barely weighed one hundred pounds. There were also more students at the high school, approximately four hundred students. Livingston High School drew students from nearby feeder schools in Arena, Atwater, Ballico, Cortez, Cressey, Delhi, Fruitland, Whitmer, and Winton. While I knew some of the upperclassmen at Livingston High who had gone to Livingston Elementary School and the forty-six classmates graduating with me from the eighth grade, most of the four hundred students were completely new to me. No longer was I the confident "big man on campus" of my elementary school days. I was now just another incoming freshman who felt dwarfed physically and emotionally in his new academic surroundings.

Despite my initial feelings, the larger new high school and the physical size of its students did not continue to intimidate this little freshman. During my elementary school days, I found that I was academically competitive. I soon learned that my scholastic achievement carried over to the high school classroom; as far as grades were concerned, I was as good as the big boys and girls. I also threw myself into extracurricular activities, such as Freshman Reception and Sophomore Return. I not only attended these social functions but took on significant committee assignments as well. But good grades and high-profile school participation alone were not the only reasons I attracted attention. I was already unique. I stood out because of my short stature, because I was one of only three Filipino students in the school, and because I was also an incurable show-off. I cracked corny jokes, liked to tease, and developed a contagious cackle of a laugh. Most important, other students seemed to like me.

I soon found myself catapulted to the position of president of our class. At the time, I believed I was elected simply because I was popular. But as I look back at that election now, I believe I had actually stumbled upon a campaign strategy that would prove useful in my years of political involvement. First, I made sure I held on to a strong, built-in voting base, in this case, those students, more than a third of the freshman class, who had been in my eighth-grade graduating class. Then, I courted a small number of students from each of the other voting segments, who came from other communities. It worked—I won the election easily.

In the years preceding high school, I developed a strong interest in baseball and football at the national level and considered myself a sports fan. During the 1944–45 school year, the New York Yankees were a championship dynasty, and Notre Dame had already enjoyed several undefeated years. Livingston High School's sports programs were also doing well. The Wolves football team lost only one game during my first year, twice beating the big-city, big bad Bears from Merced High School. In basketball, the Wolves were league champions as well as champions of the postseason Gustine Tournament. I went to every game I could and was among the most faithful of Wolves fans.

Because I was smaller than other students and already had reached my full height, my participation in high school sports was largely limited to being a spectator. However, I did make the C basketball team as a freshman; this team, the lowest level of competition, usually included the smallest and least athletically gifted boys. It became evident in my second year that my small size would keep me on the C team for the rest of my high school career. I initially tried out for basketball in the hope of earning an athletic sweater but soon found out that these were awarded only to varsity, or A team, players. There seemed to be no way I could ever earn a coveted Block L school sweater.

Mama always reminded me, "Where there is a will, there is a way." The varsity football team had a manager who earned a Block L, albeit one with a small "Mgr." printed on the letter. "Manager" was a fancy name for the boy who carried the water bucket to sweating football players during time-outs. The manager also performed other menial tasks in the locker room, such as handing out towels, being a gofer, and holding players' valuables. In my freshman year, I became manager of the varsity football team and later performed manager's duties for the varsity basketball team as well. By my senior year, I would earn enough letters to qualify for a purple and gold Block L sweater and a school sweater with three stripes. Becoming manager and possessing a Block L helped me become the littlest "big man on campus."

When summer vacation came around, I was prepared to go back to my usual summertime job as a farm laborer. As it turned out, I did not have to work in the hot fields after all. I spent the summer of 1945 in Washington, D.C., thanks to Mama's brother, Silverio. Uncle Silverio had lived in Washington from the time he and Mama immigrated to the United States in 1929. Through the years, Mama rarely heard from him. But a few days after my freshman year ended, Uncle Silverio suddenly arrived on our doorstep. He was now working as a teletype operator for the War Department by day and as a taxicab driver by night. He shared many stories and pictures showing the excitement of wartime Washington, D.C. He said he was able to spend only a few days with us but offered to pay the train fare for one of the Jamero kids to come and spend the summer with him and his family. As the eldest and the only teenager at the time, I was the obvious choice to accompany Uncle Silverio. I gathered the few good school clothes that still fit my maturing adolescent body and packed them into a small battered suitcase.

The train trip would take six days and five nights. Uncle Silverio and I boarded the Southern Pacific train at the Turlock station, ten miles north of Livingston. Since we were in the midst of World War II, men and women from every branch of the armed forces filled the train. At each stop, USO hostesses greeted all those in uniform with complimentary hot coffee, hot food, fruit, and dessert. I was envious of the greater eating opportunities for the military. Civilians riding coach, like Uncle Silverio and me, who could not afford the expensive dining car, were limited to purchasing bland cold sandwiches. As an impressionable fourteen-year-old, I thought sailors were the most glamorous. They all seemed so cocky and to be constantly surrounded by pretty girls.

Riding coach class on the train meant we had to sleep sitting up in our seats. During wartime, the trains were invariably filled to capacity. Only on rare occasions could I find an empty double seat where I could lie down. These were also the days before air-conditioning. Windows stayed open to keep cool, and black soot permeated the air. This was particularly annoying to sailors who had made the mistake of wearing their tropical white uniforms, which quickly turned a dingy gray.

When we reached Sacramento and veered eastward, the train line changed from Southern Pacific to Union Pacific. I was a country boy who had never been outside of California. The sights and sounds of the different towns and the ever changing terrain along the train route fascinated me. I had never seen mountains as big as the Sierra Nevadas and the Rockies or lakes as large as the Great Salt Lake. We were crossing the Great Salt Lake at dawn when I saw a lone coyote roaming the dry salt beds. Seeing the familiar coyote reminded me of Livingston and made me homesick.

Traveling to Chicago by train was an adventure in itself. Never had I seen as many people in one place as I did at the Chicago train stations. At the western terminal was Union Station, where all locomotives rolled onto a turnaround for the return trip west. There, passengers boarded Parmelee buses that took them to Grand Central Station and continued their trips east. Uncle Silverio warned me to remember which ticket I would need for which bus. He then said, "Peter, you have to memorize the changes backward. When you go home in a few months, you'll be making the trip back to California by yourself." This was the first time I realized I would be traveling back alone. Terrified at the possibility that I might get lost in Chicago, I concentrated long and hard on memorizing the complicated return route.

Uncle lived in an apartment at 2109 Eighteenth Street NW. The apartment was in a middle-class neighborhood in transition from being whites only to being populated by a mix of ethnic groups, including Filipinos. The nearest black neighborhood in the segregated Washington of 1945 was ten blocks away. Uncle's apartment was on the first floor of a four-story apartment building, in a neighborhood of similar apartment buildings, close to shopping, buses, and trolley cars.

Uncle Silverio had been married to the much taller Aunt Lucy for only a few years. Aunt Lucy was a prim and proper white woman who spoke with a strong Southern accent. She grew up in Somerset, Virginia, a Deep South community near the former Confederate capital of Richmond. She was very prejudiced against blacks and never hesitated to rail about real or imagined problems she believed they caused. I can still hear Aunt Lucy's Southern drawl, warning me every time I stepped out of the apartment, "Petuh, you be careful of those *nigras*." I often wondered how someone with such deep-seated prejudices ended up marrying a person of color such as Uncle Silverio. She exhibited none of these biases toward Uncle, however, and seemed to be comfortable in their marriage. She also accepted me into her family without hesitation.

Aunt Lucy had a son from a previous marriage, Kenneth Wilson, who was my age. Thank goodness for Kenneth. With his two jobs, Uncle was gone most of the time, and Aunt Lucy had assorted minor ailments and could not show me around Washington, D.C. But Kenneth was always eager to do things. He knew his way around the city, particularly which buses and trolleys would take us to our various destinations. Kenneth was my personal tour guide and turned out to be a perfect companion during that summer of 1945. We took in major tourist attractions such as the Washington Monument, the Lincoln Memorial, the Jefferson Memorial, the Smithsonian Institution, the Capitol, and the National Zoo. We also were regulars at the downtown movies, which usually featured live vaudeville stage shows in addition to first-run films.

I spent much of my time watching baseball games at Griffith Stadium, the home park of the Washington Senators. The Senators were enjoying one of their rare successful seasons, thanks to the pitching quartet of Mickey Haefner, Dutch Leonard, John Niggling, and Roger Wolf. Another of the team's pitchers, Alex Carrasquel, happened to live in our apartment building. I was eager to talk to him about baseball, but Carrasquel, a native of Venezuela, was not fluent in English. Uncle Silverio was an avid Senators fan. He knew the team batting averages and the players. His next-favorite team was my favorite, the New York Yankees. Occasionally, Uncle took Aunt Lucy, Kenneth, and me to weekend Senators games. Given Aunt Lucy's racial prejudice, I was surprised that Uncle always bought pavilion seats, which were occupied mostly by blacks, instead of seats in the grandstand, which was off limits to blacks but open to Filipinos. Segregation was the practice in southern baseball cities, including Washington, D.C., and Aunt Lucy and Kenneth were the only whites in the pavilion. However, she never complained.

Wartime Washington, D.C., was exciting. There was always something happening, with the comings and goings of many VIPs. I saw President Harry S. Truman at a ballgame and General Jonathan Wainwright at a parade in his honor shortly after he was liberated from a Japanese prison camp. Uncle Silverio introduced me to Philippine journalist and hero Carlos Romulo at the Philippine Embassy. Romulo is shown in a famous photograph wading ashore alongside General Douglas MacArthur at Leyte. In a few years, Romulo would become secretary-general of the United Nations. On July 19, Uncle showed me off to his coworkers at the War Department, commemorating my visit by preparing a teletyped message of the event. I still have the message among other memorabilia from the nation's capital.

Washington's Filipino community was unlike the communities I knew in California. The men all wore slacks or suits to work, rather than the dungarees of Filipino farmworkers on the West Coast. I learned from Uncle that there were three distinct groups in our neighborhood. First were the *pensionados,* young people who had been sent to American colleges by the Philippine government before the outbreak of World War II. After completing college, they were supposed to return to the Philippines and assume important business or government positions. The second group was made up of refugees from the Japanese invasion of the Philippines, mostly government officials and professionals. Many members of these two groups, now exiled, were from *illustrados,* or wealthy *mestizo* families, and hoped to return to the Philippines after the war. In the third group were men from peasant families, like Uncle Silverio, who, inspired by what they had learned from American teachers, came to further their education. Because of discrimination, most of them worked in menial jobs, as domestics, restaurant workers, and cab drivers. Uncle Silverio mingled freely with all three groups, although he seemed to spend most of his free time with fellow Visayans in neighborhood restaurants and clubs.

At the Bohol Club, Uncle introduced me to Bienvenido Santos, who went on to become an award-winning author. Most of the short stories in his book, *Scent of Apples,* were poignant accounts of the different social classes of Filipinos in wartime Washington, D.C., based on his experiences.

My most exciting experience in Washington, D.C., was VJ Day, the spontaneous celebration that followed the Japanese surrender on August 15. Kenneth and I joined the thousands already in the streets. Servicemen walked around in a happy daze, many with liquor and beer bottles in their hands. On the city's main thoroughfare of F Street, just about everyone was kissing, not just on the cheek, but long kisses on the mouth. Even teenage innocents, like Kenneth and me, were kissed by overjoyed women. As pleasantly shocked as I was by the kisses, I should not have been surprised. The ratio of women to men in Washington, D.C., was ten to one. Not only were most of the men away, serving in the military, but the federal government employed a record number of workers in the nation's capital, most of whom were women. The few males who remained were in high demand, regardless of marital status and, sometimes, age. Once, on the way to a Maryland beach, one of Uncle Silverio's female coworkers started to seduce me in the backseat of his cab. Luckily (or perhaps unluckily), the backseat was too crowded for the seduction to go very far.

During that summer, I also was exposed for the first time to overt racial discrimination. On a visit to Aunt Lucy's family home in Somerset, Virginia, I experienced the segregated practices of the Deep South. Water fountains, restaurants, and restrooms had "White Only" and "Colored Only" signs. When Kenneth and I boarded the Virginia bus, I started to go toward the rear, but Kenneth suddenly pulled me back, saying, "Only *nigras* sit back there." The South recognized only two races—white and black. Filipinos and other people of color were white as far as segregation was concerned. I was not white and felt uncomfortable about being a make-believe white person. Fortunately, Aunt Lucy's Southern family readily accepted me. Uncle Silverio had paved the way, since they all seemed to hold him in high regard. I may not have fully understood their beliefs on segregation or their discriminatory practices, but I felt comfortable among those gentle, soft-spoken people of the Deep South.

Just before the end of my summer in Washington, D.C., I spent a week in nearby Baltimore with Uncle Calixto and Aunt Colleen, the same Aunt Colleen who rejected Mama in 1929. They lived in an apartment in an established middle-class neighborhood on North Charles Street, famous for its spick-and-span marble steps. Uncle worked for many years as a domestic servant for former Maryland senator Ovington E. Weller. Beautiful antiques and furniture, which Senator Weller had given Uncle Calixto in appreciation for his long and faithful service, adorned the apartment. I found Uncle Calixto to be an easy-going person with a wonderful sense of humor, almost a direct opposite of his more serious brother, Silverio. Uncle Calixto and Aunt Colleen made sure I was not bored. Not a day went by without some kind of planned activity. We saw the Baltimore Orioles play at Municipal Stadium, went sightseeing, and took in the offerings at Carlins Amusement Park. They also gave me generous amounts of spending money. I enjoyed my week in Baltimore. However, I had the uneasy feeling that Aunt

Colleen was going out of her way to make my visit as pleasant as possible, as if treating me well could somehow make up for her treatment of Mama.

Shortly after my return to Washington, D.C., it was time to go home. To my relief, the return trip to California went smoothly, including the dreaded transfers I was required to make between Chicago's two major train stations. I never knew how much I missed Papa, Mama, and my brothers and sisters until I saw them at the Turlock train station. Although my trip to Washington was the most enjoyable summer I ever experienced, I was relieved and happy to be home.

I had a special reason to look forward to my second year of high school. This time, I had a travelogue of my own to share with my classmates. But after talking about my trip a few times, I grew weary of the topic and turned to other interests.

My sophomore year was perhaps my smoothest year of high school. I was no longer in the lowest grade on campus, and, more important, I now knew most of the kids in school. I continued to get good grades in solid courses, including biology and English, and also earned A's in elective courses such as typing and physical education. I participated in even more school activities and won election as class president for a second straight year. I also became a member of the Rally Committee, a highly visible body responsible for planning, organizing, and conducting rallies and events promoting school spirit.

Speaking of visibility, I was quite a sight at the annual Tacky Day Parade in downtown Livingston. For this event, put on by the high school, students wore their tackiest clothes and decorated cars and floats in the silliest manner imaginable. I rode on the Rally Committee float dressed as a baby, clad only in a makeshift diaper, and threw candy to young spectators. Both participants and parade watchers enjoyed the event, with one exception. My brother George, only seven at the time, told me years later that he denied knowing me when one of his friends asked, "Isn't that your brother?" George's response: "I don't know him. My brother Pete would never do anything so dumb."

I also became more involved in peripheral, sometimes mischievous, activities such as burning a Block L insignia on the lawn of archrival Merced High School. Male students commonly indulged in such pranks as a way of showing their school spirit. There were perhaps twenty-five of us who stealthily went to Merced under the cover of evening. Several boys carried cans of gasoline and hastily poured out the contents in the shape of a giant L. The rest carried matches. Everything went smoothly until we lit the gasoline. The plan called for us to jump over the burning L and then run back to our waiting cars. I was perhaps the slowest runner in the group, and by the time I got there, the L was blazing high. I made it safely amid laughter from the other pranksters.

Ten Japanese American classmates, who had recently returned from their wartime internment, rejoined our class. Most of them— like Hubei Kaji, Lucy Kishi, Nobu Mitobe, and Mary Shoji—were classmates from my earliest school days. I was happy to see my old friends again. Another classmate, Pat Suzuki, later starred in the 1958 Broadway musical *Flower Drum Song*. These Japanese Americans did not speak of their internment or of the gunfire from hostile white Americans that they experienced upon their return. At the outset, most students were guardedly accepting of their Japanese American classmates, but a few were openly hostile. One day, on the football practice field, the star quarterback purposely spiked the team's only Japanese American player. Sadly, those who witnessed the attack simply watched, without comment. Japanese American students chose to keep their feelings to themselves. To their credit, they soon became active in virtually every aspect of school life. By our senior year, they were participating fully in athletics, school plays, student government, and scholastic endeavors.

Toward the end of my sophomore year, I had an experience that would have a profound effect on my life. Our class was in the process of planning academic schedules for our junior and senior years. I had noted on my planning form that I was interested in pursuing a college preparatory curriculum. After reviewing the form and obviously ignoring my record of academic achievement and school involvement, the teacher asked, "Why do you want to enroll in college prep? Your kind belongs in agriculture or machine shop, not college." I was so hurt, on the verge of tears, that all I could do was walk away in shock. I told no one about this incident, not even Mama.

I should not have been surprised by this teacher's attitude. Students in his classes regularly had to sit silently and listen to similar racist comments. Fortunately, other teachers did not have the same attitudes. Some were openly supportive of my aspirations for college. My civics teacher, Mr. Lloyd, wrote prophetically in my yearbook, "You go to Georgetown or at least a State Department job or I'll be sore at you." My English teacher, Mr. Corbett, inspired my interest in Shakespeare, commending me for my reading of Shylock in *The Merchant of Venice*. Perhaps it was not coincidental that I received A's from both of them. This was the exactly the kind of support that sustained me in my educational and career pursuits.

A few days after summer vacation started, I went to Yosemite National Park with the 4-H Club. I joined the club, not because of an interest in agriculture or livestock, but for the opportunity to take out-of-town trips. We went to San Francisco several times and to Fresno. But the biggest incentive was the Merced County 4-H Clubs' annual camping trip to Yosemite National Park. The beauty of Yosemite was everything I had heard it would be. I never imagined a more beautiful and inspiring view of mountains, lakes, and waterfalls. I must admit, however, that I was more interested in the social opportunities offered by the camping trip. I was approaching sixteen and was as hormonally driven as any boy of that age. We were always closely chaperoned by adult 4-H leaders, so there were no improprieties. Mostly, it was nice to be able to talk, joke, and laugh with other kids in a setting that was entirely different from that of school.

During my junior year, I was involved in nearly every school club and organization. Many of my activities involved sports. I continued to work with the Rally Committee and became even more visible at game day rallies. Again, I was the manager for a varsity team—this time, the basketball team—which earned me a third varsity Block L. I was now eligible for a school sweater with three stripes and could not wait to wear it to school. I became treasurer of the brand-new Block L Society, open to all boys who earned a D, C, B, or varsity sports letter. I also announced varsity baseball games at the nearby ballpark.

With my election as student body vice president, I attained the second-highest position in student government. I enjoyed the excitement of the campaign and the competition of the election process. The position brought with it membership in the student council. I quickly found myself immersed in the council's two priorities—writing the school constitution and arranging for a trophy case to house the school's many awards. My election reflected not only my popularity but my steadily growing personal drive, dating back to my grade school days, to pursue leadership positions and take on greater responsibilities.

Of all the classes I took in my junior year, I enjoyed my journalism class the most. I wrote human-interest stories, reported breaking news, and had my own sports column in the *Sandpiper*, the school newspaper. By the second semester, I was editor of the *Sandpiper*. Perhaps more significant, I also became assistant editor of the *Livingstonian*, the high school yearbook, which traditionally meant that I would be the editor the following year.

The next year I selected Bob McDonald, my closest pal and classmate from grammar school days, to be assistant editor of the *Livingstonian*. Bob and I were taking many of the same courses, and we both aspired to acquire a college education. We had much in common but were different in disposition. I was outgoing and gregarious, while Bob was quiet and painfully shy. His nickname, Cado, came from a clumsy movie character of the time. He was the youngest child of a hardworking Scottish family who had a farm a few miles away from the Jamero camp.

I continued my mischief-making ways. One Halloween, I joined other boys in toilet-papering the main street of Livingston and knocking over outhouses in the countryside. During harvest season, we made night raids on berry and melon fields. One night, a farmer, waiting under cover of darkness, fired several rounds from his shotgun at us. We did not raid his farm again. In view of my mischief making, I was lucky I was never caught by the authorities.

For most juniors, the junior prom is the social highlight of the school year. But for this naive and idealistic sixteen-year-old, the prom turned out to be a painful social lowlight instead. I had never asked anyone out before. Like other boys in my grade, I nervously considered prospective dates. I did not believe it would be difficult to find a willing date since I was popular and an academic high-achiever. I was wrong. I was not like the other boys in the junior class after all. I was Filipino and brown, and the mores of the time did not permit interracial dating. Other boys of color had told me about the social taboo of dating a white girl, but until I was repeatedly turned down in my search for a prom date, I stubbornly refused to believe them. I could have asked one of the few Filipinas my age or a Japanese, black, or Mexican girl; however, I felt I should take someone I usually socialized with at school, someone I especially liked. In the end, I chose to stay home rather than be told whom to bring to the prom. This was a painful revelation for me. I looked at my image in the mirror and tried to wash my brown color away, but no matter how hard I scrubbed, the color was still there. The overt racism I had seen in Virginia may have been more blatant, but that same attitude was alive and well in California. Filipinos were just as susceptible to the pain of discrimination.

A serendipitous development helped me get over the hurt. I became a charter member of the Livingston Filipino American Youth Club Dragons. The club was the creation of Frank Padin, a World War II army veteran with ties to other returning veterans in California. The youth club movement began in 1939, when five young Filipino Americans from San Francisco's racially diverse Fillmore District formed a basketball team to play other Bay Area Filipino teams in informal pick-up games. That was the beginning of the Filipino-Mango Athletic Club of San Francisco. World War II temporarily slowed its growth, but thanks to the vision of its charter members and returning veterans such as Julian Calagos, Antonio "Dixon" Campos, Felix Duag, and Joe San Felipe, the Mangos grew into an impressive club that would number forty members by 1947.

In the late 1940s, other youth clubs emerged in Livingston, Salinas, San Jose, Stockton, and Vallejo, organized largely by Filipino American World War II veterans. Clubs representing virtually every Bay Area and Central Valley community with a significant Filipino population soon followed. Youth clubs sprang up in Antioch, Fremont, Isleton, Lodi, Oakland, Pittsburg, Sacramento, and Walnut Grove. The clubs gave Filipino American young people an opportunity to participate in social and recreational activities that were denied them in mainstream America. With the clubs' focus on athletics, young males were able to participate in team sports, which were generally closed to most of them because of their relatively small size. Almost every month, youth club teams participated in basketball, softball, or volleyball tournaments organized and funded by the host club, usually without adult help or sponsorship.

Earlier, the Filipino-Mango Athletic Club had approached its local Filipino association for sponsorship, only to be rebuffed because youth clubs were considered too radical in their interests and activities. Other clubs had similar experiences with Filipino community organizations. But these rejections had unexpected positive results. Club members had to learn to make their clubs financially independent and accountable, and they had to organize themselves more effectively. Once learned, these skills would not be forgotten.

Through the youth clubs, we young Filipino Americans met our peers from other towns and found that we had much in common. We clearly identified as Filipinos and followed most Filipino customs and cultural norms. For example, we ate steamed rice with most of our meals, savored traditional Filipino dishes like adobo, and called our elders "Manong" or "Manang" or "Uncle" and "Auntie," never by their first names alone. At the same time, our language of choice was English, we liked jazz, and we loved hamburgers and hotdogs. We were definitely Americans, but with a difference. We were brown Filipino Americans, with our own identity and peculiarities. We spoke in a tongue no one else understood—G-language, whose structure was inspired by the pig latin that was then in vogue among young Americans. We created the off-beat and adopted it along with the cha-cha as our dances, coming up with our own steps and movements. We called ourselves "Flips." We had our own clubs and athletic tournaments.

We also found that our generation had little or no interest in what was happening in the Philippines. We did not share the Filipino passion for cockfighting. We were not superstitious. We resisted our parents' efforts to get us to join fraternal Filipino organizations such as the Legionarios del Trabajo and Caballeros Dimas Alang. Perhaps most important, we did not buy into the biases of Filipino regionalism. Unlike our parents, we were inclusive. It did not matter that one was of Ilocano, Visayan, or Tagalog background or *mestizo*, Latino, black, Asian, or Caucasian. To be Filipino American, all that mattered was to want to hang around with other Filipino Americans. Our generation also rejected our parents' adherence to Filipino practices of colonialism. At parties, we did not automatically seat white persons at the best tables just because they were white. We did not assume that white people were superior or blindly accept their views. We did not believe that only whites were American. After all, we were Americans, too. Yet we interrelated well with white classmates, even though we knew we were not always welcome to mix with them socially. We also interacted easily with other ethnic minorities.

We found out that we had our own intraethnic biases. We resented the condescending attitudes of some Philippine-born people who were disdainful of our generation's failure to learn Cebuano, Ilocano, or Tagalog or who conversed rudely in their native dialects while in our midst. In cities, open conflicts occasionally broke out between American- and Philippine-born young Filipinos. The youth club athletic tournaments provided a venue in which some of these conflicts could be resolved. Through increased interaction, young Filipinos learned that they had far more in common than they had differences. Soon, teams consisting predominantly of Philippine-born Filipinos were participating regularly in the tournaments.

We did not know it at the time, but this was the beginning of the Bridge Generation. The camaraderie and close bonds we developed as youth club members would continue into adulthood, thus making an indelible contribution to our identification as second-generation Filipino Americans.

Our experiences were not unique. In talking with other ethnic Americans of my generation, I have found that they had similar experiences. They, too, went through a generation gap and created their own subculture. They, too, had their own youth clubs, where they developed life-long bonds and friendships. They, too, participated in mainstream America through their youth club activities.

I did not have as much fun at the 4-H Club camp at Yosemite in the summer of 1947, although I still managed to get into mischief. One night, two small bears woke the camp, noisily rattling garbage cans as they foraged for food. Our 4-H leaders warned us to be wary of bears since they were just waking up from their winter hibernation and were hungry. But the next day, along with several other boys, I carelessly entered a dark cave. We did an abrupt about-face when a gigantic bear emerged from the cave and began to chase us. I do not remember ever running as fast as I did on that day. We learned later that the bear was still a bit drowsy from its hibernation. It probably was too weak to chase us, was not as enormous as we had imagined, and probably was not very dangerous either. You could have fooled me.

During my senior year, I continued to be active on the Rally Committee, where Mr. Smith, one of the newer teachers, was the new adviser. Mr. Smith began teaching at Livingston High School during my junior year and quickly became my favorite teacher. He taught U.S. history with wit and a fascinating Boston brogue that made his lectures about early American history seem much more authentic. He was the first person from New England I had met. Of all my teachers, Mr. Smith was probably the most supportive of my college aspirations. At the end of the year, he wrote "High

Man '48" in my copy of the *Livingstonian*. Oh yes, I managed to get A's in his classes.

Except for my relationship with Mr. Smith, I did not have a particularly happy senior year. Perhaps I was still bitter about the racial discrimination I'd experienced with the junior prom, or maybe it was a natural part of growing up. It may have been my fear of approaching adulthood. Whatever the reason, all I know is that I had changed. I was no longer the happy-go-lucky boy with the funny laugh of previous years. The popular "big man on campus" had turned into an arrogant "big head on campus" in his relationships with students and teachers. While I used to have the reputation of being friendly to all students, I now often ignored underclassmen. I became cliquish and socialized almost exclusively with a handful of boys, such as Bob McDonald and football players Clyde Collard, Joe Lema, and Bob O'Dell.

Clyde Collard was a relative newcomer, having moved to Livingston from Los Angeles in our sophomore year. I was the first classmate he met, since he lived nearby. Clyde had moved around a great deal and until Livingston had never really fit in well at school. But he loved the atmosphere of Livingston High School and quickly immersed himself in school activities. Clyde was a welcome addition to our group. He was fun-loving and intelligent and regaled us country boys with interesting stories of big-city life. Joe Lema lived on a dairy farm only a few miles away from me. He and his brother Johnny rose at five in the morning and milked the cows twice a day. From time to time, I helped them pitch hay but always resisted their invitations to sit down and milk the cows by hand. I related well to Joe, whose Portuguese family had immigrated from the Azores Islands. While he was not as smooth an athlete as his brother Johnny, a star quarterback, Joe had a well-earned reputation in football as a tough competitor who backed down from no one. Girls found his rugged good looks irresistible. Moreover, he liked to have a good time. Bob O'Dell was also renowned for his fun-loving ways. He fit the stereotype of the Irish mischief-maker perfectly, had a contagious cackle, and was an imaginative prankster. Bob went to elementary school with us but moved south to Bakersfield in the seventh grade. He came back in our freshman year at Livingston High School, and we rekindled our friendship, seemingly without skipping a beat.

Although I spent much of my time with this close-knit group, I also engaged in mischief with others. Now, however, the mischief was often malicious and self-destructive. I was sent to the office on numerous occasions for excessive talking, disrupting class, and defying teachers. One day, my antics caused the study hall teacher, Mrs. Hurlbutt, to leave the room in tears after I repeatedly pronounced her last name with a strong accent on the second syllable. On another occasion, after a basketball game, I was one of a number of boys who vomited on the bus after chewing smokeless tobacco.

Perhaps the most serious incident of misconduct was when I led a group that crashed the Freshman Reception. I had crashed the previous year's function as a junior, and the principal, Mr. Cleary, had warned me not to do it again. This time, he suspended me for three days. On my first day at home, I told Mama I was sick, but on the second day, I tearfully admitted to her what had really happened. None of the other students was suspended, and Mama could not understand why I was singled out. While she did not condone my actions, she concluded that the punishment was too severe, given the circumstances and my excellent academic and extracurricular record of the past three years. She went to the high school with me in tow and asked for an immediate meeting with the principal. Mr. Cleary had not expected that an immigrant parent would dare question his decision; neither was he quite prepared for the eloquent argument Mama made on my behalf. He immediately lifted my suspension, and I returned to my classes that afternoon.

Shortly thereafter, Miss Middleton, who taught the publications class, removed me as editor of the *Livingstonian*. Was this a coincidence? I believe the notoriety I received from crashing the Freshman Reception provided a convenient reason for Miss Middleton to rescind her earlier decision elevating me to editor. I had sensed she was uneasy about the promotion, which came only after the class unanimously recommended me for the post. Moreover, I had long sensed she was uncomfortable around people of color. Her failure to give me a clear explanation told me all I needed to know.

This would not be the last time I had differences with Miss Middleton. Traditionally, the last edition of the *Sandpiper* ran a tongue-in-cheek column in which graduating seniors willed something to underclassmen. I chose to will my nickname "Wino" to Joe Lema. Miss Middleton ordered me to remove the item. When she read the final edition and saw that I had defied her order, she gave me an F for the semester. I told her I did not care. I had enough units to graduate.

My change in attitude extended to other areas as well. I chose not to apply to the academically prestigious California Scholastic Federation, although my grades fully qualified me for membership. I lost the election for second-semester student body president, at least in part because students perceived that I had changed. Edith Ann Downey, a classmate since the first grade, would tell me years later that my behavior during senior year worried her greatly, as I had become so unlike the person she had known for twelve years. Milt Manoukian, who went on to become a prominent Reno attorney, wrote in my copy of the *Livingstonian*, "When you regain your senses, you are going to be the only senior to go anywhere." At the time, his message was lost on me.

In March 1948, I joined the California National Guard along with my pals Clyde Collard, Joe Lema, Bob McDonald, and Bob O'Dell. The National Guard offered the opportunity to make a few dollars. More important, it strengthened the plan Bob McDonald and I had made to join the U.S. Navy. I was only seventeen and needed parental permission to enlist. I told Mama I did not feel I was emotionally ready to go to college, as she wished, and she would be wasting her money on me if I did go. I argued that I could save some money while I was in the service. Besides, it was peacetime. After getting me to promise that I would go to college after serving my time in the navy, Mama agreed to give her written permission.

I believe Mama consented because of the change she had seen in me over the past year. I was still bitter about the racist treatment

I had received at school and was increasingly hard to live with. It was also clear to my parents that their firstborn son was not cut out for farmwork. I had neither the interest nor the inclination to spend the rest of my life on the farm. One day, I angrily told Papa, "I'm glad I'm going into the navy so that I'll never have to work in the fields again." In retrospect, I don't believe my anger was really meant for Papa; instead, it reflected my unhappiness over Mama's college plans for me and Papa's disappointment with my disinterest in being part of his grape farm and labor contracting businesses. Under the circumstances, enlisting in the navy was probably my best course of action.

I graduated from high school on June 10, 1948. A week later, I was serving with the U.S. Navy, about to embark on yet another adventure.

# 6 Join the Navy and See the World

A WEEK AFTER HIGH SCHOOL GRADUATION, BOB McDonald and I enlisted in the U.S. Navy for three years. During World War II, we were bombarded with enticing recruitment posters boasting of the legendary adventures of American sailors. We were not disappointed—at least for the first few days.

Our first official day in the navy was June 17, 1948. Bob and I boarded the Greyhound bus in Livingston, bound for San Francisco. Several other recruits from Fresno were already on the bus, and more recruits from the Central Valley and northern California joined us. By the time we got to San Francisco, we all had become bosom buddies, or, in the vernacular of the navy, shipmates. We stayed overnight at the Army-Navy YMCA on the Embarcadero. Early the next morning, we took the ferry to Oakland, where we boarded the train that would take us to San Diego, our eventual destination. So far, our time in the navy had been a great adventure. We'd made new friends and slept and dined at the YMCA. We took our very first boat ride on the ferry from San Francisco to Oakland and were now on the way to another exciting port.

The fun and games stopped as soon as we arrived at the U.S. Naval Training Center in San Diego. This was boot camp, where we were to be trained and oriented—not the right way, not the wrong way, but the "Navy way." We immediately went through the navy's depersonalization process. To begin with, we could no longer use our own names. Instead, we had service numbers, which had to be memorized. Mine was 799-14-52, a number I have never forgotten. Next, brutal barbers shaved off all the hair on our heads, and we were issued ill-fitting uniforms. Most demeaning of all, we could not initiate conversation with anyone who was not a recruit. When addressed by a non-recruit, we had to respond with "Sir." There were rules on the proper way of wearing our white hats and strict times for chow, reveille, and taps. Failure to abide by these rules resulted in demerits and loss of privileges. For punishment, sometimes the entire company had to march on the "grinder"—the navy's term for its asphalt parade grounds—until we dropped. These rules may have been intended to instill discipline in a bunch of raw recruits, but most of us were totally unprepared for the demeaning manner in which we were treated. On the first night in our barracks, as we lay in our sacks, or bunks, homesick and disenchanted recruits muffled sobs and cries for "mom."

Recruits from California were assigned to the first platoon, Company 195, along with recruits from the southwestern and Rocky Mountain states. Almost all the recruits in the second platoon were from the southern states of Florida, Georgia, Louisiana, and Tennessee. Each platoon numbered 60, for a total company complement of 120. Company 195 was more than 90 percent white; the remainder was mostly Hispanic, with one black and a lone Filipino, me. Only a handful had reached the age of twenty-one, and the rest were still teenagers. Some of my new shipmates joined the navy as an alternative to serving time in jail. Our two company commanders were imposing, career chief petty officers who boasted numerous hash marks on their left sleeves. In accordance with boot camp protocol, we referred to them as "Mr. Martin" and "Mr. Kohlmeyer."

The cultural makeup of Company 195 was interesting. On the one hand, most of my new shipmates were poor whites from southern and Dust Bowl states; they were similar in background and customs to the kids in Livingston whose parents had migrated from Arkansas, Missouri, Oklahoma, and Texas during the Great Depression. I felt comfortable with them. It was almost like being back home. On the other hand, it was difficult to understand the Cajun boys from Louisiana who spoke a peculiar mix of English and French. They had French names such as Archambeau, Beauford, Boudreaux, and Dupree. In time, I was able to understand the Cajuns' speech and went on to make friends with a number of them.

The only aspect of my shipmates from the South that made me uncomfortable was their deep racial prejudice against blacks. There was only one black person in Company 195—Charles Ellers, from New Orleans—since President Harry Truman had ended racial segregation in all military units only that year. While I had run into similar attitudes when I visited Virginia in 1945, I was not prepared for the verbal and physical abuse Charles endured almost daily. These acts bothered me, but I was not quite able to confront my Southern shipmates. I tried to relate on a one-to-one basis with Charles, but my efforts had only mixed results. My failure to be more forthright in my feelings about racial discrimination disturbed me, and I hoped I would be able to deal more effectively with it in the future.

Company 195 marched everywhere—to the chow hall, to the dispensary, and to the weekly parade of recruit companies. We spent hours every day marching on the grinder. As the right guide with the first platoon, I marched alone, just behind and to the right of the recruit company commander and immediately ahead of the company's right column. The right guide's function is to maintain a moderate pace so that those who are following can keep step. Otherwise, there would be uneven lines, and those in the rear would have to struggle to keep up. The tallest recruits marched in the first row of the four columns, and Max Evans of Fresno headed the right column just behind me. He was so tall that during the first few weeks, when we were still learning to march as a unit, I often had sore heels from being stepped on by the long-legged Max. The right guide was usually the shortest recruit in the platoon, which qualified me immediately. It also helped that I was already acquainted with marching in ranks because of the months I had spent in the National Guard. Company 195 developed into one of the best marching companies in boot camp, earning several awards at the weekly parade of recruits. I felt proud that I contributed to attaining that record.

I was also proud of my personal performance at boot camp. Considering my short stature, I was not always certain that I could compete with the other recruits, but I surprised myself. I overcame the obstacle course—a physically exhausting event that involved scaling walls, jumping over pools of water, and leaping over barriers—which many recruits were unable to complete. I also was among the first to qualify on the rifle range, thanks to my years of hunting rabbits and birds. The only difference was that I was firing an M1 rather than a .22-caliber rifle. My proudest moment came on the day everyone in Company 195 received four inoculations, two in each arm. I not only didn't faint, as did several recruits, but was among the few to remain standing after the company was immediately ordered to the grinder for an hour-long march under the hot July sun.

After a month of confinement to the base, we were allowed to go on liberty, the navy's term for a twenty-four-hour pass. There we were, 120 spit-and-polish sailors, wearing our dress blues for the first time, and eager to be among civilians again. But reality soon set in. Compared to the old salts we saw in San Diego, we were hardly the "girl in every port" sailors we thought ourselves to be. Our white hats did not quite fit over our shorn heads, and our dress blues were baggy. We were just a bunch of wide-eyed teenage navy recruits in the big city for their very first liberty. Nevertheless, we all had fun eating hot dogs and hamburgers, going to movies, checking out the YMCA on Broadway, strolling through the U.S. Grant Hotel across the street, and ogling the burlesque dancers at the Hollywood Theater. The few company recruits who were over twenty-one sampled the bars on Fifth Avenue, while the rest of us could only peer in from the outside. We were given liberty every weekend throughout the remainder of boot camp as long as we did not break any rules. Sadly, some sailors went AWOL, were sent to the brig, and were either dishonorably discharged or reassigned to other duties.

We graduated from boot camp in nine weeks, three weeks earlier than scheduled. Because of escalating tensions in the Middle East—Israel had just become an independent country in May—we had to make room for the increase in new recruits. We were now full-fledged sailors. Most of us began to look the part, including me. I did not grow taller, but boot camp added twenty muscled pounds to my maturing body.

On one of my liberties, I looked up the Antipordas, a Filipino-Jamaican family I met the year before when they visited Livingston, and was pleased when they immediately invited me to their home. Mrs. Antiporda, whom I called "Auntie Pearl," was especially hospitable. She seemed to sense how homesick I was and wanted me to feel free to visit any time I wished. During the years San Diego served as my home port, the Antiporda home was my home away from home, where I could eat Filipino food and steamed rice after a steady diet of American food. The Antiporda kids—Frank, Lydia, and Linda—introduced me to their circle of friends. Before long, I was involved in the Sampaguita Club (*sampaguita* is a sweet-smelling flower, native to the Philippines), a Filipino American youth club. One of the club members was Jose De Vega, who went on to star as Chino in the original Broadway and movie versions of *West Side Story*.

Through the Antipordas, I met a sailor from the Philippines named Andy Oliva. He was older and definitely an old salt. We took an immediate liking to each other. For reasons not entirely clear to me, Andy took me under his wing, like a protective big brother. He brought me to Saturday night dances at the Filipino American Veterans Association hall. Simply by saying, "He's all right," Andy made sure the regulars at a tough downtown bar accepted me. Andy was a leader among his Filipino contemporaries, and consequently they followed his example and also looked after me. Most of his navy friends were in their late twenties and early thirties. I was grateful to Andy and his shipmates for their camaraderie, mentoring, and protection. It reminded me of high school, where my network of friends consisted largely of athletes who were similarly protective.

Andy was a steward's mate, just like practically every Filipino from the Philippines who joined the U.S. Navy. There were Filipino steward's mates on virtually every ship and base. They were the latest of several generations of sailors from the provinces of Zambales and Cavite, where American naval bases were located. The navy assigned American-born Filipinos according to their individual interests and skills—the same way it handled assignments for other American sailors. However, Filipinos from the Philippines had no choice but to perform menial jobs as steward's mates; otherwise, they could forget about joining the navy. Only Filipinos and blacks were assigned to be steward's mates, who were essentially the personal servants of naval officers. They served the officers' food, shined their shoes, brought them refreshments, and cleaned their living compartments. Even if they were highly educated, had other marketable skills, or served in the navy for twenty years, few Filipinos from the Philippines ever got into another line of work. This discriminatory treatment was just one example of the pervasive racial prejudice I found in the navy. I knew then that there was no way I could ever make the navy my career.

My close association with Andy and other sailors from the Philippines widened my understanding of the culture and people of my ancestral land. My previous contacts with Filipinos had been limited largely to people from the central Visayas, the islands my parents and their *kababayans* called home. Now I was in the company of Filipinos from other parts of the Philippines, mostly Luzon, the nation's largest island. While there was an unmistakable common thread, distinctly Filipino, between these sailors and the familiar Visayan culture, there were also differences. Most obvious, the sailors spoke Tagalog or Ilocano to one another. They were also considerably younger than my parents' Manong Generation. And there were other, subtler differences, particularly in the customs and mores they brought from their home provinces. Nevertheless, I was comfortable in their presence and came to understand their dreams and aspirations, their frustrations and anger, as I had those of the farmworkers in the Jamero camp. In return, I was treated as I had hoped to be treated—like any other Filipino.

I had taken a battery of tests at boot camp to help determine the line of work I would take up in the navy. I scored well in the clerical battery and received orders to report to Yeoman School, at the

Naval Training Center. For the first time since our enlistment, my Livingston pal Bob McDonald and I were no longer together. Bob went his separate way, to Storekeeper School. (I would see Bob only a few times after that. In 1957, at the age of twenty-seven, he died tragically in an automobile accident on a foggy night on Livingston's dangerous stretch of Highway 99.)

At Yeoman School, liberty was extended to forty-eight-hour weekend passes, not quite enough time to go home but certainly enough time to get better acquainted with San Diego and its many attractions, such as the world-famous zoo. During this time, I also rediscovered jazz. By chance, I stopped at a local club and saw the Walter Fuller Band; the band's musical style was similar to that of the nationally known Louis Jordan Jazz Band. On another weekend pass, I saw the Woody Herman Band, playing in its influential bop style, at the Balboa Ballroom.

The twelve weeks of Yeoman School passed quickly. On November 19, 1948, I received a certificate of satisfactory completion, which declared that I was now a Seaman Apprentice, Yeoman. I looked forward to the orders that would take me to my first permanent duty station. I wondered what kind of ship I would be serving on. I knew it would not be a submarine. Submarine duty, considered hazardous duty, entitled sailors to a 50 percent pay bonus. Only volunteers could serve on submarines, and because of the incentive pay, most sailors considered it a highly desirable assignment. My small size was an asset in these compact vessels, and I was asked to volunteer for submarine duty. However, I found the tiny spaces too confined and scary, particularly when the vessel was underwater. I much preferred a destroyer, cruiser, battleship, or aircraft carrier as the navy ship that would let me "ride the waves and see the world."

So instead, I found myself carrying my heavy seabag through the gates of the nearby Amphibious Base in Coronado, just across San Diego Bay. I had orders to report to a unit known as ComPhibPac (Commander, Amphibious Forces, Pacific Fleet). ComPhibPac, under the command of Rear Admiral Rodgers, included all amphibious vessels and bases operating in the Pacific Ocean area. I was assigned to Admiral Rodgers's immediate staff of more than eighty officers and enlisted men and worked as a yeoman in the Operations Office. Despite my initial disappointment, ComPhibPac turned out to be a great assignment. The Operations Office was responsible for deploying and providing instructions to all amphibious vessels on various missions and maneuvers throughout the Pacific. I was among a handful of yeomen doing clerical backup. The office had a large magnetized board with a map of the Pacific Ocean drawn on it, and pins that looked like miniature ships were used to track the locations of ComPhibPac vessels. One of my daily tasks was to move the pins to the ships' latest locations. As I moved the pins around the board, I often fantasized about being on these ships at their exotic ports of call.

Because we worked for a high-ranking admiral, the officers and men with ComPhibPac were required to observe strict standards of dress and naval protocol. Fraternization between officers and men was officially discouraged. However, our interpersonal relations were civil and often quite friendly. I particularly admired Lieutenant Commander Emrich, the second in command in the Operations Office. He was a gruff but likable fifty-year-old career man who had come up through the enlisted ranks. While he always observed protocol, he was unfailingly empathetic in his dealings with the enlisted men.

Although ComPhibPac was located on a base, we were entitled to a 25 percent sea pay bonus. As long as Admiral Rodgers flew his official ComPhibPac banner on any vessel under his command, even though it was anchored in San Diego, his immediate staff was technically on sea duty and automatically eligible for sea pay. I was grateful for the unexpected bonus, since I was sending most of my monthly paycheck to Mama to help pay for Herb's college education. Yet I was rarely low on cash. I was lucky in friendly poker games, a regular pastime of ComPhibPac's enlisted men.

ComPhibPac provided its men with a seventy-two-hour weekend liberty once a month, which meant I was able to visit home regularly. I traveled by bus, a twelve-hour trip, leaving on Friday night and returning Sunday afternoon in order to maximize the time I could spend with family and friends. One weekend, I did not have to take the bus back. Joe Lema and Bob O'Dell decided they would drive me to San Diego and take in Tijuana at the same time. I certainly appreciated this kindness from my old high-school friends. At first, I spent a lot of time with the old gang on my weekend visits. Eventually, however, these visits became less frequent as they got married or left the area. Joe and Bob wed their high school sweethearts, and Clyde Collard went off to college.

There were still many social activities to fill my time when I went home. Athletic tournaments hosted by Filipino youth clubs were in their heyday, and there was usually a basketball, softball, or volleyball tournament going on. The tournaments were a popular place for Filipino young people to meet and attracted scores of nonplayers as well as athletes. In the evening, the tournaments were followed by a dance and a ceremony for awarding individual and team trophies. For me, the dance was an opportunity to see so many beautiful *pinays* and handsome *pinoys* all together in one place. It was a time to socialize, to make new friends, and, for some, to meet future husbands or wives.

Every six months or so, ComPhibPac relocated its headquarters to one of three flagships—the USS *Estes* (AGC-9), the USS *El Dorado* (AGC-11), or the USS *Mt. McKinley* (AGC-12). An AGC (Auxiliary General Communications) was a World War II troop ship that had been converted into a communications ship. I spent most of my naval career aboard this type of vessel. I loved sea duty. There was something about the sea air and the gentle roll of the ships that always seemed to energize me. I ate heartily and slept well despite the uncomfortable four-tier racks we used for beds. My sleeping rack was on the lowest level, easy for a short person like me to get into and out of. The downside was that other sailors had to step on my rack to get to theirs.

My first cruise was on the USS *El Dorado* in October 1949, when we engaged in amphibious war games off Hawaii. We spent the weeklong war games, Operation Miki, bombarding the bombing range on the uninhabited island of Kahoolawe and conducting amphibious landings of LSTs and LCMs, two types of navy landing craft. For me, the best thing about Operation Miki was that it was scheduled around Honolulu's festive Aloha Week.

I spent the following weeks mostly ashore in Honolulu. My wish to visit an exotic port had finally come true. Sam Agpawa, a Filipino tournament acquaintance who played for the San Francisco Mangos, was stationed aboard an aircraft carrier docked at the Pearl Harbor pier next to the *El Dorado*. Sam was nicknamed "Toscani" because his boastful mannerisms made him resemble caricature *manongs* who were partial to the Italian small cigar. His sister lived nearby and knew the community well. Through Sam, I soon became involved in the social life of young Filipinos. We were welcome in the Filipino neighborhoods of Kalihi and Farrington, although the navy had declared these areas off-limits. We attended weekend picnics and played volleyball at Ala Moana Park, ate at Filipino restaurants on Beretania Street, took in the bawdy attractions of Hotel Street, and frequented the *pistas* (fiestas) at adjoining Aala Park. On Saturday nights, we danced in the armory at Fort DeRussy.

One hot and humid afternoon while Sam was off visiting his sister, I ran into a "local boy" pal of Sam's. He suggested that we go to his place and rest before we went to the dance. When we got there, I began to peel off my clothes because of the heat and thought it was strange that Sam's friend immediately left the room. Later, at the dance, I learned why. According to Sam, his friend was a *mahu*, the Hawaiian pidgin term for a homosexual. Sam's friend was not a male at all but a lesbian camouflaged in a loose-fitting Hawaiian shirt. No wonder she left the room.

On June 25, 1950, only five years after World War II ended, the United States was again at war. This time, it was part of a United Nations effort to end the territorial struggle between North Korea and South Korea. The Korean War was unpopular because most Americans did not understand why we were involved. Moreover, it was officially called the "Korean Conflict," which was generally taken to mean that this was simply a skirmish and not at all comparable to World War II. Years later, the bloody and unpopular nature of the war caused many Americans, especially Korean War veterans, to call it "the first Vietnam War." In the beginning, I was inclined to support the war, although I, too, did not fully understand the reasons for our involvement. But as I experienced the true costs of war firsthand, I began to seriously question our country's involvement.

ComPhibPac and the amphibious forces under its command were heavily involved in the Korean War. General Douglas MacArthur, the famed liberator of the Philippines, masterminded the successful amphibious landing at Inchon from our flagship at the time, the USS *Mt. McKinley*. The reality of war disenchanted me. What I experienced was far from the brave patriotism of Hollywood movies. Most of the new officers were World War II reservists who had been recalled to active duty. They did not want to be in Korea and did not care who knew it. Some were ill-trained and totally unfamiliar with the technically advanced armament and equipment aboard navy ships. Once, when we were in enemy waters, a lieutenant, who was supposedly knowledgeable about antiaircraft guns, asked me, a lowly sailor, how to fire the guns. His ignorance frightened me, particularly when I realized our lives depended on the leadership of officers like him. Ashore at Inchon, I witnessed some American soldiers pointing their M1 rifles at a group of small Korean children who had been orphaned by the war and threatening to "kill the little gooks" for allegedly stealing their personal effects.

The incident that disturbed me most during the Korean War, however, concerned the small contingent of U.S. Marines assigned to ComPhibPac. Traditionally, fleetwide commanders like Admiral Rodgers have marines attached to their commands for security reasons and for ceremonial functions. These men were spit-and-polish marines, embodying the highest standards of military service. Immediately after the outbreak of the war, they received orders to report directly to the Korean front but were given no additional training to prepare them for what they would face in battle. Sadly, all were casualties.

Like other young Americans of the time, Bridge Generation

Filipino Americans were heavily affected by the Korean War. Many enlisted in the armed forces. Others were caught by the draft and had their livelihoods or educations interrupted. Like other young Americans, Filipino Americans became war casualties. Libby Bacaylan, from the town of Hilmar, ten miles from Livingston, was killed in action. Raphael "Bee" Raagas from Oakdale, the town of my birth, was wounded and received a Silver Star for valor. My old Livingston schoolmates Dick Supat and Joe Cabrillas also saw action but came home unscathed.

The Korean War did have its light moments. When we first entered the port of Pusan, then encircled by enemy forces, we were greeted by a small band playing "If I Knew You Were Coming, I'd Have Baked a Cake."

My Korean War experience left me disillusioned, not because it did not measure up to the glamour and valor of Hollywood movies, but because of what I consider the futility of war. No one won in Korea. It certainly was not the people or the orphaned children, who are the real victims of war. It certainly was not North Korea or South Korea; they continue to be bitter enemies, divided by the same 38th parallel. It certainly was not the United States—54,000 Americans lost their lives. Subsequent wars in Vietnam, Kosovo, and Iraq have not changed my views. If I needed another reason for my disillusionment, it came soon after I returned home from the service. There, unsympathetic and uninformed people taunted Korean War veterans by saying that we had only been in a "police action," not a real war like World War II.

My three-year enlistment was due to expire on June 16, 1951. However, I spent my scheduled discharge day drowning my sorrows in a dusty enlisted men's beer hall in Korea, thanks to the one-year extension President Truman imposed upon all enlistees. In some ways, though, I suppose I should be thankful, since the additional year gave me the opportunity to visit other exciting ports of call. Besides Korea, I went to places in Japan such as Beppo, Kobe, Sapporo, Sasebo, Tokyo, Yokohama, and Yokosuka as well as to the Aleutian Island of Adak. After my transfer to the heavy cruiser USS

*Baltimore*, I went to Cuba, Panama, and the American ports of Boston, San Francisco, and Seattle. My daydreams about going to many ports of call came true after all.

I was honorably discharged in Boston on April 10, 1952, with the rating of Yeoman, Petty Officer Second Class. It was an early discharge because the USS *Baltimore* was scheduled to be in the midst of a cruise to the Mediterranean Riviera on my original discharge date of June 16. Consequently, the navy decided it would serve no meaningful purpose to transfer me to another duty station for such a short time and offered me two choices: an early discharge or another one-year extension of my enlistment. The extension would have enabled me to go to Europe on the *Baltimore*. And since I had already passed the fleetwide competition for yeoman first class, it also would have given me the time required for promotion to the second-highest rank for enlisted personnel. Moreover, at the end of the extension, I would have accrued five years in the navy, one-fourth the minimum required for retirement. It was tempting. I considered extending for another year—but only for a moment. I remembered I had promised Mama that I would go to college and opted for an early discharge.

A few days before my scheduled discharge, I listened excitedly to alto saxophonist Charlie Parker, the jazz great, at Storyville, a nightclub located in Boston's notorious Scollay Square. During a break, we stood next to each other at adjoining urinals in the club's restroom and spoke about his music. To be more accurate, I spoke about his music. Parker mostly grunted back in acknowledgment.

With my discharge papers held tightly in my hands, I could not wait to get home. Rather than take a long cross-country train ride, I decided to use some of my discharge money and fly. I caught a plane to Oakland and from there hitchhiked to Livingston. I was home again.

# 7  College Days

IT WAS GOOD TO BE A CIVILIAN AGAIN. THE FIRST thing I did was to buy Mama and Papa a pair of red metal rocking chairs for the patio. Now in their early fifties, Papa and Mama had acquired a mutual interest in gardening, and they could admire their handiwork while sitting comfortably in their patio chairs. The rest of my discharge money went to buy a year-old 1951 Chevrolet Bel Air. It was the first car I ever owned. When I was in high school, I was one of the few students with regular access to a vehicle and often drove Papa's 1932 Model A converted pickup. The Bel Air was clearly a major step up.

Thanks to the GI Bill, I enrolled as an incoming freshman at San Jose State College in September 1952, along with Junior, who had just graduated from high school. Like millions of returning World War II and Korean War veterans, I took full advantage of the bill, which provided $80 a month for a full-time student enrolled at an accredited college. The GI Bill virtually assured my going to college. I did not save money during my years in the navy, although I regularly sent money home to Mama to help with Herb's college expenses. Moreover, it is doubtful that Papa and Mama had enough money to send Herb, Junior, and me to college at the same time. I will be forever grateful to the GI Bill for giving me the opportunity to go to college.

For someone who had long planned on going to college, I found myself poorly prepared. It was a good thing Herb was there to help show me the ropes. He was in his junior year at San Jose State, majoring in social work. I did not even know what a major was, let alone what social work was all about, but I also declared myself a social work major since I had no idea what I wanted to do. Besides, I knew I could always change my major later. As it turned out, I enjoyed the course work in my accidental major. The curriculum required classes on social issues, race relations, psychology, and cultural anthropology. All had great appeal for me, undoubtedly because of Mama's example, my experiences with discrimination, and my desire to deal more effectively with social injustices. I stayed with social work, a decision I would never regret.

Herb, Junior, and I lived in a large flat above a grocery store operated by my Ninang "Bali" Todtod in San Jose's Japantown. We shared the flat with three other roommates—Ray Paular and brothers Epiphanio "Fonnie" and Raphael "Bee" Raagas from the Central Valley, whom we met through the Filipino American athletic tournament circuit. We all shared in the upkeep of the flat and in cooking meals—except for Ray. His father operated a restaurant in Stockton, but strangely, Ray never learned how to cook. Therefore, he became our designated dishwasher. As the only roommate without a sibling present, he also was the target of pranks. We "short-sheeted" his bed and often sneaked up on him to scare him when he was studying. Ray was good-natured about the pranks, and this only challenged us to come up with new ones.

Ninang Bali lived in Oakdale at the time of my birth and served as my godmother at my baptism. I had rarely seen her in the intervening years. She was now in her sixties, and while she may have slowed physically, she still put in a full day as proprietress of her mom-and-pop grocery store. Her daughter Pacing lived nearby and was a frequent visitor. She was renowned in the Filipino community for her singing role in the John Wayne movie *They Were Expendable*, which was set in World War II Philippines and had been seen many times by proud Filipinos. I hoped to hear about Pacing's days in Hollywood, but she seemed not to want to speak about that part of her life.

I renewed my acquaintance with our cousins, the Galanidas. They lived in Sunol, about twenty miles from San Jose, in a camp populated by Filipino families who worked in the adjoining strawberry fields. We knew the Galanidas through semiannual meetings of the Garcia-Hernandez Association, a mutual aid organization of former residents of Mama's and Papa's hometown. Aunt Emma, who was of German ancestry, met Uncle Usting in her home state of Montana during the 1930s, when he migrated there from California to work. Fortunately, they were able to wed in Montana, which did not have anti-miscegenation laws prohibiting marriages between Filipinos and white women, as California did. I admired the positive manner in which Aunt Emma handled her mixed marriage and raised their six children. She familiarized herself with Filipino culture and customs and excelled at Filipino cuisine. Aunt Emma and Uncle Usting passed on their culture and culinary skills to their daughters, Jean and Helen. Since Sunol was along the way on our weekend trips to and from Livingston, it became a regular stop for the Jamero boys, as we found it hard to turn down the Galanidas' warm hospitality and delicious cooking.

I found course work at San Jose State to be relatively easy and breezed through the first year with a B average. Surprisingly, I got an A in biology, but I knew I was rusty when I could only get C's in English. That I managed to earn a B average despite my poor study habits was sometimes irritating to my roommates, particularly when I tried to talk them into a game of cards or to go out for noodles at a nearby Chinese restaurant.

My college life was limited to classes. I was a veteran and four years older than most students. I could not relate to student social life and interests that seemed juvenile to me. Moreover, I sensed that most white students did not seem particularly open to socializing with students of color. It was a time when many Americans verbalized beliefs in the melting pot theory and in cultural assimilation but did not necessarily practice what they preached. These were beliefs that I had long disavowed. (I likened American ethnic diversity to Filipino *pinakbet*, a tasty dish in which the various vegetables retain their distinct flavors and textures.) By this time, however, I had become so cynical about lofty-sounding but disingenuous expressions of fairness that I no longer reacted viscerally to the hypocrisy. These were also the benevolent years of the Eisenhower presidency, when the country's many war veterans were more interested in getting on with their education or professions than in concerning themselves with social issues. I was no exception. I tried to mind my own business and did not make waves.

During the summer, I worked at the Levy & Zentner packinghouse. Ruben Ragsac, a neighbor and fellow student, helped me get the job. Ruben operated the nailing machine that secured lids on celery crates as they came off a conveyer belt. My job was to take the nailed crates and place them in another machine for washing. In an attempt to break up the monotony, we traded jobs every hour or so. Compared to other tedious jobs at the packinghouse, our assignments were relatively easy. More important, the jobs paid better.

Ruben and I hit it off from the time we met during our first year of college, perhaps because he was a fun-loving prankster. His antics were often outrageous. One night, as we were leaving after an evening of study at the college library, Ruben suddenly emitted a burst of pent-up intestinal gas loud enough to make everyone in the library sit up and take notice. He then pointed to me and ran out the door, leaving me alone, embarrassed, to endure the snickers and dirty looks of other students.

When I began my second year of college, Ray and Fonnie were no longer at San Jose State, having graduated at midyear. Herb, recently married to his sweetheart from Merced, Jeanne Balanon, suggested that we, his former roommates, also move into the duplex he had just rented. Sharing expenses with the newly married couple made a lot of sense to Bee, Junior, and me since we were all trying to stretch our scarce dollars. We moved into a two-bedroom duplex in southeast San Jose in April, and less than a week later, we faced eviction. Thus began a bizarre series of events that forever changed our lives. The landlord's son-in-law delivered the eviction notice, since the landlord, an immigrant from Portugal, had difficulty with the English language. He told us we had to move because neighbors allegedly were disturbed about the change to their all-white neighborhood. We were given a month to leave the premises.

Junior was the only one at home at the time the eviction notice was delivered. Everyone else was either in class or at work. I was the last to arrive home and found the rest of the group in various stages of despair and anger. When I learned of our eviction, I did not feel a thing for a long moment. I could not believe that our brown skin was so important that it would cause this total disruption to our lives and hopes. We all went through a period of cussing and figurative kicking of walls followed by far longer moments of abject silence. Herb and Jeanne were in tears. Bee, a football star in high school and the most physically imposing member of the household, was also in tears. Junior remembered how saddened and shocked he was to see "Big Bee" break down. A recipient of a Silver Star and a Purple Heart, he had survived bullets and shrapnel in faraway Korea only to find he could not dodge this attack at home.

It was particularly galling that there seemed to be no recourse for us. (Legal protections and civil rights for ethnic minorities would not come for another ten years.) Finally, someone suggested that we compose a letter and send it to local newspapers. Identical letters went to the morning *San Jose Mercury*, the afternoon *San Jose News*, and the *Spartan Daily*, the campus newspaper of San Jose State. Everyone contributed. Bee and I signed the letter, since we believed that a letter from two patriotic Korean War veterans would get sympathetic attention. The following letter went to the newspapers on April 22:

FILIPINO STUDENTS ASKED TO MOVE:
ASK, "IS THIS WHAT WE FOUGHT FOR?"

We are two veterans who are in dire need of some information. We realize that you are a very busy individual and would not ordinarily bore you with mere trivialities. But the problem we are about to relate to you, we feel, is of a large enough scope to warrant your attention. Perhaps you are aware of the existence of this problem but perhaps do not realize that it is so close to you and your fair city. In short we are referring to the problem of racial prejudice. Evidently, we happened to be born with the wrong color of skin. No, we're not black; nor are we white. We're both of Filipino extraction, brown-skinned. As we have already stated, we are ex-GIs, both veterans of the Korean conflict, which our country is presently engaged in. After our discharge from service we enrolled at San Jose State to pursue an education. We both come from the rural valley of the San Joaquin where people evidently judge a person for what he is and not by what his skin color happens to be. This is not the situation in this section of San Jose. Consequently, we heretofore have not encountered such a problem, nor do know how to cope with it.

Earlier this week, we moved to 725 E. Taylor Street together with Mr. and Mrs. Herbert Jamero, a newly married couple, and his brother, who are also Filipino. We rented this home with the idea of having some place of residence while we continued our studies at the college. In addition, Mrs. Jamero is working at the First National Bank. Today, we were informed by our "good American white neighbors" that our presence on their block would not be tolerated. These neighbors did not have the intestinal fortitude to inform us personally of their attitude to persons of another color. Instead, they started a personal boycott against the landlord of our home who in turn was forced to inform us of our neighbors' attitude. We have no ill feelings against the landlord for he took it upon himself to tell us the situation before the neighbors resorted to more drastic action. Actually, we do not have any ill feelings against the neighbors. We just feel sorry for them, but we also are a little puzzled.

How can supposedly educated people reared within the confines of a country that advocates democracy and freedom be of such a hypocritical opinion? Is this what we fought for? What and who were we protecting in the far-off land of Korea? We thought we knew what we were fighting for then, but this incident has left us with some doubt. And what about Herbert Jamero and his brother, who are both 1-A in the draft and subject to call at any moment? Will they be serving a country they are proud of or will they have some misgivings about their role in the fighting? We feel that this discrimination is not only unfair, but also contrary to the ideals and teachings of the country. There was no racial discrimination in the combat we experienced. We did not hesitate to assist a wounded American because he was white, black, brown, yellow or because he happened to be a Jew. All we had to know was that he was an American. It didn't stop there either. Many of the wounded enemy were also treated for their injuries. Why must cooperation among different races be confined only to the field of battle? It should be achieved here at home where it would do the most good. Perhaps our good neighbors should be reminded of the old proverb "Practice what you preach."

Again, we would like to ask the question "What did we fight for?"

PETER M. JAMERO AND RAPHAEL RAAGAS

On April 23, several carloads of San Jose State students staged a demonstration. By today's standards, the demonstration was tame. There was no violence, no obscenities, only crude, handmade signs. Thanks to subsequent stories carried by the *Mercury* and the *News*, a number of community organizations offered support and assistance. At first, I felt vindicated by the expressions of support, but now I consider the community response to have been an ineffective reaction. There was nothing in the way of lasting change. No one in the neighborhood came forward in support or to join in opposition. No official from San Jose State offered assistance. Civil rights organizations such as the National Association for the Advancement of Colored People and Japanese American Citizens League were conspicuous by their absence. Most frustrating was the absence of support from San Jose's well-established Filipino community. After the exhilaration wore off, I soon faced the sad and sober fact that this incident was of significance only to us.

Our experience was similar to that of Bridge Generation World

War II veterans when they returned home. Dixon Campos, the respected charter member of the Filipino-Mango Athletic Club of San Francisco and a decorated veteran, and his new bride, Lisa, were barred from purchasing a house after the salesperson saw that Dixon was a brown person. Thanks to the GI Bill of Rights and their perseverance, Dixon and other returning Bridge Generation veterans were able to level the playing field. I could only hope that our 1953 experience in San Jose would turn out as well.

Following the publicity generated by the demonstration and newspapers, the landlord's account of our eviction underwent a series of bizarre changes. At first, he attributed the eviction to the racial discrimination of neighbors. Subsequently, he told the press that the duplex was too small to accommodate five adults. Later, the landlord reported that the neighborhood objected to the noise we made in the duplex. This was ludicrous. We spent our weeknights studying, and on weekends, most of us went home to help on the farm. Besides, we had been in the duplex for only a few days. How much noise could we have made in such a short time? In another newspaper account, the landlord's wife said that she had no objection to our occupying the duplex. She said her husband wanted us out and conveniently seized on his perception of neighborhood racial intolerance as a way of breaking the rental agreement. In yet another version, the landlord maintained he thought he was only renting to Herb and Jeanne. With the almost daily changes in the landlord's account, it became impossible to determine the reasons for our eviction. And the stark reality was that we did not wish to stay where we were not welcome. A few days later, we voluntarily vacated the duplex.

During my second year at San Jose State, I grew more comfortable in handling my course work. I took many more classes than the minimum required for my social work major. I also began to form my own likes and dislikes when it came to my professors. Dr. Alexander Vucinich, who taught sociology and anthropology, was the one I liked the most. He emigrated from his native Yugoslavia after World War II and spoke English with a decided accent. Perhaps because he was still uncomfortable with English, he relied heavily on well-organized outlines. Dr. Vucinich's tests were based exclusively on his lectures. If one took good notes, went to all of his classes, and studied, one would very likely get a good grade. Over the next few years, I took every class Dr. Vucinich taught and usually got an A. Dr. Vucinich was one of the few professors who took an interest in me. During the summer quarter of 1955, he urged me to go to graduate school and agreed to monitor a three-unit correspondence course I needed for graduation. After this, I went on to attend the University of California, Los Angeles. I will forever be indebted to people such as Dr. Vucinich and my high school teacher Mr. Smith for recognizing my potential and believing in me. Americans often talk about pulling ourselves up by our own bootstraps, but I learned from Dr. Vucinich and Mr. Smith that we also need help along the way.

About this time, I began seeing a girl who would be the love of my life—Teresa Elizabeth Romero. I first met Terri soon after my discharge from the navy. She and several of her siblings had accompanied their mother, Esperanza Cabrillos, to visit the Jamero family. Their visit was prompted by her mother's desire that Terri's half siblings, Dolores and Frankie Ladaga, meet their relatives (Dolores and Frankie's deceased father, Timiteo, was Papa's first cousin). I was pleased to meet my young relatives. However, I found Terri far more interesting. She lived in the quaint Sacramento Delta town of Isleton and was in her senior year at Rio Vista High School. Perky and energetic, she was an academic achiever who also kept busy with school and extracurricular activities. My sister Pula had gushed over meeting Terri earlier in the year at Asilomar Convention Center, when they both were student delegates to the state conference of Future Homemakers of America.

Terri's vivacity and love of life fascinated me. While there was no blood relationship, we both referred to each other as "cuz." I liked my new cousin. I was particularly pleased that Terri seemed to be impressed with my plans to attend college in the fall. (A few months later, she would admit that she had not been impressed at all. Not realizing I had spent four years in the navy, she thought I must not be very bright since my younger brother Herb was already two years ahead of me in college.)

After graduating from high school, Terri moved to Sacramento, having obtained a civilian job with the U.S. Air Force at McClellan Field. On our first few dates, I tried to make the best possible impression on her. I let her believe I had a lot of money to spend since I drove a fairly new car. I even insisted on paying for everything. One day, hot and hungry after a long afternoon ride, we went to a drive-in restaurant in Sacramento. I asked, "What would you like, Terri?" expecting that she would order a hamburger. She ordered prawns, the most expensive item on the menu. I calculated that I barely had enough money to pay for Terri's meal and told her I was no longer hungry. On our next date, I finally admitted I was simply a cash-poor college boy trying to make a good impression on someone I liked. Fortunately, Terri was interested only in me, not in my riches.

I was aware of my growing affection for Terri. She was mature beyond her years. She genuinely understood that my struggle for a college education was a necessary first step for a better life, and she was not materialistic. Moreover, she liked me. On a cold and windy day at the Alameda County Fair in Antioch, we found ourselves in each other's arms, ostensibly to keep warm. However, there was no denying the meaning of the resulting chemistry between us—Terri and I were romantically attracted to each other. We began going steady.

I brought Terri home to Livingston to meet the family. She fit in well. She already knew Pula, and she had become better acquainted with Herb, Junior, and George through Filipino tournaments. Terri made an immediate positive impact on nine-year-old Luna when she took the time to comb the knots out of my sister's unruly hair. Although they did not admit it, Papa and Mama were pleased that I had found someone, especially a *pinay*. I had never had a serious relationship with a Filipina. Occasionally, Papa and Mama had tried to arrange a romance with a girl whose parents were close friends or *kababayans*, but none of these attempts ever led to anything serious. Their matchmaking actually had the opposite effect. Whenever I sensed Mama and Papa were trying to fix me up, I made a pact with the girl that we should pretend to get along just to please our parents.

Given the moral climate of the times, Terri and I began to feel guilty about the intense level of our relationship. We began talking about marriage. We wanted to be married in the Roman Catholic Church, but neither of us was willing to go through the months-long waiting period the Church required. One evening, over a romantic dinner at a pricey Chinese restaurant in downtown Sacramento, we decided to elope to Reno. On the morning of October 3, 1953, soon after the Washoe County Courthouse in Reno opened, Terri and I were married before a justice of the peace. I was so nervous that I almost forgot to pay the justice the $10 fee for performing the service.

We had left so hurriedly, and with so little preparation, that we barely had enough money to pay the court fee and buy enough gasoline to get back. We had not eaten since the previous evening. Suddenly, I remembered that the Manoukian family had recently moved from Livingston to Reno. We had grown up with the Manoukian kids and always appreciated the great hospitality of the family whenever we visited. Mr. and Mrs. Manoukian were immigrants from Armenia. Like Filipinos, Armenians followed the custom of always offering visitors something to eat. Terri and I gratefully accepted their kind invitation to breakfast.

Following our elopement, the plan was for me to continue college and live in San Jose while Terri worked and lived in Sacramento. We wanted to keep the marriage secret until we both talked to our parents and could make the necessary arrangements to be married in church. In the meantime, we could legally live as husband and wife. Our carefully laid plans went awry just a week later. I got a phone call from Mama, who said, "We need to talk about your wedding. I already buy your present." Mama did not sound angry or disappointed. As I listened, still in shock, she went on to tell me that she had learned of our marriage through Bob McDonald's mother. Neither Terri nor I realized that Reno marriages were routinely reported to the county of the husband's residence. After reading the marriage notice in the *Merced Sun-Star*, Mrs. McDonald called Mama to offer her congratulations.

I drove to San Francisco a few days later to meet Mama, who was there to attend the Legionarios del Trabajo convention. She indeed had bought our wedding present. It was a living room set— a chartreuse fold-out couch, a matching chair, a coffee table, and a pair of end tables. As we began discussing the wedding arrangements, I became apprehensive. But I had no reason to be fearful. Mama seemed to be comfortable with the elopement; she just wanted to get on with making plans for the wedding.

The church wedding was in Livingston's St. Jude's Church on January 2, 1954, at 10:00 A.M. on a cold and foggy morning. The parish priest, Father Thomas Higgins, dictated the unusually early time after deciding that we were not entitled to the full rites of the Catholic Church because we had eloped. He also ruled that Terri could not have bridesmaids, nor could she have flowers. Terri was very disappointed at the priest's strict application of Church rules, especially since a Sacramento priest had made no mention of such restrictions. While I was disappointed, too, I was not surprised. Father Higgins's strict ways were well known to parishioners in Livingston. Despite everything, Terri and I were grateful that the Church formally blessed our marriage. Herb served as my best man, while Sally Crujido, Terri's former roommate in Sacramento, was the maid of honor. We did not let our disappointment dampen our spirits on our big day. Terri and I had a wonderful time at our wedding reception. Guests feasted on Filipino delicacies such as *lechon* and adobo along with all the delicious side dishes. A bebop trio from Stockton provided the music, headed by piano player Mike Montano, who went on to a successful career touring with comedian Jack E. Leonard and later became musical director at the Flamingo Casino in Las Vegas.

Terri and I established our first home at 710 North Sixth Street, a rented two-bedroom duplex in a Filipino neighborhood, a few blocks from San Jose's Japantown. We shared the duplex with my brother Junior, Felipe "Flip" Dangaran from Hawaii, and Peter Handa from Livingston. We got along well, although strange noises often permeated the quiet of our evenings. Junior often talked in his sleep, Flip gnashed his teeth, and Peter snored. Moreover, because of ill-fitting boards, our bed would fall down at embarrassingly inopportune times—to the suppressed laughter of our male housemates. It may not have been an ideal situation for a newly married couple; economically and realistically, however, it made all the sense in the world.

Married life was also good for my grades at San Jose State. When I was single, I earned an acceptable but unspectacular grade point average of 2.1, on a scale of 3. My very first quarter as a married man, I earned a near-perfect 2.8.

At the end of my second year of college, I returned to my old summer job at the Levy & Zentner packinghouse. Once again, Ruben Ragsac and I worked on the celery crates together. Ruben's family, who lived in the same neighborhood, had always treated me as one of the family, and the family extended its hospitality to Terri, particularly Ruben's mother, Manang Mary Cabebe. Terri was alone in a new community, without a network of family and friends, while I was in class all day for most of the year. It was comforting to know that she had someone like Manang Mary close by.

Manang Mary got Terri a job on the conveyer-belt line at the packinghouse. The job required her to stand for eight hours, and Terri was in her first trimester of pregnancy. I could only watch as she worked without complaint at her tedious task. We were both relieved when our summer jobs ended. We looked forward to the birth of our first child, but we were also mindful that a baby would tax our limited means. I received only $100 a month from the GI Bill. The savings that Terri and I had accumulated were rapidly dwindling. I got a part-time job as a warehouse janitor to supplement the GI Bill. In addition, each weekend during the 1954 fall quarter, we went to Livingston, where I picked grapes from dawn to dusk on Saturday and for half a day on Sunday. I took home $30 for my weekend work.

Terri made as much money selling homemade muffins to the *munongs* for $.50 apiece, thanks to Mama, who donated the baking mix. The sympathetic men, noting that she was in her last trimester, generously bought the muffins. Some told Terri to keep their change. Others paid for the muffins but wouldn't take them, saying they were not hungry after all, thus enabling Terri to sell the muffins more than once.

Several *manongs* were not as sympathetic to me as they were to Terri. They felt that my primary responsibility as a husband was to provide for her and the coming baby. According to them, instead of carrying books for study, I should be carrying tools for work; instead of having my pregnant wife make muffins, I should get a full-time job. I did not argue with their point of view. Their beliefs on what constitutes a husband's duty were deeply ingrained in Filipino culture. But Terri and I were both strong believers in the long-term benefits of a college education. Nevertheless, the words of the *manongs* hurt me deeply.

Terri's pregnancy went relatively well. She gained forty pounds, more than advised by her doctor, but the baby was developing normally. Finally, on a rainy November evening, she calmly announced that it was time to go to the hospital. Her labor pains were coming at five-minute intervals. I was so nervous, I could not think straight. Fortunately, Terri could. After noticing that I was having difficulty seeing the rain-swept road, she suggested that I turn on the windshield wipers. Later at the hospital, I experienced another episode of nervousness. When Terri's water broke, I ran through the hallway in a panic, yelling at the top of my voice, "Nurse, help us, help us!"

Terri endured fifteen hours of labor before Karen Noreen Jamero finally emerged into the world on Thanksgiving Day, November 25, 1954. Karen was a healthy, happy baby whose development went according to the Dr. Benjamin Spock baby book we followed religiously. Her only difficulty was an allergic reaction to cow's milk, but her eating problems disappeared after we shifted to a messy soybean-based formula.

In the summer of 1955, Terri was pregnant again, but she had to go back to work. She found a job as a clerk-typist for the motor pool at Parks Air Force Base, thirty miles away. Her pregnancy and the long commute were difficult for her. In addition, we had to move to a converted one-car garage behind the Sixth Street duplex after the landlady suddenly informed us that they would be reoccupying the space. The converted garage was tiny, with only enough space for a single bed, Karen's crib, a hot plate, and a small refrigerator. Luna, age twelve, lived with us so she could take care of Karen for a few hours. We then moved to a basement apartment at 644 North Seventeenth Street. This was my last term at San Jose State, and only a short time remained until graduation.

San Jose State granted me nine elective units for courses I had completed in the navy. The windfall units, earned by carrying seventeen to eighteen units for several quarters, and the three-unit correspondence course Dr. Vucinich had monitored, enabled me to graduate early, in three years. On September 2, 1955, I received a bachelor of arts degree, cum laude, with Terri, Karen, Mama, Pula, and Luna looking on. My family was proud of my accomplishment, especially Mama. While she never complained, I knew she still felt the hurt of being denied the opportunity to go college. Now that her eldest son was the first in the family to graduate from college, the hurt dissipated.

Still smarting from the scolding I had received from the manongs for allegedly failing to support my family properly, I planned to get a job immediately after graduation. However, thanks to Dr. Vucinich, who advised me to consider going on to graduate school, my plans suddenly changed. He pointed out that scholarships sufficient for a family of three were often available for deserving students. I followed his advice and applied to the University of California at Berkeley and at Los Angeles. Both schools accepted me. Just as important, I won a State of California Child Welfare Scholarship for $1,700 a year, considerably more than what I received under the GI Bill. Terri encouraged me to go to graduate school. We both knew it would be a continuing struggle for the next two years but realized a graduate degree would be best for us in the end. I chose to go to UCLA, not for academic reasons, but because it had a national championship football team and because Terri and I thought it would be a nice change to live in southern California.

A few days after graduation, we hauled our belongings onto a truck borrowed by Papa for the long ride to Los Angeles. We also borrowed the muscles of my brother George for the arduous job of loading and unloading. After they left, Terri and I suddenly felt alone and apprehensive. At the same time, we felt a definite sense of excitement about what awaited us at UCLA.

One of the benefits available to me as an ex-serviceman was affordable living quarters at Veterans Housing, on Strathmore Drive, at the edge of the UCLA campus. The complex consisted of fifteen two-story wooden buildings, each with fourteen units. Each unit had two rooms—a small bedroom and a combination kitchen, dining, and living room. Our unfurnished unit was located on the lower level. We bought a dining table and a small refrigerator at a used furniture store. Together with the furniture we brought with us, we had all the necessities. Terri sewed café curtains, purchased an inexpensive folding room divider for the combination room, and added several other decorative touches to transform the unit into a homier space. It may have been small, but thanks to Terri, it was comfortable for our family.

Surrounded on each side by Sorority Row and Fraternity Row, Veterans Housing was euphemistically termed Maternity Row, and for good reason. It seemed that wherever one looked, there was an expectant mother—including Terri. We were much more relaxed about the baby this time around. At the hospital, I did not panic as I had with Karen. However, I was too squeamish to accept the invitation of the UCLA Medical Center, a teaching hospital, to witness the delivery. Cheryl Louise was born on January 3, 1956. We had hoped for a boy but did not feel disappointed. It was more important that Terri and Cheryl were both healthy following the delivery.

One of my major reason for selecting UCLA instead of UC Berkeley was UCLA's nationally ranked football teams. However, the most memorable football game I attended at the cavernous Los Angeles Coliseum was a game featuring the University of Southern California and Notre Dame. It was memorable because it was Papa's first college game. Papa was wide-eyed. He could not believe that 100,000 fans had come to witness the clash between the two football powers. He kept looking incredulously around the stadium, muttering that there were more people there than in Livingston, Merced, and Stockton combined. He was so impressed with the mass of humanity that the football game clearly was of secondary interest. Even after we arrived back at the apartment, he continued to rave about the large crowd.

While I had not necessarily chosen to attend UCLA for academic reasons, the School of Social Welfare turned out to be a great learning experience. The graduate school had been in existence for only a few years and was located in temporary quarters in several Quonset huts in the middle of the campus. Its faculty was top-notch and included internationally known author Dr. Karl DeSchweinitz; Dr. Donald Howard, who headed the European refugee resettlement program after World War II; and Dr. Judd Marmour, a respected southern California psychoanalyst. Just as important, our class numbered only eighteen students, thus assuring students of valuable individual time and attention from the faculty. The small class size contributed greatly to learning. Students spent a lot of time together, not only in valuable discussions about the subject matter, but also in social interactions, since most of us were from outside the Los Angles area. I became particularly close to Paul Chikahisa, a single Japanese American. We two were the only ethnic minority members in the class. He was often a visitor to the house, became close friends with Terri, and delighted in entertaining Karen and Cheryl.

My first-year field placement was fortuitous. I was assigned to the Los Angeles County Department of Social Services office in West Los Angeles, where I carried a small caseload of general welfare cases. Not only did I gain practical experience in working with poor, mostly female, welfare recipients in the Venice Beach area, but at the end of the placement, I received an offer for a summer job. The salary was $350 a month, the most I had ever earned.

Students were solely responsible for keeping up with the heavy academic workload at the School of Social Welfare. I spent many hours in the library, which was within easy walking distance of our housing. When I was not at the library, I studied in the space that Terri fashioned out of a small closet. Karen and Cheryl usually were in bed early, which helped me get in the necessary study time. I spent so much time studying that I finally had to get prescription glasses.

On the rare occasions when we could afford to go out, Terri and I would take in some jazz. Los Angeles was the center of West Coast jazz during the 1950s. We were able to enjoy such well-known musicians as Conte Condoli, Stan Getz, Dizzy Gillespie, Jimmy Guiffre, the Lighthouse All-Stars, Shelly Manne, and Shorty Rogers. Unfortunately, their appearances were not usually well attended, since the rock-and-roll craze had taken over the country. And I always made time to follow the New York Yankees. On October 8, 1956, glued to a black-and-white television in the crowded UCLA Student Union, I excitedly watched Don Larsen pitch the only perfect no-hit, no-run game in World Series history.

My second-year field placement was at the Vista Del Mar Child Care Center, a Jewish agency with a good professional reputation for providing residential and counseling services. A number of well-known figures from the entertainment industry were on its board of directors. One of the more active board members was Dinah Shore, the singer and TV hostess. The center served largely troubled kids.

The placement at Vista Del Mar was my first real experience with Jewish people. To my knowledge, there were no Jews living in Livingston when I was growing up. I read about the Holocaust in newspapers during World War II and heard unkind Jewish jokes while in the navy. However, I was generally uninformed about them as a people. My year at Vista Del Mar was a valuable opportunity to learn about Jewish culture, history, and religion. I was particularly impressed with how their history and culture have been so essential to their survival through the centuries, despite widespread oppression and discrimination. For me, it was a personal wake-up call on the importance of knowing the history of the Philippines. More important, I made a mental note to become knowledgeable about the Filipino experience in America.

Peter Jr. was born at the UCLA Medical Center on January 13, 1957. Terri and I had planned to name a son "John," having decided that we did not want our child to be called "Junior." But when Terri first saw him, she thought he looked so much like me that he had to be named "Peter." She was right. Not only was there a close resemblance at birth, but the likeness has continued through the years. And Terri made sure that everyone knew about our son's preferred name.

Terri had the major burden of caring for our three kids, all under the age of two. It was not easy. Peter was a colicky baby, particularly at night, and Terri was understandably tired. Her weight dropped to less than a hundred pounds. I did not make it any easier with my macho attitude about fathers and child care. Despite everything, the kids developed normally, thanks to Terri's nurturing ways.

I was still getting a Child Welfare Scholarship from the state of California. Unfortunately, I exhausted my educational benefits under the GI Bill at the end of my first year at UCLA. To help with finances during my second year of graduate school, Terri hocked the expensive Zeiss-Icon camera she had received as a gift from her brother Bob. Every month, when my scholarship money arrived, she redeemed the camera at the pawnshop. Sadly, she had to sell the Zeiss-Icon at the end of the school year to pay bills.

Although we did not directly ask them for assistance, Papa and Mama somehow sensed our financial situation and periodically provided help in the form of food, which we referred to as our "care packages." (Papa received a strong clue on our economic circumstances during our first year at UCLA when he made an unexpected visit. As was his custom, he opened the refrigerator and saw that it contained only food and milk for the kids.) Sometimes, Papa and Mama drove down from Livingston with rice, canned goods, chicken, and meat as well as goodies for the kids. Whenever they learned that someone was planning to come to Los Angeles, they made sure that these visitors delivered care packages to us.

As welcome as the care packages and the extra cash from Terri's camera may have been, I felt bad about my inability to do more to support my growing family. I looked forward to graduation so that I would be able to get a full-time job. In 1957, people with masters in social work were in high demand in California. As a condition of my Child Welfare Scholarship, I was obligated to work for two years in a county welfare department. I received a number of tempting offers before deciding on Sacramento County. Sacramento seemed perfect for us. Terri was from the area, and we would be within an hour or two of family. Moreover, Sacramento County offered the most money—$455 a month. I wired my acceptance immediately.

Before I could finalize the Sacramento offer, however, I had to graduate with a master of social work (MSW) degree. I was comfortable with my second-year class work and felt I would not have any trouble completing the requirements for the degree. I was wrong. On the first day of finals, I froze. I stared at the essay questions but couldn't think of anything. After what seemed like an eternity, I came up with a blur of responses. In retrospect, I believe I froze because so much was at stake. Not just getting the degree and a job, but also the future of Terri and the kids and Mama's and Papa's dreams for their firstborn. I ran home to Terri, crying, "I failed you and the kids. Since I did so badly, there's no point in my going for the second day." Terri persuaded me to return for the last day of finals. This time, I did not freeze. And despite my panic on the first day, I managed to pass. It was a good learning experience.

Papa and Mama, George, and Uncle Onsing came down from Livingston to celebrate my June 5 graduation. Herb, in his first year of graduate school at UCLA, Jeanne, and their family were there. Terri surprised me with a gift of a beautiful wristwatch, suitably engraved. She got the money for the watch by diligently saving Karen's and Cheryl's stools for several weeks and selling them to the UCLA Medical Center for a research project. I was grateful, not only for the watch, but also for Terri's creativity in coming up with the necessary means to solve a problem.

Although Papa and Mama did not say much at the graduation ceremony, I knew they were proud of my receiving a master's degree. I did not know the extent of their pride until Mama showed me several newspaper articles reporting on the accomplishments of their children. A lengthy article in the *Merced Sun-Star* bore the headline "Dreams Come True in Livingston Family." The *Modesto Bee*'s article was headlined "College Going Family's Son Gets Master's Degree." It seems Mama had called Margaret Cassell of the *Livingston Chronicle*, and Mrs. Cassell, also a contributing reporter for the *Bee* and the *Sun-Star*, did the rest. The articles were generous in their coverage and their praise of the family. We all took pride in the unexpected publicity.

Graduation day was also moving day for us. The ceremony was at midday. After sitting through boring speech after boring speech, it was finally over. I immediately shed my cap and gown and rushed home to help George and Uncle Onsing load our belongings onto a truck. At dusk, Terri, Karen, Cheryl, Peter, and I boarded my '51 Bel Air Chevrolet, on our way to our next adventure—Sacramento and my first real job.

# III

## EARLY CAREER

### 1957–1970

DURING THESE YEARS, AMERICA EXPERIENCED A mixture of hope, violence, and social justice. John F. Kennedy's election as president in 1960 gave the country an invigorating sense of hope. In the dynamic JFK, the youngest president ever elected, and Jacqueline, his sophisticated wife, people saw the ideal couple to lead them toward a new beginning. The great promise of his presidency was shattered with his assassination in Dallas on November 22, 1963. It would not be the only assassination of a national figure. Martin Luther King Jr., the civil rights leader, was shot down as he stood on a hotel balcony in Memphis, Tennessee, in 1968. Soon after, presidential candidate Robert F. Kennedy was killed during a campaign stop in Los Angeles. Initially, the assassin was mistakenly identified as a Filipino fanatic. Following Dr. King's assassination, violence broke out in many large cities, including Detroit, Los Angeles, and Washington, D.C. The greatest acts of violence during this time period, however, were the unpopular Vietnam War and the growing antiwar demonstrations at home.

The fight for social justice achieved a number of significant victories with the enactment of voting rights legislation and a host of civil rights programs to benefit blacks and other disenfranchised minorities. Social programs underwent similar growth. Landmark programs in the Social Security Amendments of 1962 included medical assistance and provision of social services to the needy.

As the nation was going through a new beginning in the Kennedy era, I was embarking on my professional career. Just as I had been naive in venturing out into the real world, so, too, was I naive in my first few ventures into the job market. I found, for example, that attaining positions of leadership was not necessarily a matter of merit but was often decided by one's membership in the "old boys' network," which, in turn, depended on one's skin color. Brown was definitely not the right hue. I also found that professional credentials and many years of program experience did not necessarily guarantee fair treatment. For me, it was a time of lessons learned, growing self-confidence in the workplace, and professional-reputation building. I learned the benefits of taking risks, became aware of the good fortune of being in the right place at the right time, and came to trust in my own skills, abilities, and judgment. Happily, I became much more comfortable with my Filipino identity. No longer pained by my brown skin color, or conflicted in my status as a Filipino American, I began to embrace identifiable American interests, attitudes, and behaviors typical of other Bridge Generation Filipino Americans. ❦

## 8 My First Real Job

TERRI AND I BEGAN OUR SACRAMENTO HOUSE
hunt with mounting excitement and anticipation. We scoured the
newspapers for an affordable two-bedroom rental in a neighborhood that seemed tolerant of children. We had a good idea of neighborhoods to consider, since Terri was familiar with Sacramento, and
confined our search to a few promising prospects. Our excitement
quickly turned to anger. On one of our first rental inquiries, an elderly white woman met us. Smilingly, she said, "I'm so sorry—the
house was just rented." I sensed she was not being altogether forthcoming and went to a nearby phone booth. When I asked if the rental
was still available, she replied in the same saccharine voice, "Yes,
would you like to see it?" I then told her she was a "lying SOB,"
identified myself as the brown person who had been on her doorstep a few minutes before, and slammed the receiver down before
she could answer. Again, I experienced the pain of being denied
housing—not because I could not afford it, but because of my brown
skin. I was so angry that I broke down in tears.

We finally found a place on 2009 Fifteenth Street, just minutes
away from work. The house was of circa 1920s vintage but clean
and inviting. With a formal dining room, a fireplace, and an enclosed
backyard, it was by far the fanciest place Terri and I had ever lived
in. Thanks again to the help of my brother George, we moved our
belongings to our new home.

My first real job was with the County of Sacramento, as a child
welfare worker in the Adoptions Unit. I reported for work in the
middle of June, just two weeks after earning my MSW from UCLA.

I was eager to start my career and provide for our rapidly growing family. The Adoptions Unit consisted of a supervisor, five social workers, and two clerical employees. I was the first male to work for the unit in the history of the program. This was not surprising, since adoptions, like social work in general, was traditionally a woman's field. I was also the first person of Filipino ancestry hired in adoptions. My coworkers were white, except for Louise Robinette, an outgoing black woman who had received her graduate education at the prestigious Atlanta University.

Louise took me under her wing soon after she learned of my enlightened attitudes regarding ethnicity. The Adoptions Unit often based its collective decisions on stereotypical and racially biased factors when selecting adoptive parents and placing babies. Much to my dismay, I found that some of the adoption workers relied on unscientific criteria, such as an applicant being "too dark" or a certain ethnic group "not being intelligent enough." My coworkers all had the benefit of higher education and should have known better. Louise was an intelligent and assertive person who was effective with her coworkers, but she obviously needed an ally. She was often a lone voice, and I was happy to help out.

Adoption workers were not limited to making placement decisions as a group but were involved in all facets of the job. We counseled unwed mothers, obtained signed relinquishments from natural parents, took relinquished babies from the hospital to temporary foster homes, supervised kids in foster care, performed adoptive parent studies, supervised adoptive placements, and prepared court petitions legalizing adoptive placements. I was the exception to this generalist approach. My assignment included two specialized responsibilities: to obtain relinquishments from incarcerated fathers and to supervise the "hard-to-place children" caseload.

The task of obtaining relinquishments from incarcerated fathers took me to county and city jails and to state institutions like San Quentin and Folsom Prisons. It was obvious why I had this assignment. Prisons can be intimidating and formidable for anyone but were more so for the women. My female coworkers were relieved that I had taken over the assignment, believing that, as a male, I would be more comfortable with it. I found the prison visits challenging and interesting. However, my female coworkers were wrong. I was seldom comfortable, particularly when the prison doors clanged shut loudly behind me. I also had to be alert to potential hostility from the prisoners I was supposed to interview. These men were usually not the biological fathers, and in most cases, they were unaware of their wives' infidelity until my visit. As legal husbands, however, they were the legal fathers. Their signed relinquishments were necessary before babies could be legally adopted. Under these circumstances, I was aware of the possibility that they could direct their anger over their wives' indiscretions at me. Fortunately, the prisoners always agreed to sign the relinquishments. They were actually pleasant to work with for the short time we were together. But I did not forget for a minute that most of them were there for committing violent crimes.

Almost all the couples seeking children for adoption preferred healthy white infants. Accordingly, other adoption workers dealt exclusively with babies. My caseload was far different, made up of kids who were older, physically disabled, or of minority background. My assignment was to try to find permanent homes for these children, who were considered less desirable by most adoptive parents. It was an often discouraging assignment, and placements were few. However, every success, and the resulting happiness for each child and new adoptive parents, made up for any discouragement. Knowing that I had played a role in their happiness was enough.

The most satisfying and heart-wrenching case involved Richie, a five-year-old boy who had been in the same foster home since infancy. When he was a baby, the Adoptions Unit was reluctant to place him because he was perceived as developmentally slow. The concerns turned out to be unwarranted. By then, Richie was no longer an infant and thus not highly desired by potential adoptive parents. He received good care in his foster home and enjoyed a loving relationship with his foster parents. While they expressed a wish to adopt Richie, they were in their sixties, too old by existing standards to be considered as adoptive parents.

From a list of recently approved studies of applicants, I found a warm middle-aged couple who appeared to be a good match for Richie. After having him in their home on several trial visits, they declared their strong interest in adopting him. However, I first had to help Richie and his foster parents accept the reality of a permanent separation, a process that took several months. The day I came to take him away from his foster home was a tearful experience for everyone. Richie pleadingly asked me, "Mr. Mero [he wasn't able to pronounce my last name], do I have to go?" Richie and I had developed a trusting relationship. I convinced him that the placement was in his best interests, and he was able to leave the security of the only parental figures he had ever known. The placement in his new home turned out to be an unqualified success. I have been forever grateful.

We lived in the Fifteenth and T Street house for only a few months, too brief to call it home. Despite our initial belief that two bedrooms would be sufficient, there clearly was not enough room for our growing family. Besides, our family was set to expand yet again. Terri and I were about to be parents for the fourth time in four years. Another reason for our decision was the availability of housing. The post–World War II boom in new housing starts had continued after the Korean War. I took advantage of my eligibility for low-interest loans under the GI Bill and bought a three-bedroom home in a new subdivision. The price was $12,000, with a down payment of $99. The house, at 2070 Berg Avenue, was among the first houses built in the subdivision, which was located behind the Bing Maloney golf course and Sacramento Municipal Airport. My brother George again helped us move. This time, we stayed for a while. Berg Avenue would be our home for the next seven years.

Terri and I began the slow process of furnishing and landscaping our new house. When I was a student, our economic situation permitted little but the bare essentials. The living room set we received from Mama and Papa as a wedding present was virtually all the furniture we owned. In the course of the following months, we had to buy a bed for ourselves to replace the foldout divan we'd been using for the past few years. We also purchased bunk beds for the kids, a small dinette set, an inexpensive stove and a refrigerator, and a washer for the endless loads of dirty diapers and laundry. We put in our own lawn and a few plants in the yard, including an apricot tree that in a short time supplied delicious fruit and shade in the hot summers. Terri's brother Eddie helped put up a fence. Once again, Terri demonstrated her creativity with the tasteful interior decor. It may have been a lot of work, but it was definitely worth it. We had a home, not just a house, and one large enough to accommodate our family.

Not long after our move, Terri and I noticed that we were the only family of color in the new subdivision. Recent legislation prohibited discrimination in housing, especially against veterans, but we knew that the real estate industry often used less obvious means to discriminate. Why were we the only exception in the subdivision? What should we do? We decided to turn the other cheek. We had three toddlers to care for, we had finally bought a house, and I was just starting out in a new career. It was not worth rocking the boat. The rationale made sense. Nevertheless, I felt guilty. Six months later, several minority families moved into new houses on adjoining blocks in our neighborhood—much to our relief.

Many families in the neighborhood had children the same ages as ours. Our kids were usually outside playing with their friends, which made Terri's busy life much more bearable. She had the major burden of caring for the kids, no small task considering that our children were so close in age. I could have been of greater help to Terri, but I was preoccupied with my budding career. At the time, I also was too much of a macho man. I felt that my role was to provide for the family, not to take care of the kids.

On May Day 1958, Julie came into our life swiftly and with little warning. Terri and I mistakenly thought we were prepared for anything that might develop. But Julie was so ready to come into the world that there was not even time for Terri to go into the labor room. She was wheeled directly into the delivery room. After thumbing through only a few pages of a magazine in the waiting room, I was told I was the father of a healthy baby girl. Considering that Terri had just had her fourth baby in four years, I was thankful the delivery had gone well. Her obstetrician, Dr. Dimik, commented that her delivery was so smooth it was "like the textbooks."

Now that we were living in the familiar environs of Sacramento, Terri and I began seeing old friends. We also made a number of new friends in the area. All were Bridge Generation Filipino Americans. Before long, we were involved in their get-togethers. We joined the Filipino Bowling League, which met at the downtown Sacramento Bowl. I was encouraged to take up golf but could never generate much enthusiasm for the sport, mainly because I considered it a rich man's game that violated my farmworker roots. I shrugged off invitations to join my friends on the golf course, saying, "Golf clubs aren't made for guys my size." Someone gave me a five iron for my birthday, thinking that this would surely help change my mind. It did not.

Terri and I also began seeing old friends on the Filipino tournament trail. We rooted for our old clubs, the Livingston Dragons and the Isleton LVM Girls team (LVM stood for Luzon, Visayas, Mindanao—the three major areas of the Philippines). Livingston had developed into a major power in the *pinoy* basketball tournaments, quite a change from the team's first year of competition, in 1948. Then, the newly organized team had lost most of its games, despite the addition of experienced players such as Richard Gacer and Raphael Raagas from nearby Oakdale. Now, ten years later, the team was composed of younger, taller, talented players from the Livingston area. These included Patrick Alcordo, Apollo Bacaylan, my cousin David Galanida, Flo Hipolito, my brother George, and Sonny and Fred Pomicpic (the sons of Hildo Pomicpic, who drove me home after I got lost on the bus in the first grade). Veteran tournament players from other towns—Al Baguio from Salinas, the East Bay's

Don Del Pilar, and Joe Muca of Vallejo—were also recruited to play for the Dragons. My playing days were long behind me, but Terri was still in her prime. She played on the Livingston Dragonettes volleyball team and was a physical and inspirational factor in its success. At the Bethel Island volleyball tournament, she was voted most valuable player. When we moved to Sacramento, the city was not represented in Filipino tournaments. Youth clubs of earlier years had folded for a number of reasons. The sizable Bridge Generation population that resided in Sacramento had a strong interest in joining the tournament circuit again. With our established participation in *pinoy* youth clubs, it was perhaps inevitable that Terri and I became involved in forming a club in Sacramento. In 1958, the Sacramento Filipino Youth Association (SFYA) became a regular participant in tournament play.

Jazz offerings were scarce in Sacramento compared to Los Angeles, but Terri and I tried to see and hear as many acts as we could. We took in Stan Kenton and his orchestra when they played at the posh Senator Hotel. We also made several trips to San Francisco and saw Dave Brubeck, Paul Desmond, Shelly Manne, Cal Tjader, and other musicians at the Blackhawk nightclub. With the exception of the Kenton performance, there was little in the way of big-name jazz in Sacramento. It was in Sacramento in the late fifties, however, where I first met a couple of Bridge Generation jazz pianists, both of whom would become our close friends. The first was Joseph "Flip" Nunez, who grew up in San Pedro and got his start performing in black nightclubs on Central Avenue in Los Angeles. Flip was a gifted bop pianist whose style was reminiscent of the well-known Carl Perkins, his southern California inspiration. The other Filipino jazz musician I met was Cornelio "Corney" Pasquil. I first met Corney in the Strawberry Patch, a north Sacramento club. Connie Viernes, a close friend who grew up in nearby Walnut Grove, introduced Corney to Terri and me. Corney was the only Filipino from Kansas we ever met. He grew up in Junction City, the son of a career army soldier. His phrasings and chord progressions reflected his training in classical music, and his style reminded me of the great Bill Evans.

We had a terrible scare in December 1959. Peter was stricken with the flu. He became dehydrated, and we took him to the emergency room of the county hospital. However, after Peter failed to respond to treatment and the dehydration worsened, I decided I could no longer rely on the hospital's medical staff and placed a frantic call to Dr. Brainerd, who was considered perhaps the foremost pediatrician in Sacramento. I knew Dr. Brainerd through my work in the Adoptions Unit, where he was an examining physician for relinquished babies. He responded immediately to my plea and quickly diagnosed the problem: Peter had developed an immunity to penicillin. Our son made a swift recovery after the switch in medication. According to Dr. Brainerd, Peter was treated just in time. He had already become dangerously dehydrated, and further delay without proper treatment would have been fatal.

I continued to progress in my position as an adoptions worker, consistently receiving "good" to "excellent" ratings in performance evaluations. My starting salary of $357 per month in June 1957 increased to $540 by the end of 1959. I had two modest career goals when I graduated from UCLA. The first was to earn a five-figure annual salary, and at $6,480 per year, I was almost two-thirds of the way there. My second career goal was to be able to go to work wearing a business suit, white shirt, and tie, which I had done on my very first day of work with Sacramento County. I felt good about my achievements, and I liked my job. At the same time, I realized that a higher salary, more than I could ever make as an adoptions worker, would better meet the needs of my growing family. To add to my concern, I learned that Terri was expecting again, with the next baby due in July 1960. I began to explore other alternatives.

I learned of an opening for a supervisor in the Aid to Needy Children (ANC) Division, California's controversial welfare program for families. Although I had worked for a summer in the General Assistance welfare program in Los Angeles, I had no experience with the ANC program. I was also concerned that, as the only employee with an MSW, I might be resented by supervisees who had more experience but no graduate training. I decided to talk to Jack Corey, the department director, to see if either of these concerns was a drawback. I was impressed with his forward thinking and ideas for the department. He also had an MSW and had already expressed his desire to bring more professionally trained staff to all of the department's divisions. Jack encouraged me to compete for the position. He suggested that I read up on the ANC program so that I could pass the written examination. He also felt that, despite an initial learning curve, I would be able to fulfill all the requirements once I was on the job.

Although it was not a factor in my final decision, I thought about the attitudes of most Filipinos regarding welfare, especially Papa and Mama. During the Depression, Filipinos expressed pride in working rather than accepting relief, or welfare. They derided anyone who took advantage of public monies to support their children. I could understand their feelings, particularly in light of their cultural beliefs and their work ethic, but I had a different perspective. I believed there were circumstances beyond a person's control that contributed to a parent's inability to support his or her children. I believed children should not be punished for the real or imagined failures of their parents. And I believed in the Aid to Needy Children program, the public program that helped provide children with the basic needs of food and shelter.

I discussed the pros and cons of the ANC position with Terri. She supported my plan to compete for the job and urged me to take it if it was offered. There was one other hurdle. No, it was not the written examination, which I passed. It was the oral interview. I had contracted a bad case of the flu just before the interview and was still drowsy and nasal-sounding. Despite my condition, however, the oral board passed me. Soon thereafter, I received an offer to work as ANC unit supervisor, an offer I did not refuse.

Jacqueline was born on July 2, 1960, nearly two years after Julie. When she was just a few weeks old, I shed my macho ways and took on a greater share of her care. We were financially strapped due to the rapid growth of our family, and Terri found an evening job as a clerk-typist for the state. At night, I was responsible for

Jackie and her four siblings. Thanks mainly to Terri, the older kids were on an early-to-bed schedule and were able to handle most of their own needs. This enabled me to devote the necessary time to the baby. It also helped that Jackie was a happy baby and easy to care for. In later years, Terri and the kids would tease me that Jackie was my favorite. I would never admit to it, but if it were true, it may be because of the closeness that developed between us when she was an infant.

# 9 Moving Up

MY PROMOTION TO UNIT SUPERVISOR AT AID TO Needy Children was an example of being in the right place at the right time and demonstrated my growing confidence in taking risks. Jack Corey was eager to bring more MSWs into his department, particularly in the difficult ANC program, which had no MSW staff at all. I was the only one on the promotion list. The opportunity was there, and I was ready to risk moving into a completely new situation.

Because I was apprehensive about my lack of experience as a supervisor, I gave careful consideration to how I would approach my new job. I decided to use the problem-solving approach that had been drilled into me at graduate school. This disciplined approach had worked well for me in the Adoptions Unit, and there was no reason why it should not be applicable to my new position. I helped staff identify problems, consider alternatives, analyze the pros and cons of the alternatives, and, finally, guide their clients through an appropriate plan of action. Unit social workers were receptive. They already felt that the agency's prevailing practices—ferreting out welfare cheats, closing as many cases as possible, and keeping welfare payments to the minimum—did little to resolve family problems. They were ready to consider a more positive approach in working with the families on their caseloads.

I was pleased with the six social workers assigned to me. They were eager to learn, wanted to be of greater help to clients, and had a positive outlook. They were relatively young, just a few years younger than I was. They offered to help me learn the technicalities of ANC. Like Jack, they felt this aspect of the job should not be a problem for me, and they were right. The staff was looking to me for help with the people problems in their caseloads, not the technical aspects. I was very happy to help.

Gary Mead, an affable, easygoing country boy from Oklahoma, was the most outgoing of the unit staff. He took the lead in explaining the technical details of the program, which consisted of determining budget needs for families. While Gary was not the most senior member in the unit, he was the unofficial leader of the group. He once sold shoes for a living and often expressed the happiness he felt now that his job did not require him to kneel down before his customers. If Gary was the most outgoing among the staff, Simon Dominguez was easily the quietest. Si came from a proud Hispanic family with a long history in California. He cared deeply about the mothers and children on his caseload and had a deep understanding of the problems they faced. I was not surprised to find that Si was ready to consider ways to be of greater help to his clients. He proved an apt student.

Gary and Si were the first of a dozen staff members that I recommended to graduate schools of social work while I was at the Department of Social Welfare. Gary received an MSW from the University of Utah, and Si got his master's from the University of Southern California. At the same time, I also helped them obtain financial stipends from the state. The stipends required that they return to work for Sacramento County on a year-for-year basis— a win-win situation for all of us. Employees got master's degrees, and the agency got back trained staff people who could deal more effectively with the department's clients.

My immediate supervisor was George Cunningham, ANC division chief. George had come up through the ranks and was thoroughly knowledgeable about ANC. He did not have graduate training in social work, and I wondered if he would resent my degree. Fortunately, such was not the case. A loyal company man, he could always be counted on to get behind department initiatives.

The country's civil rights unrest was starting to produce reforms in social welfare programs. Congress passed the landmark 1962 amendments to the Social Security Act, which legitimized the provision of social services to the ANC program. Previously, ANC had taken a standardized approach based on eligibility and family-budget determinations. The Sacramento County Department of Social Welfare entered a phenomenal growth period, adding numerous programs and financial resources, and a second ANC division emerged to accommodate the growth. I decided to compete for the new position of division chief. My success as ANC supervisor convinced me that I could do the job. Perhaps as important, I had learned that I derived enhanced job satisfaction from the power and status of an administrator. I had liked my old position in the Adoptions Unit but, from time to time, had not given it my best. As a supervisor, however, I was more enthusiastic and motivated.

In July 1962, after serving as supervisor for one year, I was promoted to chief of the Division of Special Services. I was pleased that my old unit was among the ANC units transferred into the new division. In addition, I was to implement the new Homemaker and Rehabilitation programs, which were designed to help welfare mothers become financially independent. From supervising one unit of seven social workers, I had gone to being in charge of five units and a staff of thirty.

The expectation behind my promotion was that I would provide new direction for the rapidly changing ANC program. My response was to develop a division that was more service oriented instead of focused simply on establishing eligibility for financial assistance. Using the problem-solving approach that so far had served me well, I recruited workers who showed they had the potential to understand family problem situations. I developed my own casework-training curriculum for the division and negotiated specialized training for my staff with the new School of Social Work at Sacramento State University. The excitement generated by these initiatives was not lost on staff assigned to other divisions of the department, and I received many requests for transfers to the Division of Special Services. My new initiatives began to achieve the desired program results. Staff members became more effective in working with families yet maintained their efficiency in dealing with the practical aspects of financial eligibility. Perhaps as important, staff cohesiveness and morale improved—important sources of needed strength, particularly when under the stress of meeting deadlines.

As division chief, I was part of the executive staff that met regularly with department director Jack Corey. At first, I was anxious about these meetings. Not only was I the newest administrator; I was also the youngest and the only ethnic-minority member of the group. (This was my first Filipino First. No person of Filipino background had risen to this level in Sacramento County government.) As it turned out, I experienced no problems whatsoever and quickly became comfortable at the meetings. My position as division chief also began to broaden my perspective, since I was now exposed to the various community and political forces associated with public programs. Initially, I was not comfortable with these outside groups, particularly when they expressed their own ideas of how welfare programs should be administered. As far as I was concerned, the department had knowledgeable and experienced leaders who needed the support, not the criticism, of laypersons. I would soon find, however, that working with outside groups was a necessary skill for an administrator.

My immediate supervisor was Orlando (Del) Delliquadri, assistant director. Also an MSW, he came from a family of professional social workers (a brother was dean of the University of Michigan's School of Social Work). Del strongly supported my ideas for the division. He also proved helpful in my interactions with other administrative staff, community representatives, and outside political people. Del's everlasting contribution, however, benefited my love for jazz. He had purchased an expensive high-fidelity set when hi-fi first became popular. However, the novelty of listening to the sound of freight trains—his reason for buying the set—soon wore off. I had often dreamed of owning a quality hi-fi so that I could listen to jazz but could never afford to buy one. Del offered his set to me at a bargain price.

The years 1963–64 found me busy with the implementation of new federal provisions designed to help clients gain financial independence. Funding incentives were in place to continue the initiatives I had begun a year earlier. These incentives, called "Federal financial participation," were available at the rate of 75 percent in reimbursements for staff who provided social services and only 50 percent for staff assigned to establish eligibility. The federal government further mandated that a social service caseload should not exceed sixty cases and that no more than six social workers were to be assigned to each supervisor. Another federal provision was a new Unemployed Fathers program, which authorized payments to intact families whose fathers could not find work. The immediate impact of these new provisions greatly expanded the ANC program, now known as Aid to Families with Dependent Children (AFDC). The Division of Special Services was the main beneficiary of the rapid program growth and soon doubled in size, to ten units, with a staff of more than seventy.

Implementing the Unemployed Fathers program was by far my most difficult challenge. The local community, unable to accept that able-bodied men could not find jobs, actively opposed the controversial program. The County Board of Supervisors directed me to provide weekly reports, which received extensive media attention. Despite the satisfactory responses I gave the board, it still doubted the value of a service-oriented approach with AFDC fathers. To complicate matters further, the division was under a deadline to eliminate the long waiting list of applicants. Thanks to the dedication and hard work of the staff, we met the deadline. When the last person on the waiting list had been assigned, I got up on a nearby desk and thanked the staff for a job well done. An impromptu, boisterous celebration ensued. The seventy staff members fully understood that they had performed well despite adverse conditions and were proud of their accomplishments. I shared their pride. I was also grateful that their earlier training and direction had paid off in a big way.

The Unemployed Fathers program did not enjoy wide public support. Taxpayers resented having their hard-earned money go to provide assistance to families because fathers were not able to support them. I was personally involved in a dramatic, and somewhat humorous, example of that resentment. Uncle Onsing had given me his 1940 Dodge coupe as a second car for commuting to work. Our children were then so small that we all could fit in the car. One Saturday, dressed in my grubbies after working in the yard, I took the family grocery shopping in the Dodge. As we got out of the twenty-four-year-old car, people, particularly women, gazed sympathetically at Terri and our five little kids, who also were not dressed in their Sunday best. They then turned and gave me the dirtiest looks I have ever experienced. It dawned on me that they thought I was one of those notorious lazy fathers with a family on welfare. I could only chuckle to myself.

My increased responsibilities required that I travel to other parts of the state for conferences and meetings. I was at a conference in San Jose on November 22, 1963, the day President Kennedy was assassinated. The intense business discussions of just minutes before suddenly seemed unimportant. All we could think on our somber ride back to Sacramento was, "How could this happen?" and "What will happen to the country?" In the wake of the assassination, there was a rush of civil rights legislation, a legacy to President Kennedy's all-too-brief presidency. I was gratified by the national response to civil rights. The fight for social justice was now almost ten years old. There was no question of where I stood. When Dr. Martin Luther King Jr. led the famous march on Washington, D.C., in 1963, my white colleagues asked me, "Pete, what will you do if there is a black against white war?" Without hesitating, I replied, "Fight with the blacks, of course." My swift response surprised me—at first. However, I had no reason to ponder my response. My views on race relations were established. Growing up brown had taught me about the ugly realities of living with discrimination and prejudice. There could be no other response to the question.

I was not a 1960s activist. With one exception, I did not participate in marches or demonstrations. Instead, I expressed myself through organizations such as the Sacramento Chapter of the

National Association of Social Workers, where I was treasurer. In 1963, in concert with other community and professional organizations, the association sent an official letter of protest to the Sacramento School District for its practice of de facto segregation. Our collective protests convinced the school district to redraw its attendance boundaries. I also engaged in discussions about civil rights with whites. Whenever I mentioned my personal experiences with racial discrimination, they typically commented, "I didn't realize that kind of thing happened to you. It's hard to believe." I doubt I really changed their basic attitudes. Nevertheless, I felt it was positive to discuss these matters in the open; it was also a kind of catharsis for me.

I am proud to have marched in one Sacramento demonstration. In 1965, Cesar Chavez led a march of mostly Mexican farmworkers to protest working conditions in the fields of California. The march originated in Delano and was to end on the steps of the state capitol in Sacramento, two hundred miles away. Given my farm-labor background and commitment to civil rights, I decided to join the march when it reached the outskirts of Sacramento. Chavez, like civil rights leader King, also believed in nonviolence. We sang songs such as "We Shall Overcome" and chanted in unison. It was an emotional, unforgettable experience. That evening, I met Chavez. He was about my height. Enormous leadership in such a small person—I was impressed and inspired.

Chavez is correctly credited with leading the National Farm Workers Association (NFWA) against the conglomerate agricultural interests in Delano. However, it is a little-known fact that the NFWA actually owes its existence to Filipino labor leader Larry Itliong. Earlier in 1965, Itliong led the Agricultural Workers Organizing Committee (AWOC), a Filipino farmworkers union, on a sit-down strike in a wage protest. AWOC joined with Mexican farmworkers under Chavez to form the National Farm Workers Association (later the United Farm Workers), which began the epic farmworkers' struggle. Chavez was elected president, and Itliong became one of two vice presidents.

On a weekend visit to Livingston shortly after the 1965 AWOC sit-in, Papa remarked to me that he had serious questions about the wisdom of the strike. He did not doubt that Filipinos should fight for higher wages. He simply believed that this matter should be discussed at the negotiation table, as he had done with local farmers, and not decided on the streets. What I did not fully understand at the time, however, was that Papa's situation was different from that faced by Itliong's Filipino farmworkers in Delano. The farmers Papa dealt with all these years were small ranchers who only wanted to have their crops picked in return for a fair wage, not the giant Delano conglomerates, which tried for years to squeeze every dollar from farmworkers.

I was to meet Itliong in 1971. He was still a charismatic labor leader, still energized by the gains that farmworkers had made since the 1965 AWOC strike. However, he had severed his ties with the UFW after he became disillusioned with the UFW for failing to pay sufficient attention to the needs of Filipinos. By 1971, the ranks of Filipinos within the union had been reduced by old age, and Filipinos were a small minority among union members compared to the much larger number of Mexican farmworkers. With the exception of erecting Agbayani Village, in Delano, to house aging Filipinos, the UFW continued to emphasize the priorities of Mexican farmworkers at the expense of Filipinos. Itliong died a few years later without realizing his dreams for his people.

Family matters continued to receive much of my attention. Our sixth child, Jeanine, was born on May 13, 1965, five years after Jackie. At seven pounds and seven ounces, she was Terri's largest baby at birth. Our family physician, Dr. Nitoma, selected Jeanine's birth to demonstrate an ideal delivery for a group of student nurses. Jeanine and Terri did not disappoint.

The phenomenal growth of the Division of Special Services left me little time for boredom. There always seemed to be a new program to implement, staff to hire or fire, community people to satisfy, explanations to be made to the board of supervisors, and endless oversight of division activities. I relished the challenges. Moreover,

I was proud of what I was accomplishing on the job. My superiors were supportive. My staff grew increasingly able and competent, and about a dozen of them went on to graduate school. I was proud of yet another accomplishment. In 1964, I reached the second of my modest career goals when my annual salary surpassed five figures.

My duties as division head brought me in touch with many business and community leaders. During my naive years, I believed that people attained positions of leadership because of their superior abilities and qualifications. Otherwise, why were they often members of prestigious country clubs and other prominent community organizations? Once I began working with the mostly white people in leadership, I found they often lacked the requisite skills and knowledge for their positions. While my knowledge and skills compared favorably with theirs, I doubted I would ever rise to equivalent positions of power. To begin with, membership in country clubs and other such organizations in which business is often transacted were closed to people of color. In addition, there often was an old boys' club, a relative, or an influential community member behind their appointments. As a brown Filipino, I had no such advantage. I knew I had to be better than, not just equal to, my white competitors.

Under this system, people of color were on the outside looking in. My success in the world of work occurred without affirmative action, since the program would not exist for a few years. The unfair advantage that came with access to influential whites had long been a prime reason for the lack of ethnic minorities in leadership positions, including the public sector, which supposedly assured fairness through civil service protections. I thought of the *manongs* I had grown up with who spent their entire lives in farm labor and had no opportunity to enter other lines of work. The very fact that a Bridge Generation person like me had only just now attained a leadership position was clear evidence of discrimination against Filipinos. European immigrants who arrived in America during the same period as Filipinos were able to enter the mainstream much earlier. Although I subsequently achieved a number of Filipino Firsts in my career, it has been a bittersweet success. My people are still on the outside looking in.

Four challenging and stressful years after my promotion to division chief, I should have felt like I was on top of the world. But instead, I felt a generalized anxiety that often made me unnecessarily brusque and impatient at work and at home. The term "burn-out," which was yet to be coined, would have been a perfect description of what I felt. This burn-out, along with my growing confidence in my abilities, led me to explore other alternatives. I applied for a White House Fellowship in Washington, D.C., and for other county and federal administrative positions. The federal government made me an offer.

Terri and I often dreamed of living and working in San Francisco. We had spent our honeymoon there, gone to jazz clubs, and enjoyed the rich cultural and entertainment life of the metropolitan city. I felt mounting excitement as I drove to the federal office building in San Francisco's Civic Center. My excitement rose further when I was offered the position of Social Services Administrative Advisor (GS-13), instead of the GS-12 level I'd expected. The offer of the higher-level position was part of a recent effort to recruit younger candidates with administrative experience at the local level—people like me. Again, it appeared that I was in the right place at the right time. I was prepared to accept the offer until I learned that the job was not in San Francisco after all but in far-off Washington, D.C.

I was not sure that accepting a position in Washington, D.C., was in our best interests. We would be three thousand miles away from family and friends, and we did not know anyone there. Our children were too young to make a major move. There were risks to taking a job with a completely new employer. But Terri put things in perspective for me. She minimized my fears of the effect the move would have on her and the kids. In addition, she reminded me that I had never been afraid to take risks. And finally, she said, it was my decision to make, not hers.

I accepted the federal job offer in June 1966 and prepared to report for work in August. We had much to do in just a short time before we could make the cross-country move. Our biggest concern was what to do with our house. Corney Pasquil, my jazz pianist pal, who was married to our friend Connie Viernes, came up with the solution. He owned several rentals and offered to take our house as an additional property. I sold our 1963 Chevrolet station wagon to Gary Mead. Alicerae Hanley, who worked for me as a supervisor, arranged through Congressman John Moss's office for a realtor to help us find a suitable place to live in Washington, D.C. Uncle Silverio, who had moved from Washington, D.C., to California, called a *kababayan* to pick us up at the airport. With all the help from our friends and relatives, Terri and I were able to take care of the other details. Since I was still working in Sacramento, Terri shouldered much of the workload, arranging for a moving van, contacting the children's schools, and packing. Fortunately, the federal government was paying for all our moving expenses.

There was one more obstacle. Most of the airlines were on strike, and we could not get a nonstop flight. The best we could do was to fly with several airlines, with a transfer at Chicago's O'Hare Airport, the busiest airport in the country. Before we departed for Washington, D.C., we took the kids to visit our favorite city, San Francisco. "How ironic," I thought. "Now we are only visitors. Just a few weeks earlier, we believed San Francisco was going to be our new home."

Finally, the day arrived for our move to Washington, D.C.

# 10  Washington, D.C.

IT WAS A BRIGHT, SUNNY AUGUST DAY AT THE SAN
Francisco International Airport. We were all dressed in our best
clothes. Terri wore a fashionable outfit, and the girls were adorned
in new dresses, bonnets, and gloves. Peter, wearing a suit and tie,
was a smaller version of his father. Herb, Jeanne, and their children
were there to see us off. Mama and the rest of my brothers were
also there. My sisters Luna and Pula, who was eight months pregnant with her second child, had not arrived by boarding time. As
the plane taxied on the runway, we finally caught sight of them.
They had arrived on time but parked by mistake at the opposite
end of the airport. When Pula and Luna finally got to the gate, all
they could see were the white-gloved hands of our girls waving
good-bye.

This was the very first flight for Terri and the children. I had flown
a few times, but I was hardly a veteran flier. The flight to Chicago
was unremarkable. However, starting with our late arrival in
Chicago, the rest of the day was hectic and stressful. First, we found
that our Eastern Airlines connection at O'Hare was at a distant terminal, and we had only a few minutes to catch our plane. We rushed
through the crowded airport. I carried Jeanine, Terri held Julie and
Jackie by the hand, and Karen, Cheryl, and Peter held hands with
one another. We all toted miscellaneous carry-on baggage. We barely
made the flight.

Our stressful day was just beginning. Because we were late to
board, we had to sit at the rear of the plane. The inefficient air-
conditioning system had little effect on the humid conditions. We

were not only out of breath after running through the airport but also uncomfortably hot. Once we were airborne, the air-conditioning finally began to cool us off. However, we were not prepared for the lightning storm that hit shortly after takeoff. The remainder of the two-hour flight was frightening, particularly for neophyte flyers like us, as the plane alternately dipped and rose amid the thunder and lightning.

We landed at Washington National Airport—harried, disheveled, but grateful to be on solid ground again. After gathering our luggage, we ventured outside to look for Manong Constancio Bucia, Uncle Silverio's *kababayan* who was supposed to meet us. I had never met him, but I was not worried. How many Filipino cab drivers could there be? However, after what seemed to be an eternity of waiting, I began to feel concerned. Mr. Bucia finally appeared, much to our relief. Washington's infamous humidity was getting to all of us. We literally piled into Mr. Bucia's air-conditioned cab, but only after he had used every inch of the trunk to accommodate our luggage. He commented quietly in his gentle Cebuano accent that he had not realized there would be so many of us. Uncle Silverio had somehow failed to tell him that we had six children and three times that many bags.

Washington, D.C., was a cultural shock for all of us, particularly the kids. They were silent and wide-eyed as we drove through the different sections of the city. The brick buildings and the landscape were unlike anything they had ever seen. Manong Bucia lived with his brother in a public-housing development in the city's ghetto. The density and the racial makeup of the residents were also new for the kids. Most of the residents were black. The kids had never seen such a concentration of black people in their lives. Mr. Bucia's housing unit was neat, clean, and inviting. He was a quiet man from Bohol, the home province of Papa, Mama, and Uncle Silverio. He arrived in the United States during the 1920s and had been living in Washington, D.C., since that time. He remembered seeing me when I spent the summer of 1945 with Uncle Silverio. Manong Bucia was an excellent cook whose adobo and rice helped make all of us feel much more comfortable. He proved to be an ideal host and was a good resource for us as well. In the several days we stayed with him, he helped us buy an affordable station wagon, find a reputable bank, and get in touch with Mrs. Augliere, the realtor Congressman Moss's office had asked to assist us with finding housing.

Mrs. Augliere's territory was the Arlington–Falls Church area of Virginia, across the Potomac River and about ten miles from the District of Columbia. Earlier, Terri and I had decided we should rent, perhaps with an option to buy. The Washington, D.C., area was the highest-priced housing market in the United States. We wanted to feel more secure before we purchased a home. We finally decided on a two-story, three-level brick house in the Seven Corners area of Falls Church, at 3023 Castle Road. The house had four bedrooms plus an enormous master bedroom with its own fireplace. It was located in a quiet, woodsy neighborhood of similarly large homes. However, the house rented for $299 a month, about three times more than our house payment in Sacramento. According to Mrs. Augliere, the rent was a bargain. The neighborhood was also prestigious. For example, our next-door neighbor, Henry Byroade, was a career diplomat and in just a few years would become U.S. Ambassador to the Philippines.

August 17, 1966, was my first day as a federal employee. I reported to Field Services Branch III, Division of Program Operations, Bureau of Family Services, Welfare Administration, Department of Health, Education, and Welfare (DHEW). With five organizational levels, DHEW was the largest bureaucracy I ever worked with. Field Services Branch III was responsible for regional offices in Dallas and San Francisco, which oversaw state welfare programs. The department offered a generous GS-13 incentive to recruit young professionals like me. It did not take long for me to figure out why. Staff members at the Bureau of Family Services had entered federal service soon after the 1935 Social Security Act and were mostly in their fifties and sixties. These veteran staffers were knowledgeable and effective, but the bureau clearly needed an infusion of younger blood. Again, a job seemed to have come my way because I was in the right place at the right time and was willing to take the risks involved in accepting it.

Marcelle Clark, assistant chief of program operations, was my immediate supervisor. The plain-spoken, gruff, but kindly social worker from South Carolina had a reputation for augmenting her vast program knowledge with practical common sense. She was highly regarded by everyone, including those in the highest echelons of the department. I could not have had a better supervisor for my first federal-service job. Moreover, she and I hit it off from the beginning. Marcelle seemed to appreciate my sense of humor; I liked her homespun wisdom and quick wit. Other members of the branch were Irmgaard Taylor, born and raised in Germany, who still spoke with an accent; Luisa Iglesias, a New Yorker of Puerto Rican background; and Bob Brown, a black newcomer to federal service.

Of all my fellow workers, Irmgaard developed the closest relationship with me and my family. At first glance, this may have seemed somewhat surprising because of our ages and backgrounds. She was of retirement age, Caucasian, and European born and raised; I was thirty years younger, Filipino, and American born. What brought us together was her passion for hiking. Irmgaard regularly hiked the surrounding hills of Maryland and Virginia and knew all the trails. Terri, the kids, and I often went with her on weekend outings. Because the children were so small, Irmgaard took us on walking trails that were easy for all of us—except for Jeanine, a toddler, whom I had to carry. At the end of each trail, we usually got an unforgettable view of the valley below. The prettiest view was from Panorama Peak in Virginia's Shenandoah Mountains. Another unforgettable hike was to Sugarloaf Mountain in Maryland, where we could see parts of five states—Delaware, Maryland, Pennsylvania, Virginia, and West Virginia.

The kids adjusted well to their new environment despite their unusual first day of school. When I asked them about it, their unexpected response was, "It was strange. We didn't expect anyone to know us, but we don't understand why most of our classmates didn't know one another either." We would learn later that this was the first day of desegregation in the Commonwealth of Virginia, which caused widespread changes in school attendance boundaries. Actually, desegregation helped with our children's adjustment to their new school because everyone else had to make adjustments, too. Moreover, since they were neither black nor white, they did not carry the racial baggage of their classmates. However, they did have to deal with occasional taunts of "Chinks" and "Kongs." To their credit, they were able to educate their schoolmates about their Filipino identity, and in a relatively short period, they had almost as many friends in their new school as they had in California.

For the children and me, school and work provided built-in places for meeting new people, but Terri had no such source for socialization. She busied herself with caring for our family and making our home comfortable with her customary flair. However, from time to time, I noticed that she missed the companionship of relatives and friends in California. She filled some of the void through her interest in the arts. She took advantage of Washington's many art galleries, with us in tow. We also went to a number of pre-Broadway shows at Washington's National Theater. The children also developed an appreciation for culture. While I was always part of these artistic adventures, I did not have the same passion for the arts.

On weekends, we enjoyed the historical and tourist attractions of the Washington, D.C., area, particularly during the first few years we lived in the East. Although I had visited Washington in 1945, I had forgotten how beautiful and awesome the various buildings and monuments were. We visited the Capitol, the Congressional buildings, the Lincoln and Jefferson Memorials, the Washington Monument, and the White House. By the awed looks on our children's faces, I knew they were impressed as well. The myriad exhibits of the Smithsonian Institution, particularly the futuristic space-age exhibits, broadened our view of the world. Nearby Civil War sites such as Bull Run and Gettysberg were vivid reminders of the thousands of lives that were lost in the conflict. We also took longer trips to early American historical sites at Jamestown, Williamsburg, Yorktown and to Thomas Jefferson's palatial home at Monticello. On an extended vacation, we swam and sunned at Virginia and Buckroe Beaches. One remarkable aspect of living in the area was that we were able to experience the historical significance of the Revolutionary War, the Civil War, and both World Wars and also enjoy the beach and the mountains. At the same time, we lived in the metropolitan area of the nation's capital, where history was made daily.

We also took a number of trips to Baltimore to visit Uncle Calixto and Aunt Colleen. I was shocked when I first saw them. Their living situation had deteriorated from the last time I had visited them in 1945. They lived in a run-down apartment in a poor part of town, quite different from their former North Charles Street middle-class neighborhood. Their apartment was sparsely furnished. Gone were most of the furniture and artifacts from Senator Weller, Uncle Calixto's longtime employer. Most shocking of all, they both seemed to be in poor condition, physically and emotionally. Uncle Calixto was no longer the smiling, happy person I remembered, and Aunt Colleen was incoherent at times. I soon learned that Uncle Calixto suffered from diabetes, and Aunt Colleen had a serious drinking problem, so serious that over the years, she had sold much of their furnishings, many of them valuable antiques, for alcohol. I wondered how many bottles of cheap wine Aunt Colleen had exchanged for their antiques.

In 1967, Uncle Calixto suffered a stroke and had to be hospitalized. I had kept Mama and Uncle Silverio regularly informed about their brother's situation from the time of my first visit to Baltimore. When Uncle Calixto became bedridden, they decided to move him and Aunt Colleen to California so that they could take better care of him. Mama and Uncle Silverio flew in immediately to make the necessary arrangements. Uncle Calixto's health had deteriorated to such an extent that he would live for less than a year. Afterward, Aunt Colleen would return to Maryland, where she would pass away shortly from complications of alcoholism.

It was good to see Mama again. As the first family member to visit our new home, she received a warm welcome, particularly from the kids. By now, they were familiar with the city's attractions and excitedly showed their grandmother around town. We also stopped in at the Catholic National Shrine, to which Mama had made a small contribution some years back. She was awed by the impressive facility with its various chapels and religious shrines. As it turned out, Mama's visit with us was rushed and far too short. She stayed for just a few days, only until Uncle Silverio completed arrangements to take Uncle Calixto and Aunt Colleen back with them to California.

I admired Mama's unwavering decision to come to the aid of her brother and his wife in their time of need. Considering that Uncle Calixto and Aunt Colleen refused to assist her when she first arrived in America in 1929, no one would have blamed her for doing the same to them now. But I was not surprised by her decision. Her faith had much to do with choosing to forgive her brother and his wife for their actions. A more important factor, however, was the Filipino value of *walay ulaw*. She could not bring shame on her family by disrespecting her sibling and turning her back on him. I never heard Mama speak ill of her brothers, nor did she ever talk about the shabby treatment she'd received in 1929.

Another Californian came to visit us shortly thereafter. Pat Suzuki, from my Livingston High School graduating class of 1948, spent a wonderful Saturday afternoon with us. She was costarring with Robert Reed in the stage play *The Owl and the Pussycat* at the National Theater, where Terri and I had seen her the evening before. Pat starred on Broadway in the original cast of *Flower Drum Song* and had a successful television and recording career. She clearly was the most famous member of our graduating class. We had not seen each other since we were both at San Jose State in 1953. I remembered Pat as a vivacious and outgoing girl who interacted comfortably with all ethnic groups in high school. As such, most of her Nisei classmates, more conservative and inclined to socialize only with other Japanese Americans, ostracized her. She was now a widow, the mother of one son, and a confirmed New York City resident. It was like old times. Pat and I swapped many stories and reminisced about the "good old days."

I almost did not get to visit with Pat. While getting ready to pick her up at her Washington hotel, I noticed that the station wagon needed washing. After all, I was going to pick up a big star of the entertainment world. I got on top of the car, water hose in hand. Suddenly, my bare feet slipped out from under me, and I fell to the ground. My first thought was that I was lucky to land on my feet. Jackie, who was watching me, asked, "Daddy, what is the red stuff coming from under your feet?" I had landed on my feet all right, but on the sharp edge of a rock. A pool of blood formed quickly under my feet. Terri drove me to the emergency ward, where I was told I had to wait my turn. However, when the staff noticed that my bleeding was making a mess of the hospital waiting room, they quickly gave me a shot and stitched up my foot.

In the wake of President Kennedy's assassination in 1963, a number of social welfare reforms and civil rights legislation became law under President Lyndon B. Johnson. When I joined the Division of Program Operations, it was engaged in the continuing development, oversight, and implementation of the 1962 Social Security Amendments. One of my major assignments was to review California's proposed plan for medical assistance, known as MediCal, a task I relished since it brought me back in touch with state officials I knew in Sacramento. California's plan was one of the more comprehensive proposals yet submitted and would shape decisions made on the plans of other states. I threw myself into the assignment, much to the delight of my superiors. My performance in reviewing the MediCal proposal enhanced my growing reputation within the Division of Program Operations.

As part of a major departmental reorganization, I received a promotion on April 1968, less than two years after coming to work for the federal government. Again, I was in the right place at the right time. My new job, as branch chief of the Division of Program Operations, brought me into the midst of federal policy making and came with a corresponding increase in salary. In this position, I was responsible for supervising a staff of four. My specific assignment was to provide central office direction to regional offices in Dallas and San Francisco. This was my first experience in developing policy that would influence nationwide programs.

The promotion also meant I would be traveling to California, where I would have a chance to visit family and friends. As it turned out, my first business trip after my promotion was a three-month assignment to New York City. Scandal and financial improprieties had recently rocked the city's welfare programs, and I was assigned to a special investigative unit that would be reviewing the city's practices. My job was to interview welfare mothers and verify decisions made on their cases. The territory I was supposed to cover included some of the toughest neighborhoods of New York City—the Bronx, Brooklyn, and Harlem. Many of my interviewees lived in public-housing high-rises with reputations for drugs and violence. As if this was not daunting enough, I often had to trudge up multiple flights of stairs to ice-cold rooms because employees of Consolidated Edison were on strike. The assignment opened my eyes to the harsh realities of living poor in a large city. It also made me appreciate the complexities of administering welfare programs in such an adverse environment. In comparison, my earlier experience with the ANC program in Sacramento seemed much simpler.

On a lighter note, the New York City assignment gave me the opportunity to get acquainted with the city's many attractions. I became a savvy subway rider, developing the ability to read a tabloid newspaper with one hand while holding onto a strap with the other. I also found my way to the various ethnic neighborhoods and city districts and familiarized myself with jazz clubs such as the Blue Note.

In Washington, D.C., my leisure activities usually involved baseball, Little League and major league. The game was important not only to me but also to Peter, who was developing into a skilled infielder with his Little League team in Falls Church. At the end of his last year in Little League, Peter was selected for the all-star team and participated in the Virginia State Championship playoffs, where his team was eliminated in the second round. Peter had the largest and loudest rooting section, led by Terri and his sisters. He could always count on getting a big ovation when he came up to bat, got a hit, or made a good fielding play.

Whenever we attended Saturday afternoon games of the Washington Senators, it was a Jamero family outing. We took full advantage of the Senators' promotions for afternoon games, which enabled families to sit in the unreserved section for only $2, including parking. We went to D.C. Stadium early so we could claim the seats right next to the reserved section. Terri packed a lunch and brought refreshments for all eight of us, so the $2 fee was practically the only expense we incurred during these outings. Not surprisingly, we saw as many New York Yankees games as possible. Unfortunately, these were not banner years for the longtime champions. They finished in the second division during the entire time we lived in the Washington, D.C., area. The great stars of Yankees glory had either retired, been traded, or were only a shadow of their former selves. In 1968, Mickey Mantle was in his last year as an active player. Injuries had slowed him down so that he could not hit or field well. Anyone who had watched Mantle in his productive years would have found it sad to see him so ineffective. Terri took some movies of him on his very last game in Washington, D.C. To this day, I still cannot bear to watch this version of the player who was once the most feared hitter in major league baseball.

We became a small piece of history when Terri and I were part of an official White House reception hosted by President Johnson for West Germany's chancellor Konrad Adenauer. We watched as the two tall, ramrod-straight world leaders made brief remarks to the attentive audience. The reception was in the Rose Garden on a beautiful spring day. How did we manage to be part of the reception? It was regular procedure in gathering a crowd for official Rose Garden functions to have each department, on a rotating basis, ask for volunteers from its workforce. The only other requirement was that the employee have a security clearance. Fortunately, my clearance, issued when I was in the navy, was still in force.

In 1968, I found myself in the midst of one of the ugliest episodes in America's history. Riots broke out in Washington, D.C., following the assassination of Dr. Martin Luther King Jr. in Memphis, Tennessee. The riots were centered in the vicinity of Seventh Street and Florida Avenue, the area in which Griffith Stadium, the old baseball park, had been located. Along with thousands of other federal workers, I watched the steady stream of black smoke in the distance through the windows of my fourth-floor office and listened to the radio for breaking news. Suddenly, without warning, came the announcement ordering all federal employees to go home. This turned out to be a big mistake. With everyone on the main roads at the same time, a massive traffic jam quickly developed. I had called Terri immediately after the announcement. I knew she was on her way to pick me up but wondered how she would maneuver through the confusion. She made it to my office building sooner than expected by getting off the main streets and driving on the shoulder.

I believe the government panicked and overreacted to the riots. The violence, confined to a relatively small area, was not even close to the government buildings. Moreover, the damage was limited to businesses known to have taken unfair advantage of black customers. I seriously doubt whether the same level of panic and overreaction would have occurred if whites rather than blacks had been participating in the violence. The most memorable sight of the riots for me, however, was the immediate posting of rifle-bearing militia in government buildings. It reminded me of my experiences during the Korean War. I did not like what I saw.

The riots led to the establishment of Resurrection City, a tent city occupied by members of the Southern Christian Leadership Council, who were there protesting unfair practices in the provision of social services. The temporary encampment in the Capital Park area adjacent to the Lincoln Memorial housed civil rights marchers led by the Reverend Ralph Abernathy, successor to the assassinated Dr. King. The marchers, mostly from rural areas of the South, were engaged in a nonviolent demonstration designed to elicit better services.

My assignment was to assist a cadre of federal officials in

addressing the protesters' concerns. I believed that many of their grievances were reasonable. I saw that they were weary after their long march and uncomfortable in their quarters in Resurrection City, which was muddy after days of constant rain. Most of them had not been able to communicate with their families back home. I agreed to let some of them use the telephones in our office building to call home. At the office, I was shocked by the negative reactions of a few of my fellow workers when I arrived with a group of protesters. One staffer objected, "These dirty people have no business being here." Shocked, I ignored the remarks and went ahead with assisting the demonstrators. My shock quickly turned to anger and disillusionment as I thought about the hypocrisy of these white public employees, paid to assure the provision of adequate social services to people in need. The protesters were only seeking equal treatment under the law; they did not deserve to be insulted.

I should not have been surprised at the racist remarks of the federal workers. The fight for civil rights continued to be resisted by many Americans and affected not only blacks but all people of color. When we first moved to Virginia, Terri and I went to the Department of Motor Vehicles to get our state drivers' licenses. At every slight deviation during my driving test, the white examiner sarcastically commented, "You're not in California. We don't let *you people* drive like that here." I said nothing, since having a driver's license was essential to me. I failed the driver's test after being marked down for minor or imaginary infractions. Terri had the same experience. Although the examiner referenced California, his real message was not lost on me. I was not only a Californian but a Californian with brown skin. I doubt that a white person from California would have received the same treatment.

Another racial incident occurred shortly after the 1968 riots. We were on a leisurely family outing on a lonely road in southern Virginia when I noticed a pickup in the rear view mirror. As it drew closer, I saw that its gun rack held two rifles. The pickup suddenly sped up and tried to force us off the road. It was an awkward effort that, fortunately for us, was unsuccessful. I could think of two possible reasons for this senseless act. First, we were brown and were perhaps mistaken for blacks. Second, our rear bumper bore a sticker that read "Black and White Together."

The Resurrection City experience disillusioned me about federal service. Although I was well paid, I began to consider other options. My work developing federal policies brought me into contact with many attorneys I admired, and my appreciation of the law grew. I explored the idea of enrolling at Georgetown University, which had one of the best law schools in the United States, and was encouraged by the possibilities. My plan was to attend law school at night. Terri was working at the Navy Department and we believed that law school was doable under these circumstances.

I also applied for a Career Incentive Program fellowship that awarded midcareer federal employees one-year grants to attend one of twelve quality universities in the country, all expenses paid. The fellowship was prestigious and highly competitive. For example, one of the applicants was Richard Holbrooke, who went on to become the U.S. Ambassador to the United Nations during the Clinton administration. Although I received an excellent recommendation from Steve Symonds, commissioner of the Assistance Payments Administration, I thought it was a long shot at best. I barely came under the upper age limit for the program. Moreover, I had fewer years of service than most of the other applicants.

There was another potential obstacle. Contrary to the explicit instructions on the application, which asked me to list three universities, I wrote that I would go only to Stanford University if selected. Consequently, I was surprised to receive a notice for an interview. When the interview panel asked why I had listed only one university, I decided to answer honestly. I said, "I have already put my family through a lot by moving them across the country. If we move again this quickly, it should be to a university close to home. Stanford is the only institution under the Career Incentive Program to meet this criterion." A few weeks later, I was notified that I had been accepted into the program and would be attending

Stanford University beginning in the fall of 1969. I forgot about going to Georgetown University and becoming an attorney.

Under the Career Incentive Program, awardees and their dependents received per diem allowances. When the personnel department calculated our per diem, they first thought there must be a mistake because it totaled about the same amount as my monthly salary. In the entire history of the program, no awardee with this many dependents had made this long of a move and been allowed such a large per diem. The department was reluctant to authorize the allowance. After I pointed out that the calculations were consistent with the rules, the department agreed to authorize the calculated amount. The per diem was an unexpected windfall. Terri and I decided we would bank the per diem since I would continue to earn a full salary while attending Stanford. In just another year, the accumulated per diem would be the major funding source for purchasing our next house.

Luna visited us for a few weeks shortly before we were to leave for California. Her visit turned out to be helpful for our move as well. I was to supposed to be in Stanford in July for orientation. Terri and I, particularly Terri, had a million things to do before we could make the move to California. We would be returning to the same house in Falls Church after the year at Stanford, which meant the house had to be ready for the family who would be subleasing it while we were away. We needed to determine which household goods should go with us and which should remain in Virginia. In addition, we had to sell the car. Terri thought that if the kids flew back to California with Luna, they wouldn't be underfoot, and the few free days would give us the time to take care of moving. Luna readily agreed to accompany the girls back to California. Peter stayed behind with us, as his all-star team was still alive in the Little League state playoffs.

# 11  *A Stanford Man*

WE RENTED A THREE-BEDROOM HOUSE AT 324 LA Mesa Drive in the Ladera neighborhood of Menlo Park, just west of Stanford University. At first, we considered living in married student housing on campus, but after looking at the tiny rooms, we decided to look elsewhere. Ladera was home to a number of Stanford faculty members. John Ralston, the football coach, and his family lived up the block. There was also a neighborhood recreation center complete with a pool, where the kids learned to swim. The rent was somewhat pricey, but Terri and I felt that since the house was so much roomier, it was well worth it. Besides, we would be there for only a year.

Stanford University lived up to its reputation, and then some. The academic excellence of its faculty members and the richness of its course offerings were even better than I had anticipated. During our orientation to the Public Affairs Fellowship Program, I was pleased to learn that a great number of course offerings were available to Fellows. We had only one required class, a five-unit seminar taught by Dr. Eric Hutchinson, director of the program. At the same time, we were encouraged to audit as many elective classes as we could schedule.

I looked forward to taking as many classes as I could squeeze into my one year at the university. There was so much from which to choose. Moreover, academic offerings had changed significantly. When I was in college during the 1950s, courses in such subjects as ethnic studies and civil rights were nonexistent. At Stanford, there seemed to be no end to the intriguing offerings in these and other subjects. Knowing that I did not have to worry about tests and grades, I signed up for such diverse courses as History of Portuguese Slave Traders, Constitutional Law, Business and the Civil Rights Movement, Public Administration Theory and Practice, and Nonviolent Civil Disobedience. It was a great opportunity to catch up on my knowledge. How was I able to afford the books required for so many classes? My fellowship included a government charge card for the Stanford Bookstore.

Fifteen Fellows made up the Public Affairs Class of 1969–70, representing virtually every federal department. All but two were men, and all were white except for Tony Elias and Jack Brent, who were black; Bill Babby, who was Native American; and me. At thirty-nine, I was the oldest. The Fellows were superbly articulate, intelligent, and knowledgeable about a whole host of subjects. I had never been in the company of such gifted people. We became a close-knit, compatible group, thanks to our shared background as federal employees and because we were older than most of the university students. Our closeness also grew out of our interactions in Dr. Hutchinson's weekly seminar. The seminar was loosely structured, appropriate for a group that had such wide-ranging interests and concerns. We discussed current topics such as civil rights, the emerging women's movement, and hippie lifestyles as well as traditional subjects like the role of government in a changing nation. After the seminar, we Fellows usually went to a nearby pub where we continued our intense discussions.

Of all the Fellows, I became closest to Tony Elias, originally from New Orleans, and Bill Babby, from the Big Sky State of Montana, perhaps because of our status as ethnic minorities. Through seminar discussions, we learned early on that we had the same views on race relations and civil rights. Tony's outgoing and engaging personality was not unlike my style of interacting with people. We were like kindred spirits. Bill was quiet and thoughtful, but, like me, he was a country boy who had an appreciation for rural life. Their wives, Sara Elias and Bert Babby, were compatible with Terri. We began to socialize as couples more and more.

As far as other facets of Stanford campus life were concerned, I found that my elective classes were instructive and met my desire for increased knowledge on a variety of subjects. The young students in these classes seemed to accept my active participation despite our age difference. I admit that the bra-less girls on campus initially distracted me, but like the other male Fellows, I soon got over it.

Some aspects of Stanford students were personally irritating. First, I could never quite get used to the unkempt and shabby state of many of the students. Some did not seem to bathe regularly. Most Stanford students came from high-income or middle-class families and could afford to be clean and better dressed. Logically, I knew that these students reflected the current "hippie" lifestyle, but emotionally I saw them as spoiled, rich, white kids trying to look poor at a time when disadvantaged groups were making genuine efforts to assert themselves. It further galled me that these young people tried to look poor at the same time they turned to their well-to-do parents to satisfy their every whim and want.

I also disliked their hypocritical involvement in the antiwar movement. Like many campuses around the country, Stanford was a hotbed of opposition to the Vietnam War. Many of the male students had secured draft deferments because they could afford to attend the university, yet one of their main issues was the country's unfair use of mostly poor minority men and women to fight the Vietnam War. If they felt that strongly about it, they should have enlisted; they should not have used their personal connections or wealth to get out of serving. I also continued to harbor some bitterness about continuing perceptions of the Korean War. As far as I was concerned, the war in Korea was really the first Vietnam War— the first unpopular, undeclared war with a high casualty rate. These students, like many other Americans, had somehow forgotten that the Korean War was a bloody conflict in which 54,000 American lives were lost. When Stanford closed the campus during one of the antiwar demonstrations, Terri and I, along with Bill and Bert Babby, went to Reno to get away from what we considered insincere and disingenuous protests.

There were several unexpected bonuses to being at Stanford. First, the school's football team was having one of its most successful seasons. I took Terri and the kids to several Saturday afternoon games at the 100,000-person-capacity Stanford Stadium, where we were able to get good seats at student rates. All-American quarterback Jim Plunkett and his teammates became champions of the PAC-10 and ended a great year with a win at the 1970 Rose Bowl.

The second bonus was also sports related. I had the opportunity to see one of the great UCLA basketball teams in action. I took advantage of student rates to see UCLA at Stanford's Maples Arena and bought tickets for my brothers George and Titi. The 1969–70 team featured forwards Sidney Wicks and Curtis Rowe, center Steve Patterson, and guards John Vallely and Henry Bibby. At the end of the season, Wicks and Rowe were named to the All-American team as UCLA again won the national title under legendary coach John Wooden.

The Filipino youth clubs and the tournament circuit in California declined considerably in the years we were living back east. One reason for the decline was the prohibitive cost of insurance now required by local schools and municipalities that held basketball tournaments in their gymnasiums. Perhaps a more significant reason was that the doors to many social and recreational activities, previously closed to the Bridge Generation, were now open to Filipino youth. Youth clubs and tournaments were a large part of Terri's and my lives. Although we were thankful that Filipinos had more opportunities to participate in American society, it was hard for us to accept that youth clubs, healthy outlets for our generation, were no longer part of the Filipino youth experience.

Although tournaments were in decline, they were not dead. Volleyball tournaments continued to be popular. The big difference was that there were now as many girls' teams as boys' teams. Nina Gonzalez, who grew up in the Livingston area, was living in San Francisco with her husband Sam and their two girls. Nina played for the Bay-O-Nets, one of the more successful teams in the volleyball tournaments. Remembering Terri's Most Valuable Player performance in 1957, Nina immediately recruited Terri for the team. Terri's MVP days may have been behind her, but she was still competitive. Furthermore, she had a built-in rooting section in her family, who, only a few months earlier, had cheered loudly for Peter at his Little League games.

The Bay-O-Nets hosted a volleyball tournament later that spring. The team had never beaten its archrivals, the Stockton Karaans (Old-timers) before. However, the Bay-O-Nets were greatly improved. Not only did they have Terri, but Terri, in turn, recruited my cousin Nancy Galanida. Nancy, in her early twenties, was tall and athletic, no longer the little girl I remembered as hiding behind Aunt Emma's skirts in Sunol. The Bay-O-Nets beat the Karaans to win the tournament championship.

We celebrated the Bay-O-Nets' championship at that evening's tournament dance. What turned out to be a bigger celebration, however, was being with so many of our old friends again. Terri and I had not seen many of them for at least ten years. The dance was a fun-filled reunion for us. We brought Karen, Cheryl, and Peter— now in their teens—along with us, thinking they might enjoy being there after hearing so many stories about the dances.

The only baseball I saw were San Francisco Giants games at Candlestick Park, a short drive away. Even though I could have watched the New York Yankees when they came to Oakland to play the A's, I was so disappointed by their decline that I never could quite get myself to go. The spectator sport for me in this year was football, especially the Oakland Raiders. The American Football League, of which the Raiders were a charter member, was formed in 1960. The newer league proved to be immediately competitive with the more established National Football League and won most of its games. The Raiders had exciting players, like quarterback George Blanda, receiver Fred Biletnikoff, center Jim Otto, defensive back Willie Brown, and guard Gene Upshaw—who would all be elected to the Football Hall of Fame after their playing days were over. They played across the Bay, easily accessible by way of the San Mateo Bridge. I saw them a number of times accompanied by Terri or Peter, who, like his father, temporarily changed his sports allegiance from the Yankees to the Raiders.

Terri and I also took advantage of our close proximity to San Francisco to enjoy my other love—jazz. Jimmy Tenio, my saxophone-playing cousin from Stockton, had a steady gig at a club near the Marina, which soon became a regular jazz venue for us. Jimmy's younger siblings often joined him, Josie on vocals and Rudy on piano. We also made sure we listened to pianist Flip Nunez, whom we first met in Sacramento. Flip was living in San Francisco and played regularly at one of the many jazz clubs in the city. There were so many Filipino musician-friends in town that we seldom had time to take in some of the nationally known musicians who came to San Francisco.

Shortly after the beginning of 1970, it dawned on Terri and me that we would be back in Washington, D.C., in just a few months. Unexpectedly, I received word that a new office would be opening in Seattle, part of the new Federal Region X. I was asked if I would be interested in working there and could not write back fast enough to request a transfer. That spring, I received official approval for a transfer to the new Seattle office.

The year at Stanford was one of the best years for Terri and me. I attended one of the best universities in the country. We lived in one of the most beautiful areas in California, within easy driving distance of our favorite city, San Francisco. We visited with our ever expanding families and reminisced with old friends. Moreover, we had a few more dollars to use for enjoying life, thanks to my per diem.

If we could not stay at Stanford, then the next best place for me to work was the beautiful city of Seattle. We had been very impressed with Seattle when our family visited it on vacation in 1964. Terri and I had an old friend there, Fred Cordova, formerly of Stockton. Most important, we would be able to visit family, with relatives in California only sixteen hours away by car. We were looking forward to our family's next adventure.

Again, Terri took the lead in organizing the family for the move. Although we had become veterans at moving, this one was different. We had to take care of two households—one in Menlo Park and the other in Falls Church. We also had to find a place in Seattle that would accommodate our family of eight. To complicate things further, I was required to report to my new office in Seattle no later than August 1, which meant we had to complete the various phases of our move within six weeks. The first step was to vacate the Ladera house and put our household goods in storage until we found a place in Seattle.

We decided that the remaining steps would be easier if we did not have to cart the children with us to Falls Church and Seattle. Our families came to the rescue and offered to watch the kids while we handled the moving details. Karen, Julie, and Jeanine stayed with Mama and Papa in Livingston, Cheryl and Peter were with Herb and Jeanne in Milpitas, and Jackie went to Terri's brother Bob and his family in Marina.

After arranging to pack our household effects in Washington, D.C., we flew to Seattle to purchase a home. Because we had to make a decision in only a few days, we looked for a home in a school district that offered the highest-quality education. Realty companies advised us that Bellevue, a suburb located about ten miles away from Seattle on the other side of Lake Washington, had the best schools in the area. We ended up buying a two-story four-bedroom house in Bellevue. We then flew back to California and rounded up our children. By the time we returned to California, we had not seen the kids for three weeks, our longest separation by far. We did not know whether we had missed the kids more or vice versa. All Terri and I knew was that it felt wonderful to be reunited.

Now that we were together again, we knew we would soon be on our way to Seattle. First, we rewarded the kids for behaving so well during our absence with a whirlwind trip to Disneyland, the San Diego Zoo, and Tijuana, Mexico. Then we were ready for our next big adventure. Seattle, here we come!

# IV

## THE ACTIVIST
## EXECUTIVE
### 1970–1995

DURING THE 1970S, THE UNITED STATES CON-tinued its efforts to provide civil rights protections to all Americans. As a result, affirmative action programs sprouted up in public programs across the nation and began to take root in the private sector as well. Although the civil rights movement was previously considered a black movement, it expanded to include groups such as women, people with disabilities, and other racial minorities. The feminist movement was born. Congress passed the Rehabilitation Act of 1973. There was a great awakening among other ethnic communities as Hispanics and Latinos, Asian Americans, and Native Americans—all concerned about their rightful place in America—grew increasingly activist in their political strategies.

Through their involvement with the emerging Asian American movement, Bridge Generation Filipino Americans became much more visible in the country's fight for civil rights. West Coast Filipino Americans were in the forefront of civil right demonstrations. Initially, Filipinos were part of an Asian community that had grown disenchanted with its stereotyped image as quiet, submissive Americans. In Seattle and San Francisco, Filipino Americans assumed leadership positions in the protest against mainstream intrusions into traditional Asian neighborhoods. More important, the 1970s saw the beginnings of a separate Filipino American movement. Sadly, Filipino visibility in civil rights vanished around the early 1980s. The divisiveness caused by the anti-Marcos movement in the United States and the disenchantment of activist Filipino Americans as their causes were disproportionately ignored in favor of other Asian ethnic groups combined to abort the promising movement.

During the years between 1970 and 1995, my community and political activities were a modest reflection of these larger events. No longer was I content to be a bystander in the fight for social justice. Thanks to my affiliation with the Young Turks—a close-knit, politically savvy group of Filipino Americans—I became not only an activist and advocate for the Asian-Filipino community but also a four-time political appointee and a candidate for elective office. Together, we helped make the larger community aware of a developing brown tinge in the sociopolitical mainstream of Seattle. The Young Turks became our most intimate friends in the twenty exciting years Terri and I resided in Seattle.

These were also the years when I matured—professionally, politically, and personally. Under my leadership, agencies that were new, in transition, or in serious trouble became organizationally and financially stable. Every department for which I served as director significantly increased its budget without a commensurate increase in staff. Agencies actively recruited me for vacancies in their organizations. My peers elected me to several national positions of leadership. I was considered for a presidential appointment in Washington, D.C.

Politically, I mastered the art of the doable and possible without compromising my commitment to my community. While I had attained previous jobs without outside help, I learned the value of community pressure and affirmative action in seeking positions and in building support for my programs. People from both sides of the political aisle sought me. A Republican governor, a Democratic governor, a Democratic county executive, and a Democratic mayor—all appointed me as agency head.

It was in my personal life, however, that I experienced the greatest growth. Although racial incidents still occurred, I grew up as a more secure brown person living in a country that continued to struggle with issues of fairness in its relationships with persons of color. Even more important, my children also grew up with their color brown. The values that Terri and I tried to instill in our children, that it was important to have a balanced knowledge of their Filipino culture, apparently took. To this day, they clearly identify as Filipino Americans but never use their ethnicity as an excuse for individual disappointments.

Seattle is the place where I have spent the most productive years of my life. Here, I found a mainstream community with a strong commitment to fairness and diversity, a relatively enlightened Filipino community with an unusual willingness to work with younger Filipino Americans, and the politically savvy Young Turks. All were instrumental in virtually every one of my endeavors. ❦

# 12  *Region X*

WE ROUTINELY TOOK ROAD TRIPS WHEN WE LIVED in California. Drives of two hours to visit relatives and even four to six hours for vacations to Disneyland and San Diego were commonplace for our family. However, we had never experienced anything like the trip we took in July 1970, when we drove from Menlo Park to our new home in Bellevue, Washington. The nine-hundred-mile trip in our 1962 Chevrolet station wagon took fifteen hours of straight driving, with time out only to eat, refuel, and take potty breaks. It was the first of many trips we would make between California and Seattle in the next twenty years. Thank goodness the kids were good travelers. The transition to Bellevue went so well that we still had time to take a mini-vacation. We went to Vancouver, British Columbia, a three-hour drive on Interstate 5. Only a few short weeks before, we had crossed the southern terminus of I-5 into Tijuana, Mexico. Now, here we were, crossing the northern terminus of the interstate into Canada.

After a year in academia, I was eager to get to work on my new job. I had yet to meet anyone from the new Seattle regional office and was understandably curious about my coworkers. The pre-employment process, conducted entirely with personnel staff in Washington, D.C., consisted of performing a cursory review of my central office performance and obtaining favorable references from my superiors. I thought it unusual, but also flattering, that my new employers did not even think it necessary to interview me before approving my transfer request. My job description stated that I was to serve as the primary federal representative in the region for welfare, medical assistance, and social service programs authorized by the Social Security Act. I had become knowledgeable and proficient in these programs while working in the Washington, D.C., headquarters and should be able to transfer this knowledge and proficiency to the regional level. Moreover, my former job as bureau chief of Field Operations required regular contact with regional offices in Dallas and San Francisco, which meant I already had a working knowledge of regional operations.

The job description also stated that I would be assigned to one of two state teams in the region. My state team was composed of other program specialists from the programs of aging, vocational rehabilitation, juvenile justice, and mental health plus specialists in personnel, systems, and planning. As a regional assistance payments specialist, I was the only program person, and the only member of an ethnic minority, with headquarters experience in Washington, D.C. Only two other people on the team had federal service experience. The rest came from state or local government or the private sector. I was not exactly sure what working with a state team entailed. However, given my program experience in regional offices, I felt I should be able to make the adjustment.

Of the sixteen staff members on the two state teams, four were ethnic minorities: two blacks, a Japanese American, and me. Top-level leadership at the Social and Rehabilitation Service was all white. No other DHEW region in the country operated under the state team structure. In this experimental approach, team members were responsible for all programs, not just their own primary programs. Experienced team members had the additional responsibility of preparing staff who were new to federal service. Since I was one of only three team members with federal experience, I was expected to train other staff in their programs as well as in my program. Moreover, I was to train the new assistance payments specialist on the other state team. When I pointed out that these additional responsibilities would likely affect my ability to perform my primary duties, I was told that I had to learn to be "a good team member." Despite this unusual interpretation of my responsibilities, I was not seriously concerned—at least, not initially. I came away from my first day on the job feeling that I must have misunderstood what I had heard from my new employers. Their interpretation of the state team approach seemed far removed from generally accepted management practices.

Other aspects of the transition to the Pacific Northwest went much more smoothly. We celebrated my fortieth birthday soon after our arrival. Many people regard forty as the beginning of old age, but I felt good about turning forty. I still felt young. I was in good health, and so was my family. I had matured as a husband and a father. My career had greatly exceeded my expectations, and my ability to support my family had improved considerably. I remembered how depressed I had been when I turned thirty. Ten years later, I was pleased about the turnaround in my self-assessment. I felt truly blessed.

One of the first things we did after our move was to call our old friend Fred Cordova, who invited the family for a get-acquainted visit. I knew Fred from our basketball tournament days, when he played for the Stockton Padres. The team name was most appropriate for Fred, who spent a year at seminary. We had all thought he surely was going to become a Catholic priest.

Fred and Dorothy lived in a large home in an established Seattle neighborhood adjacent to the beautiful Arboretum. We immediately felt comfortable in their presence. They were warm and outgoing, and their mannerisms reminded us of our Filipino American friends in California. Their experiences and attitudes were similar to ours. Their eight children were roughly the same ages as our kids, and the two sets of children hit it off right away. Fred and Dorothy seemed equally comfortable with us. They asked Terri and me to come to a meeting at their home to discuss plans to support a Filipino candidate for political office. They also alerted us to an invitation our kids would soon be receiving to join Filipino Youth Activities (FYA) of Seattle, an award-winning drill team. These two invitations marked the beginning of my twenty-year involvement with mainstream politics, the Filipino community, FYA, and the

Young Turks, the group of Filipino Americans who became our closest friends in Seattle.

Terri and I joined the group that met at the Cordovas' to consider supporting first-time candidate Tony Baruso, who was running for state representative. (Baruso later became infamous for his conviction and subsequent imprisonment for the 1982 murders of anti-Marcos activists Silme Domingo and Gene Viernes.) A native of the Philippines, Baruso was well known in Filipino community circles but had virtually no name recognition in the district he aspired to represent. He also had little in the way of people or financial resources. Winning the election was a long shot, but the small group that met that evening decided to mount a belated campaign on behalf of the Filipino political unknown.

I was impressed with the caliber of the group's members. Fred, the eloquent information officer at Seattle University, had written several articles on Filipinos that had been featured in Seattle's two daily newspapers. Dorothy, the eldest daughter of the Laigo family, with close kinship ties to the Filipino community, was the highly intelligent and assertive board president of FYA. Bob Santos, the gregarious executive director of an agency that provided tutoring services to inner-city youth, was the most visible member of the group because of his highly publicized arrests in civil rights demonstrations. Andres "Sonny" Tangalin, an intense educator originally from Chicago, had worked closely with anti-discrimination organizations. Roy Flores was the analytic director of the Ethnic Cultural Center at the University of Washington. His street-smart brother Larry, a recent graduate of the university, had strong ties with student activists and neighborhood youth. Tony Ogilvie, the group's young, bright, energetic idea man, was assistant director of minority affairs at Seattle University. Dale Tiffany, a soft-spoken Flathead Indian who was married to Dorothy's sister Jeannette, brought organizational skills honed during his years in a variety of business settings. Jeannette Castilliano Tiffany was key to the group's multimedia communications.

After learning of my experience as a federal official and my knowledge of various funding streams, the group asked me to join in its activist effort. Politics had long stirred my competitive juices. Besides, politics was another way of leveling the playing field. I did not hesitate to accept the invitation. As impressive as the group may have been, however, it was totally inexperienced in political campaigning. No one had ever participated in a campaign. This was clearly a grassroots effort, a maiden voyage in the rough seas of local politics. Despite our best efforts, Baruso lost the election.

An election may have been lost in 1970, but a core group of politically active Filipino Americans came together for the first time. The group represented a variety of strengths and access to resources. The Baruso campaign was the first sociopolitical activity in which the group focused its collective knowledge, professional skills, and community networks on a Filipino American issue. The seeds of the group's activism actually were sown much earlier, during the civil rights decade of the 1960s. Individual members of the group marched and demonstrated in support of causes that at the time concerned other ethnic groups. Their participation gave them valuable lessons in tactics and strategies for dealing with mainstream America. More important, Filipino American participation in the civil rights movement provided the community with early visibility and lasting credibility in working with Seattle's major ethnic minorities—black, Hispanic, Asian, and Native American. Now, group members wanted to move Filipino community concerns onto center stage in Seattle. The next twelve years would see them play a major role in bringing the Filipino community into Seattle's sociopolitical mainstream.

As impressed as I was with these activists, I was almost as impressed with Seattle's Filipino community. Unlike communities I had known in California, Seattle's Filipino community appeared to be more united, without a history of regional and petty jealousies. I do not know if this was due to its geographical isolation, in the northwestern corner of America, or to the predominance of one Filipino group in the community. (Seattle had a preponderance of Ilocano-speaking Filipinos rather than a multiplicity of regional groups, as was true in other West Coast communities.) Whatever the reason for the phenomenon, Seattle's Filipino community appeared to be unusually united. My new activist friends, aware of past squabbles, were surprised to hear my assessment. I explained that while there may have been squabbles, these did not appear to result in chronic divisions within the Seattle Filipino community as they often did in California.

The relative cohesiveness of the Seattle Filipino community was surprising, considering that its patterns of settlement and growth were not significantly different from those of other West Coast Filipino communities. The 1901 U.S. Census reported only 17 Filipinos in the entire state of Washington. Beginning in 1906, the Philippine government sent a small number of *pensionados* to the University of Washington to study, and a few elected to remain in Seattle. Shortly after the meeting at the Cordovas', I was introduced to Dr. Trinidad Rojo, one of the original *pensionados*. Dr. Rojo confirmed that the Filipino population, like other Filipino communities on the West Coast, had remained flat for the next few decades. During the 1920–30s, however, the importation of cheap labor, predominantly men, to work in agriculture and the Alaskan canneries, contributed to an unparalleled growth in the number of Filipinos in Seattle. According to the 1930 census, there were 1,653 Filipinos in Seattle, up from the minuscule number reported in earlier censuses. After the end of World War II, brides of Filipino soldiers serving in the U.S. Army began arriving along with descendants of white and black soldiers of the Spanish-American War accompanied by their mixed-race families. This postwar immigration was the first time that a significant number of women arrived in Seattle. War bride families became a notable segment of the Filipino community. Liberalized immigration laws of 1965 continued to facilitate a rapidly growing number of new immigrants to Seattle. By the time of my 1970 arrival, the Filipino population had grown to 5,823, and second-generation Filipinos, such as my new activist friends, were beginning to assert themselves within the community.

Fresh from the excitement of the Baruso campaign, our small

group of activists decided to run a slate for election to the Filipino Community Council, the governing body of the umbrella group Filipino Community of Seattle, Inc. (FCSI). There is an old saying among Filipinos, that if you put two Filipinos together, you create an organization. Seattle was no exception. Under FCSI, there were thirty-five organizations and clubs, organized largely according to regional origins in the Philippines. This number represents one organization for every 166 Filipinos—man, woman, and child—in Seattle. If we include non-FCSI organizations, the ratio becomes even greater. The FCSI had historically concerned itself with typical Filipino community activities, such as queen contests, and keeping current on events in the Philippines. Recently, however, it had begun to discuss social needs, especially concerns for the elderly. Our small group believed we had the expertise and an opportunity to make a difference. We also had built-in access to the FSCI through Fred and Dorothy Cordova. Because of their close kinship ties to many members of FSCI, they were credible and trusted. Fred and Dorothy's kinship ties lobbied hard for our slate. We received enough votes for election to the Community Council.

We now had a larger arena in which to push our sociopolitical agenda. One of our first priorities was to establish the Filipino Economic Opportunity Board (FEOB), under the FCSI umbrella, as a strategy to obtain Community Block Grant funds from the City of Seattle. I was elected as FEOB board chair. We were joined in this effort by two more Bridge Generation Filipino Americans—Marty and Dolores Sibonga, publishers of a Filipino community newspaper. Within a year, FEOB received city funding to operate the Congregate Meal Program and the Filipino Elderly Program. These two successful funding efforts solidified our reputation within FCSI. After our success in obtaining funding for Filipino elderly, we were eager to make additional contributions to the community through FCSI. However, FCSI seemed to be satisfied with its new programs and was not interested in pursuing this type of activity. We decided to serve out our terms and then pursue our goals without FCSI.

The name "Young Turks" came from Silvestre Tangalan, FCSI

president, who was impressed with the upstart group's success in obtaining resources from the larger Seattle community. The name seemed to fit. Except for me, the group's members were all in their thirties or late twenties. It also expressed the activist leanings of the group, whose members not only were progressive but had a record of civil disobedience. Their approach to community advocacy was far different from the conservative efforts of FCSI. For example, Larry Flores and Tony Ogilvie led a student sit-in at the University of Washington that resulted in the establishment of Asian American components within the Ethnic Studies and Equal Opportunity programs. Sonny Tangalin was a vocal member of anti-discrimination groups such as the Coalition Against Discrimination and the Asian Coalition for Equality. For the past few years, Fred and Dorothy Cordova, the inspirational leaders of the FYA Drill Team, had young drill team marchers carry incomplete American flags upside down, as symbols of protest, in parades throughout the Northwest. Bob Santos, executive director of CARITAS, a tutoring program for inner-city youth sponsored by the Catholic Church, was the most visible and insurgent member of the Young Turks. A veteran of civil rights demonstrations, Bob was blessed with a likable and irresistible personality, and his arrests received widespread media attention.

Bob and I hit it off from our first meeting at the Cordova home, when I suggested we "do lunch." At first, he did not understand what the term meant, but he caught on quickly, perhaps because we found out we both liked our liquor, before and after meals. We became drinking buddies, hanging out at his favorite watering hole, the Gim Ling Restaurant in Chinatown. Sonny Tangalin, who was always ready to philosophize about any subject in his distinctive high-pitched voice, usually joined us. In a few years, Sonny would be vice principal at Franklin High School, while Cheryl, Peter, Julie, and Jackie were students there. Our Gim Ling sessions often included Catholic priest Harvey McIntyre, minus his collar and black shirt; he called this outfit his "shazam" uniform, referring to the comic-book character Captain Marvel. He and Bob were respected members of the Seattle Human Rights Commission. The lone Caucasian member of the Young Turks, Father Mac became a close friend of our family's, and years later, he would officiate at several of our children's weddings. Bob's watering hole became a regular stop for me. But going to Gim Ling was not simply a social activity for us. It also provided a convenient venue where the Young Turks could strategize the next steps on their sociopolitical agenda.

Soon enough, the core group of Young Turks that met at the Cordovas' was augmented by other like-minded Bridge Generation Filipino Americans. Bob Flor, a thoughtful doctoral candidate in education, provided valuable linkages to the Democratic Party. Our wives—Terri, Evelyn Tangalin, and Angie Flores—added a woman's perspective to what often was a male-dominated agenda and could always be counted on to perform behind-the-scenes work. From time to time, other Seattle Filipino Americans offered their invaluable skills, talents, services, and access points. They included Mike Castilliano, assistant to the vice president for minority affairs at the University of Washington; Peter Bacho, who went on to a successful career as an author and university professor; Pio De Cano Jr., son of the legendary Seattle labor leader; Val Laigo, Seattle University professor; Frank Irigon, a University of Washington student whose forte was leading nonviolent demonstrations; and the aforementioned Dolores Sibonga, who went on to serve several terms on the Seattle City Council.

Before the year was over, the Young Turks spearheaded another successful funding effort, this time through the federal government. The Department of Health, Education, and Welfare approved funding for a new program, the Demonstration Program for Asian Americans, based on a proposal I helped write. Dorothy Cordova became the executive director of the program, but only after considerable arm-twisting from Terri, Bob, and me. Dorothy had never worked outside the home in her eighteen years of marriage. She wondered whether she would be able to do the job. She not only was able to perform but held the position until funding for the program ran out in the 1980s.

*Stanford Public Affairs Fellowship Program, Class of 1969-70. Peter Jamero is third from left and Dr. Eric Hutchinson, faculty director, is far right in the front row. Bill Babby and Tony Elias, Jamero's closest friends among the Fellows, are the first two from left in the back row. Stanford University, 1970*

*(Left to right) Young Turks Tony Ogilvie, Sonny Tangalin, Peter Jamero, Dale Tiffany, Peter Bacho, John Ragudos, Larry Flores, Bob Flor, and Roy Flores (kneeling). Seattle, 1971.*

*Bob Santos wearing a dashiki. Seattle, 1971.*

*Young Turk women and friends. (Left to right): Jeannette Tiffany, Dorothy Cordova, Becky Flores, Betty Ragudos, Pilar Quintero, Terri Jamero, Evelyn Zapata, and Angie Flores. Seattle, 1971.*

*Dorothy and Fred Cordova, the Young Turks' major link to the Filipino community establishment.*

*Peter and Terri's passport picture,*
*May 1971.*

*Mama and Papa's church wedding, with (from left) Aunt Feling and*
*Uncle Pastor Jamero and Luna, Terri and Peter Jamero. Tagbilaran, Bohol,*
*Philippines, July 1971.*

Peter Jamero, director of the Division of Vocational Rehabilitation and assistant secretary of the Department of Social and Health Services. Seattle, December 1971.

With Governor Dan Evans in Olympia, Washington, 1973.

*As a member of the mayor's Official Reception
Committee, Jamero greets President Gerald Ford
on his September 1976 visit to Seattle.*

*Farewell dinner with staff of the Division of Vocational Rehabilitation.*
*Jack Owens, chief of Field Services, showing a gag gift to Terri.*
*Seattle, May 1979.*

*The Peter Jamero family. Seattle, 1978.*

The early victories of the Young Turks helped bring the Filipino community into Seattle's sociopolitical mainstream. No longer did white politicians limit their visits to annual appearances at community functions wearing too-tight *barong tagalog*, the traditional Filipino men's shirt, to eat *lumpia*, or Filipino egg roll, and utter "may-boo-hay" (*mabuhay*, the Filipino equivalent of "aloha"). Now, they came prepared to discuss issues with a far more enlightened community, thanks in large part to the Young Turks. For the next twelve years, the Young Turks would continue to be influential in bringing increased access, recognition, and resources to the Filipino community. I am forever grateful to have had the opportunity to play a small part in that effort.

In the fall of 1971, I participated in my first civil rights demonstration since marching with Cesar Chavez in 1965. An ethnically diverse group of protesters, including the Young Turks, staged a number of marches against the racist pastor of St. Theresa Catholic Church. The parish community, which had become predominantly minority in recent years, considered the priest's views to be antithetical to its spiritual welfare. After three days of demonstrations, which were extensively covered by Seattle media, the diocese reassigned the priest to other responsibilities. "My attitudes toward priests had certainly changed," I thought. "When Father Higgins imposed unfair restrictions on our church marriage in 1953, protest was the furthest thing from my mind. Now, here I am, demonstrating against a man of the cloth."

Another demonstration soon followed, one with national implications. The Council of Social Work Education was having its national conference at the posh Olympic Hotel in downtown Seattle. Paul Chikahisa, my old UCLA graduate-school pal, was a conference delegate along with other Asian Americans from California. A significant contingent of Asian Americans from the Pacific Northwest, including Young Turks, also attended. Together, we formed a small but identifiable bloc among conference attendees. The conference theme was civil rights; however, the civil rights concerns of Asian Americans were given scant attention in the proceedings.

We went before the conference with a five-point resolution, which, although politely acknowledged, failed to elicit a concrete commitment for action. It was as if the council was patting us on the head and saying, "Asians have no problems." We decided to stage a demonstration during the evening general session. In front of the startled conference delegates, we marched down the aisles with makeshift signs, chanting, "Asians do have problems." We got our message across, thanks to the assembled media, which provided wide coverage of our concerns.

The protest resulted in federal financial support for five national conferences on mental health, beginning in 1972. This was soon followed by funding to establish the Asian American Community Mental Health Center in Los Angeles and the Mental Health Training Center in San Diego. I was one of several Young Turks who were asked to serve on the National Advisory Committee overseeing the centers. The demonstration's lasting legacy, however, was the ties we forged with other West Coast activists. Among our new contacts were Filipino Americans Royal Morales, whom I first met at UCLA; Rev. Tony Ubalde of San Francisco's Glide Memorial Church; and Japanese American Jim Miyano, aide to Los Angeles County supervisor Kenneth Hahn. These ties would prove valuable in years to come as we worked on Asian American issues and national political campaigns.

The colorful FYA Drill Team, which consisted of seventy youngsters from eight to eighteen years of age, was an instant success with our kids. Since its inception in 1959, the FYA Princesa Drill Team, Cumbanchero Percussioneers, and Mandayan Marchers—the team's full name—had been a fixture at West Coast parades and pageants. Their dynamic founder, Fred Cordova, the driving force behind its unique style, led the team. Its intricate maneuvers, exotic costumes, and mixed-language commands never failed to excite spectators and earned the team many awards in parade competitions.

The drill team's performances always brought a proud lump to our throats. Terri and I were impressed with the team's Filipiniana focus. Commands were given in the various Filipino dialects as well as in English. The exotic costumes were based on the Muslim dress of the southern Philippines. The famed Philippine Bayanihan Dance Troupe inspired its rhythms and maneuvers, and the driving drumbeat took its cue from the Latin jazz music of Cal Tjader. In the midst of their Saturday afternoon practices, the predominantly American-born kids took time out to listen to lectures on Philippine and Filipino American history. As parents who grew up brown, Terri and I knew the importance of understanding our own Filipino culture in a country that could often be unfriendly. Except for their relatives, this was the first time our children were in the company of so many Filipino kids. The team would become an important part of their lives. Cheryl, Peter, and Julie became team leaders, and all three stayed with the team through their high school years.

Terri and I were also impressed with the FYA practice of reaching out to Filipino American kids who might be on the periphery of the community. The group actively recruited children of mixed-race background, especially black and Alaskan Indian. Similarly, children from low-income families residing in Seattle's Central Area were encouraged to join the drill team. This socioeconomic diversity added even more to the young participants' understanding of their world.

In 1971, the drill team went on a Thanksgiving tour of California. In five jam-packed days, the team performed before proud, appreciative Filipinos in Livingston, Sacramento, Salinas, San Francisco, San Jose, Stockton, and Vallejo. I was particularly happy about being able to schedule a performance in the high school gym in my hometown of Livingston, the smallest venue of all our stops. Mama made sure that the whole Filipino community turned out. She also organized a *pista*-style luncheon reception at the Jamero camp. Most of these city-raised drill team kids were getting their first intimate look at Filipino campo life. It was a real shocker for many of them, particularly when they realized that the *manongs* they learned about in lectures were elderly men who still worked at the same back-breaking jobs.

The most dramatic and best-executed performance of the California tour took place on the evening of Thanksgiving Day at the San Francisco Opera House. The drill team performed flawlessly before an appreciative and boisterous crowd of mostly young Filipino Americans. It was an emotional experience for everyone associated with the team. To this day, Fred and Dorothy describe the San Francisco performance as the finest they had ever seen and the 1971 team as the best ever. Karen, Cheryl, Peter, Julie, and Jackie were important members of the crack drill team. Their performance brought tears of pride and joy to our eyes.

The drill team and Filipino Youth Activities were also a significant part of Terri's life. Parents were encouraged to volunteer their time and talents. Terri sewed costumes, put makeup on the girls, and participated in various fund-raising events. I volunteered to chauffeur the kids throughout British Columbia, Oregon, and Washington and lent my muscle power to move the team's equipment. In 1971, I spearheaded the successful effort to secure funding from the United Way, funding that has continued to the present time. Terri and I also sat on the FYA board of trustees, with Terri serving two terms as board president.

When we were preparing to move to the Northwest, we relied on the views of white realtors in deciding to settle in predominantly white Bellevue, which had a reputation of providing quality education. Perhaps our inquiries should have gone further. The children, who had successfully adjusted to different schools during the past few years, had mixed experiences at their new schools.

Peter got into a fight at Odle Middle School because a white student taunted him with "Ching-Chong Chinaman" and "Go back where you came from." I was proud that Peter fought back.

Soon after, Julie's homeroom teacher at Odle accused her of stealing articles from another student's locker. The teacher simply assumed that the accuser's story was true and did not even bother to ask Julie for her version of the incident. I was incensed when a tearful Julie told me about the hasty accusation, particularly since the accuser and the teacher were both white. I asked to see Mr. Sanor, the school principal. Mr. Sanor, not expecting a father who spoke flawless English, looked surprised as I arrived from work dressed in a suit and tie. He asked, "Where do you work?" I replied tersely, "I'm not here to talk about my work. I want to know why Julie is being accused of stealing." After hemming and hawing, Mr. Sanor, now visibly uncomfortable, told me he'd look into it. As I left his office, I added, "I can only assume the homeroom teacher is racist, since I didn't hear a clear explanation from you."

Julie was assigned to another homeroom. However, I could not help wondering whether the principal ever confronted the teacher about her handling of the situation. A few months later, I got my answer. The homeroom teacher also taught PE. She promised her PE class that everyone who participated in a twenty-mile walk would receive an A, and Julie was the only participant who did not receive the promised grade even though she completed the walk. To add to Julie's disappointment, the C spoiled what otherwise would have been straight A's for the term. The racist treatment Peter and Julie experienced brought back memories of my 1953 eviction in San Jose. I recalled naively thinking at the time, "Racism will not exist when I have my own children. My kids will be free from the ugliness and pain of discrimination that I have had to endure." Sad to say, I was wrong.

The incidents spurred our desire to know more about our Filipino roots, and Terri and I decided to join Mama and Papa on their planned trip to the Philippines. It also made sense to visit our ancestral land and meet relatives we had heard so much about with Papa and Mama, rather than on our own. Luna decided to go, and the three of us talked Uncle Onsing into going as well. Papa and Mama had visited their homeland several times since the end of World War II; however, Uncle Onsing had not set foot in his birthplace since immigrating to the United States in the early 1920s. Terri, Luna, and I would be visiting for the first time. In June 1971, with great excitement and anticipation, the six members of the Jamero clan made the long, sixteen-hour flight to the Philippines via Pan American Airlines.

As a boy, I heard countless stories about the Philippines, not only from Papa and Mama but also from homesick *manongs*. Their stories were still vivid in my mind. I had always wondered what the real Philippines would be like. Now I finally had a chance to find out for myself.

I had a mixed reaction to the Philippines. On the one hand, the abject poverty in some of the poor neighborhoods of Manila and Cebu City was shocking. In the notorious Tondo of Manila, for example, thousands of squatters lived in the flimsy shacks of tin and cardboard that rose among garbage-strewn paths, and near-naked children begged on the streets in Cebu City. It was hard to believe that this was the country with the second-largest Asian economy at the end of World War II.

On the other hand, Manila and Cebu boasted breathtaking cultural and historical attractions. I marveled at the architectural and historical beauty to be found inside the walled-in Intramuros fortress in Manila. In Cebu City, we saw the faithful walking on their knees to kiss Santo Niño, the image of the Holy Child Jesus presented by Magellan to Queen Juana upon her conversion to Christianity, a truly inspirational sight. From the Cebu airport on Mactan Island, I gazed at my ancestral island of Bohol just fifteen miles away, remembering that I stood on the site of Magellan's death at the hands of Chief Lapu Lapu in 1521. In the northern city of Baguio, I witnessed Igorots and Negritos coming down from their mountain homes to shop. Muslim-dominated Zamboanga, in the southern Philippines, gave me a greater appreciation of the centuries-old conflict between Muslim (Moro) inhabitants and Christian settlers, a conflict not unlike that between white settlers and Native Americans. Our ancestral island of Bohol had a famous attraction of its own—Chocolate Hills, an impressive panorama of several hundred rounded hills that turn brown during the dry summer, rising one hundred feet above the flat terrain. According to folk legend, a lovelorn giant created the confectionery sight with his tears.

Most impressive to me, however, were the resiliency, faith, and strength of the people in Mama's and Papa's hometown of Garcia-

Hernandez. The people may have been poor peasants with little of the modern conveniences we in America take for granted, such as hot and cold running water and electricity, but they seemed at ease and accepting of their way of life. They worked long hours in the rice fields and filled the parish church on Sundays. People in the town and *barrios* of Garcia-Hernandez did not complain about their lot. This was consistent with the fatalistic cultural norm of *bahala na*, the Filipino version of *que sera sera* (what will be, will be). I thought about the stresses and hurried pace of life in America, particularly in the workplace, and suddenly envied the peace of mind of the people of Garcia-Hernandez.

For me, the highlight of the trip was meeting my relatives in Garcia-Hernandez. I fully expected to meet many kinfolk, since Papa and Mama were from the same town and were third cousins. However, I was not prepared for the sheer number of relatives. On our first night, for example, I met at least thirty first cousins—an overwhelming number considering that I had met only one first cousin in my entire life (Sixto Pagaran, who immigrated to America in the late 1950s). This was also the first time our relatives met American-born Filipinos like Terri, Luna, and me. They had some preconceived ideas about us and were surprised to learn that we ate Filipino food regularly and preferred rice to bread. They were also surprised that we could understand the dialect and that I could speak Cebuano, albeit not fluently. I felt comfortable and accepted among my relatives. I was in my ancestral home, a truth confirmed numerous times by the remarkable resemblance between many of my relatives in Garcia-Hernandez and my own children and siblings in America. Most Americans have the security of belonging to an extended family. At forty years of age, I was experiencing it for the very first time.

Papa, Luna, Terri, and I stayed in the stately two-story home of Uncle Pastor Jamero, who was Papa's first cousin, and Aunt Felicia (Feling), in the Lungsod Daan, or Old Town, district of Garcia-Hernandez. Uncle Pastor had the same family build—broad shoulders and large chest—as Papa, my brothers, and me. Like Papa, Uncle

Pastor was an expert negotiator, a skill that no doubt was helpful to him during the several terms he served as mayor of Garcia-Hernandez. He was soft-spoken and well-read, as befit his career as a school principal. Aunt Feling, gentle and aristocratic, complemented Uncle Pastor perfectly with her activities in the town's religious and social circles. Their son, Pastor Junior, was a free spirit. Throughout his life, he usually got his way, including convincing his parents to pay for flying lessons. Once, he buzzed the family home in a rented plane while they were hosting a large celebration, frightening most of the guests. Their daughter Nenny was the image of her mother. Three years my junior, Nenny was the dean of students at Divine Word College in Tagbilaran, the capital city of Bohol.

At our stopover in Cebu City, I had witnessed several large demonstrations against President Ferdinand Marcos but did not fully understand the reasons behind the protest. Nenny, a close follower of Philippine politics, provided a wealth of valuable information on the current unrest in her country. According to Nenny, the Philippines was in a shambles under Marcos, now in his second term as president. Agrarian reform had failed, violence was rampant, the economy was bankrupt, and widespread starvation beset the population. The people were taking to the streets to show their displeasure.

From Nenny, I also learned that the roots of the unrest were centuries old. Beginning with the four hundred years of Spanish colonialism, through the forty years under U.S. rule, and since its independence in 1946, the Philippines has been run by a favored few. Most Filipinos are either rural peasants or urban poor. There is no middle class. The long reign of a small group of rich families originated with land grants to Spanish settlers. Over time, these families evolved into wealthy *mestizo* families, or *illustrados*, which gave rise to the oligarchic form of government that continues today. Favored families sent their sons to Europe to study. When the sons returned, they assumed positions of influence, thus increasing the power of their families. After the Philippines became a U.S. colony, the system continued through the *pensionado* program, whereby students, often selected from well-to-do families, went to America to study, with the expectation that they would become leaders when they returned. The traditions of kinship, which allowed family allegiances to expand many times over through intermarriage, and the *compadre* system, also contributed to keeping power in the hands of a few.

With the election of Ferdinand Marcos as president in 1965, the country was hopeful that the centuries-old pattern of oligarchic rule and the widening gap between the wealthy and the poor might soon end. After all, he was one of them, from a family of modest means. He was also a decorated World War II hero. Marcos did indeed eliminate the old oligarchy, but he replaced it with a corrupt one made up of his own family and cronies. Moreover, he did this by illegal and violent means. He pillaged the country, kept his booty in Swiss banks, and built a personal fortune estimated to be in the billions.

During the past year, according to Nenny, Marcos planned to impose martial law to control his enemies and remain in power. Henry Byroade, the longest-serving United States Ambassador to the Philippines since it attained independence, interceded and persuaded Marcos that martial law would only make matters worse. The Byroades had been our next-door neighbors in Falls Church. Before flying to Bohol, Terri and I paid a social visit to the Byroades in Manila. I wish I had known something about Philippine politics at that time, as it would have made an interesting topic of conversation with Ambassador Byroade.

Rosario, Uncle Pastor's niece and a student at a nearby college, was also living in his home. I noticed that Rosario did much of the housework and food preparation, much like a maid. However, she was also accorded the respect and privileges appropriate for a relative. This was my introduction to the Filipino custom of *tabang*, by which families who were better off provided financial help to poorer relatives by giving these relatives jobs in their homes and businesses in exchange for room and board and a small salary. Initially, I felt the custom was demeaning for the less fortunate relatives. However, as I observed how the system seemed to work for the mutual benefit of everyone concerned, I could better understand its value in a third world country like the Philippines. In Rosario's case, *tabang* helped her through college and then into a successful teaching career.

Mama and Uncle Onsing stayed with their respective families in the nearby *barrio* of Canayaon. My first cousin Roman Madelo and his family hosted Mama for the entire time of our visit to Garcia-Hernandez. Roman's father was one of the eldest members of the family of thirteen children, and Mama was the youngest. As a result, Roman was only a few years younger than Mama. The Madelo clan, while not as politically or socially prominent, nevertheless had much in common with the Jamero family. They looked after one another, treated one another with respect, and were devoutly religious in their practice of the Roman Catholic faith. The Madelos were a fun-loving family, and I could see how Mama became the outgoing and sociable person I knew her to be. Another first cousin, Manang Bebay, was so uncannily like Mama. She not only looked like Mama but walked, talked, and even sang and danced like Mama.

The Catholic Church did not recognize Papa's and Mama's 1929 civil marriage in the United States. Mama had wanted their marriage to be blessed by the Church, but Papa did not see any reason to be married twice. While Mama seldom brought the matter up, I always sensed she was uncomfortable with a marriage that was not recognized by the Church. Now that she was back in the Philippines with Papa, she asked Uncle Pastor for his help. Papa was close to Uncle Pastor. He admired Uncle for what he had accomplished and respected him as a man. In his gentle but skillful manner, Uncle Pastor pointed out the benefits of a Church marriage for Papa, not just for Mama. He did not push Papa into making an immediate decision but simply asked him to give it some thought and offered to discuss it further if Papa wished to do so. After a few days, Papa agreed to a Church wedding. Uncle Pastor arranged for a ceremony at the cathedral in Tagbilaran, and Papa and Mama exchanged wedding vows in accordance with the sacraments of the Catholic Church. Uncle Pastor and Aunt Feling served as witnesses, with Luna, Terri, and me in attendance. The groom was handsome, and the bride was radiant. Most of all, the bride was grateful that her wish of the past forty-two years had been fulfilled.

Following our return to the United States, I became heavily involved with planning the First Filipino Young People's Far West Convention. The convention was sponsored by FYA, under the direction of board president Dorothy Cordova, and the Young Turks played important roles. The convention theme, A Quest for Emergence, coined by keynote speaker Tony Ogilvie, expressed the Filipino response to the recent awakening of America's ethnic minorities, who were developing greater pride in and knowledge of their individual identities. Young Turks Fred Cordova, Larry Flores, Roy Flores, Bob Santos, Sonny Tangalin, and I served as panel members or speakers. The convention was a huge success, drawing upwards of five hundred young Filipino Americans from Alaska, California, Hawaii, Oregon, and Washington. The agenda included virtually every significant issue for Filipinos—from political empowerment, to education and employment concerns, to family issues and discrimination and identity problems.

Only an unscheduled demonstration by a group of young anti-Marcos delegates marred the convention's success. We had considered providing a forum for discussing the Marcos issue but rejected the idea because the topic was not consistent with the theme of the conference, which focused on the concerns of Filipinos in America. The anti-Marcos delegates demanded that their issue be given a place on an already crowded agenda. We stood our ground and ultimately prevailed.

The convention laid the groundwork for a plan to empower Filipino communities on the West Coast. A proposal submitted to the federal Community Services Administration proposed the establishment of a networking organization, the Filipino Information and Referral Center. My sister Luna and I were among the members of the proposal-writing committee. The Community Services Administration approved the proposal. Unfortunately, a last-minute cutback ordered by the administration of President Richard Nixon rescinded the approval.

The convention also gave me the opportunity to meet with other concerned West Coast Filipinos. I renewed friendships with Royal Morales and Al Mendoza of Los Angeles and formed lasting relationships with San Francisco activists Anita Sanchez and Rodel Rodis. Both Anita and Rodel were to play an influential role in my 1989 appointment to the Human Rights Commission by San Francisco mayor Art Agnos.

The satisfaction I experienced in my social and activist activities did not carry over to the workplace. My initial mixed feelings about the state team approach soon proved justified, and the job became my worst nightmare. I found myself performing work that would be more appropriate for my supervisor or the training officer. My assigned duties included orienting most of the staff on both state teams to my own responsibilities as well as to theirs. I was also responsible for assisting my supervisor, new to federal service, with his duties as deputy commissioner. My pleas for a more equitable workload distribution met with the same response from my superiors in the regional office: I should "learn to be a better team player."

I grew to resent the state team approach, which was basically management by committee and placed extraordinary burdens on a few experienced employees, like me. I resented the disproportionate share of the workload I had to assume while my superiors and peers enjoyed lower performance expectations and more spare time. In addition, I was not paid or otherwise recognized for shouldering these extra responsibilities. I felt I was being exploited and resented being treated unequally. For the first time in my career, I was not happy in my job. It began to show in my relationships with staff members. My April 1971 performance evaluation described my frustrations perfectly. My supervisor gave me superior marks, noting, "excellent technically in his program area . . . ambitious . . . could handle increased responsibilities," but added, "the only concern is his capacity to relate to others."

To make matters worse, my application for promotion to deputy regional commissioner was rejected with the terse comment "not ranked in the best qualified group." I was shocked. I had been given outstanding performance evaluations in my Washington, D.C., positions and received the prestigious Federal Career Incentive Award that sent me to Stanford University. Past supervisors and other references all praised my work and leadership abilities. In addition, with the exception of the comment about staff relationships, my April 1971 performance evaluation was similarly outstanding. The rejection made no sense to me. The poor ranking devastated me.

Subsequent efforts to understand the reasons for the rejection of my application yielded nothing new. My superiors at the regional office as well as the civil service office responded to my inquiries evasively or with bureaucratese. I could only conclude that, despite denials to the contrary, my complaints about the workload and my less-than-satisfactory relationships with other staff must have influenced the ranking.

There was much more behind the rejection—racial discrimination. The regional office leadership was patronizing in its relationships with ethnic-minority staff members. The deputy commissioner often said that ethnic minorities "should be grateful to have a job in federal service." When white staff members expressed similar complaints about their workloads, they suffered no apparent retaliation. I was the only person of color to complain about my workload, and I was the only one punished for it. I concluded that my application was rejected to put me in my place and considered filing a discrimination complaint. However, having observed the way the federal government handled complaints, I was uncertain that the process would be fair or expeditious. My superiors' failure to provide a valid rationale for rejecting my application was a clear signal that seeking a remedy through official channels was not the answer.

Before the advent of civil rights, ethnic minorities had little recourse in dealing with unfair treatment in the workplace. I found it strangely ironic that I did not turn to the legal protections that were now available to me. I also found myself wondering, "If this could happen to a knowledgeable and experienced person like me, what chance did others who knew less or had fewer resources have to achieve fairness in the workplace?" The answer to this rhetorical question is obvious. The Manong Generation certainly encountered workplace discrimination. They were systematically denied access to jobs, even if they had college degrees or had practiced professionally in the Philippines. I knew that my Bridge Generation contemporaries went through similar experiences. I had little doubt that the rejection of my application was based, at least in part, on racial discrimination.

A third factor came to my attention. Thanks to the help of a staff member sympathetic to my cause, I obtained a copy of my confidential file for the promotion. The file contained a letter signed by Larry Coleman, deputy director of the Sacramento County Department of Social Welfare, dated July 1971. Coleman was my immediate supervisor before my departure from Sacramento in 1966 and had consistently evaluated my work performance as excellent. In his letter, however, he rated my work as "poor," commenting, "after he left we found out that he seriously misused people, was less than honest and I would not rehire him in any capacity." He provided no specifics to support his generalized charges. I was shocked, even more so than when my application for the promotion was rejected. I immediately contacted my old Sacramento County director and Larry's boss, Jack Corey, who had since become the director of the Peace Corps effort in Turkey. Jack was just as shocked as I was. He wrote to the Civil Service Department refuting Larry's allegations. I also got other letters of support from Sacramento leadership staff who were familiar with my work under Larry. However, by then, the damage was done. The decision makers in Region X refused to rescind or even reconsider the official rejection of my application for promotion.

With my future in federal service in doubt, I was unsure of where to turn. Once again, fate intervened. I received a call from Mike Linn, a former colleague at Sacramento County. He was now a top cabinet adviser to Sid Smith, secretary of the new Washington State Department of Social and Health Services (DSHS). The department had been created to pull the state's diverse health and social service programs into one agency. DSHS was seeking to fill the executive-level position of assistant secretary and director, Division of Vocational Rehabilitation. Mike had seen what I was able to accomplish in Sacramento County. He also remembered that my responsibilities included a vocational rehabilitation component. Mike said he had taken the liberty of talking to Sid Smith and convinced him that I was the right man for the job. Since it was an appointive position, Sid received preapproval to hire me from Governor Dan Evans, contingent on my concurrence with the plan. Mike and I scheduled a meeting with Sid at the state capital in Olympia to discuss the matter further.

I could hardly wait to share the exciting news with Terri. We talked about some of the issues. First, the position was a political appointment and subject to the uncertainties of elections. Governor Evans was in the midst of a four-year term and had yet to announce whether he planned to run for another term. Terri and I were concerned about the impact on our family, including the possible loss of salary and medical benefits if the governor chose not to run again. At the same time, we realized that the high-visibility position would open other opportunities should a change in administration occur. The governor's Republican Party affiliation was another issue. I was a lifelong Democrat, diametrically opposed to the basic beliefs of Republicans. Governor Evans, however, was a moderate Republican who actively supported civil rights and affirmative action, which made the conflict less troublesome. A third issue concerned giving up the security of federal service, which totaled ten years, including my four years in the navy. We agreed, though, that my future with the federal government was clouded, given the events of the recent past. A fourth issue related to my lack of experience with the program I would be directing, but Terri reminded me that this was no different from any of my previous positions. After considering the pros and cons, we concluded that the advantages far outweighed the risks. If it was offered, I was prepared to accept the position.

My meetings with Sid and Governor Evans went well. Mike Linn had thoroughly briefed me on the Division of Vocational Rehabilitation (DVR) as well as the DSHS umbrella agency, and I was prepared. However, Sid and the governor did not seem to need much detail from me, having already made up their minds, thanks to Mike. Neither brought up my recent troubles at the regional office, nor did I volunteer to discuss the matter. The position came with a substantial increase in salary. I gratefully accepted the offer and agreed to report to my new job effective January 17, 1972.

Just before the Christmas holidays, I submitted my resignation to the regional office. I felt vindicated but did not voice it. Nor did I gloat. The broad grin on my face clearly communicated my jubilation, although I was going to miss some of my coworkers. The Region X decision makers were dumbfounded but polite, and my peers were genuinely happy for me. However, as far as my experience there was concerned, the X in Region X, the tenth region of DHEW, was not the Roman numeral X. To me, it was a mark advising avoidance, like the warning on a jar of poison. I said to myself, "Good riddance to Region X."

Despite my negative experience at Region X, I came away with several lessons learned. First, I knew that I had handled the situation professionally and ethically. My decision to question the fairness of the state team approach was based on principle, not on whether it would help or hinder my chances for promotion. Second, I learned that being right and being capable do not necessarily offset the power of a racist, entrenched bureaucracy, regardless of laws prohibiting discrimination. Third, it's impossible to discount fate. Without the serendipitous call from Mike Linn, I might still be languishing at Region X.

Terri and I celebrated my new position while hosting a New Year's Eve party. We invited our friends from the Young Turks to a sit-down dinner complete with our best china, silver, and crystal. We spent the rest of the evening engaging in typically loud debates and dancing. Terri and I were thankful to see another new year, thankful for our new friends, and thankful for our children. Most of all, we were thankful that fate and my willingness to take risks had given me the opportunity to embark on yet another adventure.

# 13 Umbrella Agency

ON JANUARY 17, 1972, I JOINED THE STATE OF
Washington's new Department of Social and Health Services, taking on two titles: director, Division of Vocational Rehabilitation, and
assistant secretary, Department of Social and Health Services. The
first title represented my major function, directing the vocational
rehabilitation program, but the title of DSHS Assistant Secretary
requires a bit more explanation. In that capacity, I was part of a nine-
member executive secretariat that had policy-making and administrative oversight of all the department's programs. The state
legislature created the department so that the state's various health
and social service programs could be gathered into one coherent and
more cost-effective department. In addition to vocational rehabilitation, DSHS programs included assistance payments (welfare) for
families, the elderly, and the disabled; adult corrections; juvenile
rehabilitation; public health; mental health; child welfare; social
services; and veterans' services. Most of the programs had been
departments and were now expected to function as parts of a single
department. DSHS was the largest state department, with a budget
of $2 billion.

The umbrella agency approach for the Department of Social and
Health Services—its critics called it a superagency—was one of
the first reorganization efforts of its kind in the nation. The new
department was a controversial experiment with as many detractors as supporters. Detractors resented the loss of their programs'
independence and power. They also suspected that smaller programs

such as vocational rehabilitation would be swallowed up in a massive welfare-program takeover and would gradually disappear.

I knew enough about federal law to feel certain that a welfare program could not legally take over the vocational rehabilitation program. I was also convinced after several briefings with Mike Linn and Sid Smith that a takeover was not in the plans. The state legislature's only intent in creating the new department was to achieve improved coordination among its many health and social programs, not to create an indistinguishable melting pot of programs. Nevertheless, many DVR staff and their supporters across the state felt otherwise. Rumors persisted throughout the first few years of my tenure that there would be a sit-down or other form of staff demonstration to take the Division of Vocational Rehabilitation out of DSHS. The clear challenge for me as DVR director was to keep the program operating successfully within the new department structure.

After assessing the program's strengths and weaknesses, I concluded that I could best exercise leadership over DVR by achieving two initial objectives: first, gain control over the staff and, second, improve the program's image. DVR management was in the hands of an old boys' club of white males, at or nearing retirement age, who carried out their jobs using the same old approaches and methods. To facilitate their departure, I announced that I expected them to provide their staffs with the knowledge and skills necessary to raise the number of successful rehabilitations among disabled people. I calculated that these managers would not be able to improve their effectiveness and thus would fail to develop their staffs accordingly. My second strategy was to establish affirmative action priorities requiring managers to hire ethnic minorities and the disabled, categories in which DVR had been chronically deficient. Again, I calculated that the old boy's club of managers would have difficulty carrying out this directive.

My next step in gaining control over staff was to hire a tough, no-nonsense deputy director. I hired Spence Hammond away from the governor's Office of Finance. I knew him to be a good manager from our days with the federal regional office. His assignment was to carry out much of the detailed staff work, particularly in managing personnel and establishing quantifiable program objectives. Spence and I understood from the outset that the task I was assigning him would probably not endear him to the staff. It did not.

My three-prong approach had its desired effect. Within a year, most of the original managers retired or resigned, thus enabling me to hire staff more compatible with my management style and program direction. There was another positive result, for me at least: employees now considered me more approachable than Spence, a case of "good cop, bad cop."

I was now free to work on my second objective, to improve the program's image. DVR needed to market itself as a program that had positive outcomes for disabled people, not just a program that did good things for the handicapped. The program had one of the best performance measures among health and human service programs because it kept track of the numbers of rehabilitated disabled who went on to full-time employment. However, DVR had not taken full advantage of its record to sell itself to the legislature. Consequently, support for its continued funding was a chronic problem.

I contracted with Berkeley Planning Associates, a California firm specializing in cost-benefit studies, to evaluate DVR's effectiveness. At the end of the study, the firm concluded that DVR's cost-benefit ratio ($11 in income earned for each $1 spent on rehabilitating a disabled person who gained full employment) exceeded the comparable national rate of $8 to $1. Berkeley further concluded that DVR's percentage of successful rehabilitants who were also welfare recipients was number one among the country's vocational rehabilitation programs. The firm's findings provided convincing evidence of DVR's viability in my presentations before the legislature, in public appearances, and in press releases. During my eight-year tenure as DVR director, these findings became essential selling points in gaining legislative and public support and eventually led to stabilized funding for the program.

By the end of 1972, I had achieved my two initial objectives, which greatly eased the pressure on me. I knew that staff members continued to feel discontent about DVR being part of the superagency but sensed it was diminishing. On balance, I felt good about my first-year performance.

The good start with DVR would have been moot if Governor Dan Evans had not won his bid for reelection in November. As one of only a handful of minority executive appointees, I was highly visible during the Evans campaign. Although my visibility may have been political showcasing, I was proud to be campaigning for Governor Evans. I did not feel like a token minority. Evans, unlike most Republicans, had a record of accomplishment in support of minority causes such as affirmative action. In addition, the governor had issued an executive order banning the use of private clubs for state government functions because of the clubs' exclusionary policies toward ethnic minorities. He issued the executive order in response to the efforts of advocacy groups such as the Coalition Against Discrimination and the Asian Coalition for Equality, for whom Young Turks member Sonny Tangalin was an effective spokesperson.

One of these private clubs, the Elks, was the source of a potentially embarrassing situation. On my first visit to the Spokane district office, I heard an announcement stating that a reception had been planned in my honor at the Elks Club at the end of the workday. I calmly went to the podium and thanked the group for organizing the reception but said I could not attend because of the governor's executive order. Holding the function at the Elks Club after normal work hours made it technically a nongovernment function; however, I believed it violated the spirit of the order. Another venue was immediately found. My strong position in support of the executive order earned me respect, albeit reluctantly, in a part of the state that was strongly opposed to the governor's policy. A few days later, I received a most welcome letter from a staff member, expressing her appreciation that an executive-level member of DSHS had been forthright on a matter concerning equality. How effective was the governor's executive order? All private clubs in Washington State rescinded their exclusionary policies and practices within a few years.

With the help of other Young Turks, I played a highly visible role in organizing an October fund-raising dinner for Governor Evans. Held at the elegant Sorrento Hotel, owned by Filipino Tony Del Fierro, the fund-raiser was a thoroughly enjoyable and successful event. A capacity crowd turned out in enthusiastic support of Governor Evans, proud that he had appointed a Filipino to head a major state program. Attaining the position was a Filipino First, not only for Washington but for the entire country. Shortly before the fund-raiser, my achievement received wide media attention, thanks to a statewide poster project. The State Superintendent of Public Instruction selected me for the project on prominent Asian Americans, and the posters were displayed in public schools across the state. My poster included the caption "Highest-ranking government executive of Filipino ancestry in the nation."

As with my previous Filipino Firsts, I had mixed feelings about this latest honor. On the one hand, I was happy for my people and for the recognition my family and I received. On the other hand, I could not help thinking about the historic difficulties Filipinos had encountered in winning appropriate recognition for their accomplishments. While I was growing up, I had no outside role models. Members of other ethnic groups had long ago achieved prominence in American life, including groups who immigrated after Filipinos. We were mistaken for Japanese, Chinese, or Mexican. We had been part of America for generations, yet Filipinos were seldom recognized as Filipinos let alone for their contributions to society. If life was like a stage show, we were part of the scenery but not members of the cast.

And yet, perhaps things were changing. Bridge Generation Filipino Americans were just beginning to be more visible in the fight for civil rights as they joined the emerging Asian American movement. West Coast Filipino Americans were in the forefront of demonstrations for the Asian community. Filipino Americans assumed leadership positions in protesting mainstream intrusions into the traditional Asian neighborhoods of Seattle's International District and San Francisco's Kearney Street. In the same two cities,

Filipino Americans led demonstrations at the University of Washington and San Francisco State University, calling for culturally appropriate curriculum and faculty.

Moreover, Bridge Generation Filipinos achieved a number of Filipino Firsts as they began to participate in the American mainstream. Gregg Bambo was the first Filipino American pilot for a major airline (Western Airlines). Dixon Campos received a promotion to full colonel in the U.S. Army Reserve. Two Filipina Americans became university professors—Barbara Posadas at Northern Illinois University and Deanna Daclan Balantac at California State University–Sacramento. In San Francisco, Fred Basconcillo was elected president of the Iron Workers Union. Roman Gabriel starred as the All-Pro quarterback of the Los Angeles Rams, and Dick Dagampat became the starting fullback for the U.S. Naval Academy. Filipinos took understandable pride in these achievements. To put it in proper perspective, however, these modest achievements were just a beginning. And sadly, the great majority of Filipinos were still on the outside looking in.

The performance of Washington State's vocational rehabilitation program continued to improve under my leadership, despite Congress's failure to appropriate scheduled increases in federal money for vocational rehabilitation in 1972 and 1973. DVR's record of successful rehabilitations underwent remarkable growth. Moreover, the state again was among the leaders in the percentage of successful rehabilitants who were able to leave the welfare rolls. The program reforms I instituted had clearly affected state performance, and I further strengthened staff capability through training and targeted recruiting. Under my leadership, diversity—ethnic, gender, and disabled—increased not only at the counselor levels but also in leadership positions, achieving one of the best records in state government.

Retaining John Elder as chief of Field Services was another positive step. John was the only holdover from the old boys' club whom I asked to stay. He was highly respected by the staff and knowledgeable about the program. More important, I sensed from the outset that he was ethically driven and would be loyal to me. John justified my faith in him. He helped encourage staff across the state to put aside their resistance to new leadership and the new umbrella agency. When he announced in the fall of 1973 that he would soon be retiring, I appointed Jack Owens, a tall, redheaded country boy from the Palouse region of eastern Washington, as his replacement. Jack, like John, enjoyed strong staff support and was technically and historically knowledgeable about Washington's vocational rehabilitation program. Unlike John, however, Jack was much more assertive in providing direction, a timely attribute considering the accelerated pace of operational changes I brought to the program. Jack's bold leadership would prove invaluable in dealing with several events that were just beginning to unfold.

Late in 1973, I received a copy of an unsigned, poorly written letter to the governor's office dredging up unsubstantiated allegations that I had been hired to dismantle the vocational rehabilitation program and effect a welfare takeover. The anonymous letter writer enclosed an old newsletter from a defunct organization of vocational rehabilitation counselors, lamenting my appointment to director, to support these charges. After considering the positive performance of DVR under my leadership and the fact that the letter was unsigned, the governor's office concluded that the charges were without merit.

Early in 1974, the governor's office received another critical letter, this time from a staff member at a nonprofit advocacy agency for disabled people. The letter alleged certain improprieties in my handling of a performance contract with Educational Consultants, Inc., a private employment agency located in Everett. The contract was an experiment to determine whether a private agency could be more effective in locating jobs for disabled persons. The letter also accused me of entering into a "sweetheart deal" with the agency's lobbyist, Pat Gallagher, who had been hired under a personal service contract. In fact, the purpose of the personal service contract was to help bring newly authorized federal money into the state for employment projects with private industry and was completely unrelated to the company's performance contract. Perhaps most damning, the letter writer enclosed a copy of yet another letter to the governor calling for my immediate dismissal. The second letter, from the executive director of a sheltered workshop (a facility authorized to pay below minimum wage to eligible disabled persons), raised the same charges, adding that the poor morale of counselors was resulting in poor state performance.

The charges may all have been circumstantial and unsubstantiated, but, unlike the previous unsigned letter, this letter included a signature and seemed to have a modicum of merit. I was asked to submit a written report to the DSHS secretary. While the secretary was inclined to agree that the charges were groundless, he felt that an outside review would assure objectivity and fairness. The State Audit Agency conducted the review. In the fall of 1974, the audit agency's final report cleared me of all charges. The report concluded that the performance contract and the personal service contract were completely within applicable state policies and procedures. Moreover, the report declared that all the allegedly questionable practices were fully justified given the facts and circumstances.

The audit agency's findings strengthened my position as state director. The report not only vindicated me personally but also helped validate my leadership style and the direction I'd set for DVR. Moreover, the findings cleared the DVR staff of any complicity, crediting them with working consistently in accordance with contract requirements, thanks to Jack Owens's strong leadership. The findings suggested that the sheltered workshop director, acting alone, had instigated the controversy. Apparently, he believed that contracting with a private employment agency would put sheltered workshops such as his in jeopardy. But his concerns were baseless. At the end of the one-year contract period, Educational Consultants had not performed as stipulated, clearly demonstrating that private employment agencies could not compete with DVR and sheltered workshops.

The incident involving Educational Consultants was the most

serious threat to my tenure as DVR director. In my remaining years with the program, DVR continued to build on its reputation among the nation's leading state vocational rehabilitation programs. Although I knew I was guilty of no wrongdoing, I had not been sure that the audit findings would exonerate me. The whole episode was continuously stressful. I rarely took my troubles home, however. Somehow, I had developed the gift of being able to separate work from other aspects of my life, and I have been ever so thankful for it. Otherwise, I could never have enjoyed the rewards provided by my family, my community involvement, and my social life, all of which continued to be there for me throughout this most difficult period at work.

In May 1973, we moved from Bellevue to Seattle, on the other side of Lake Washington. It made all the sense in the world to live in Seattle: our friends, our kids' activities, and our social and community life were all there. We were never comfortable in Bellevue, especially after the racist incidents involving Julie and Peter. In our search for a new home, we concentrated on southeastern Seattle, an area known for its ethnic diversity. Neighborhoods were racially integrated, including the section of prestigious homes overlooking Lake Washington. We found our perfect home at 5221 Holly Street—a five-bedroom, 3,300 square foot house. It was located in the Seward Park area and had a view of Lake Washington and Mount Rainier. This house was to be our perfect home for the next sixteen years. It became a popular meeting place for Filipino and Asian community discussions, a setting for political campaigning, and a comfortable environment for social get-togethers with our friends from the Young Turks.

Our move to Seattle was everything we had hoped it would be. The kids adjusted immediately to their schools and neighborhood. When we lived in Bellevue, they rarely brought friends to the house. In Seattle, they routinely had visitors, particularly on weekends. Cheryl, Peter, and Julie went to Franklin High School, where the student body was one-third white, one-third black, and one-third Asian. All did well academically, were popular with their peers, and did not get into any trouble. And it was comforting to know that my Young Turk buddy Sonny Tangalin was vice principal and was available if needed.

When the kids were younger, visitors to the house were mostly girls, which is not surprising, since Peter is the only boy. Now that most were teens, however, there were more boys, not to see Peter but to see our *dalagas*. The kids' friends, predominantly Filipino, were well behaved and respectful. They called us "Uncle" and "Auntie," Filipino style, and seemed to have been well briefed on the dos and don'ts of the Jamero household. We had a few simple rules. There was to be no honking of horns in front of the house to call the kids. Visitors should be introduced to all family members, parents first. Friends of the opposite sex were not to be entertained in bedrooms. When the kids went out, they were to return at the agreed-upon time. Except for the last rule, which they broke occasionally, our children respected our wishes.

The FYA drill team took up much of the family's time in the early 1970s. During the summers, the team participated in at least one parade every weekend. Except for overnight trips to Vancouver, Canada, and Portland, Oregon, most of the parades were in-state, in Everett, Olympia, Seattle, and Tacoma. The drill team's season culminated with Seattle's weeklong Seafair celebration, when the kids had a grueling schedule of one parade a day. The coveted championship trophies they won for outstanding performance were well-earned rewards for their efforts. For the most part, the summer parade performances were positive experiences. Unfortunately, the all-too-familiar racist taunts of "Ching-Chong Chinaman" and "Go back where you came from" sometimes marred the occasions. Because of such experiences, Terri and I were glad FYA placed heavy emphasis on teaching the drill team children what it meant to be Filipino. These ugly incidents also confirmed how right we were to raise our own kids so that they appreciated their ethnicity and also knew how to deal with discrimination.

Parades were not the only activities for the drill team kids. During the off-season, FYA held appreciation dinners for parents and children, complete with awards for virtually everyone. The off-season highlight was the talent show. One year, Bob Santos and I parodied a boxing match in which I knocked out the taller, more skilled Bob, who, incidentally, was an amateur boxer with the U.S. Marine Corps. Loud laughter burst out when we boxed in slow motion and showed how a few strategic punches to Bob's groin actually made the difference. The only one who did not appreciate the skit was little Jeanine, only seven years old, who cried at the good-natured booing from the crowd when I was introduced as Bob's opponent.

With my appetite for show business whetted, I got my big chance to be an extra in a movie. A Hollywood film, *Harry in Your Pocket*, starring James Coburn and Walter Pidgeon, was being filmed in Seattle. The storyline called for a gang of Colombian pickpockets, and since Seattle did not have a sizable Colombian population, the word went out to cast Filipinos as extras for the scene. Bob Santos and I showed up. As it turned out, the movie company was looking not only for Filipinos but for short Filipinos. Bob was too tall, but I fit the requirements perfectly and ended up playing the leader of the Colombian pickpocket gang. A professional "dip" (pickpocket), hired as a technical consultant, gave us on-the-job training on how to go through a crowd and pick men's pockets and women's purses. Our scene seemed simple. No lines were required. However, it took two days to film, since the perfectionist movie director was never satisfied. The repetitive process took away the glamour I had associated with appearing in a movie. A few months later, I excitedly took the whole family to a downtown theater to see my film debut. It never happened. Unknown to me, my movie debut had ended up on the cutting-room floor.

When business trips took me to California, I made sure I took the time to visit Mama and Papa. They were now essentially semi-retired, and their once bustling camp had dwindled to about fifteen to twenty steady boys, mostly the same *manongs* I knew from my boyhood days. They were all in their seventies, as were Mama and Papa. Free from the long hours required to run a labor camp, Papa and Mama spent much of their time tending the flowers and plants in the front yard. Although they were in good health, they were clearly aging. I thought about their mortality and suddenly experienced a rush of random memories of my growing-up years with Papa and Mama. I saw how influential each had been in shaping the person I had become. I remembered the sacrifices they went through as they raised eight children and sent them all to college.

For perhaps the very first time in my life, I realized how truly blessed I was to have such parents. I inherited the best that each had to offer. My passion for social issues and community involvement came from Mama. I remembered her untiring efforts to collect money for families who had lost their homes in a fire and her eloquent argument for fairness after my high school principal suspended me. My leadership qualities and cultural pride were primarily from Papa. I remembered how he had stuck to his principles after Bill Horine threatened to cut the wages of the farmworkers and recalled his effectiveness in negotiating with ranchers. My family values, rooted in Filipino belief systems, came from both Mama and Papa. To this day, such cultural beliefs as *walay ulaw* (avoiding shame) and *walang batasan* (without respect or manners) continue to influence my behavior and my approach to raising my children.

The camp's somberness also contributed to my pensive mood. Not only were Papa and Mama and their steady boys aging, so were their surroundings. The outbuildings were in various states of disrepair. The three-story bunkhouse was just about empty, with only the first level occupied by the aging *manongs*. I looked at the empty pigpen, where hogs used to slog through the mud. Even the crowing of the fighting roosters seemed somehow subdued.

Shortly after returning home from California, I began to enjoy working in the yard, perhaps influenced by Mama's and Papa's love of gardening. Up to that time, I did yardwork because I had to. Even then, I limited myself to mowing the lawn. Terri, however, loved digging in the dirt and watching plants and flowers grow. My metamorphosis into a happy gardener probably began with the need to prune the many trees and shrubs that graced our front yard and backyard. Pruning was one of the few things Terri could not do. I took on the task by default and immediately found that I enjoyed lopping off branches and limbs. Perhaps I was motivated by a need to deal with pent-up frustration and aggression, but whatever the reason, I became skilled at trimming and pruning. Before long, the trees and shrubs were as well kept as the plants and flowers tended by Terri.

My gardening prowess must have been obvious. One day, I was weeding in the front yard when a woman walked by on her way to the nearby Jewish temple for Sabbath. Thinking I was a hired gardener, she asked in a heavy accent, "How much you charge?" I looked up at her and in the best Filipino accent I could muster, I said, "Surry, I'm tu beesy." Embarrassed after figuring out that I was the homeowner and not a gardener, the woman did not go past our house again. She always walked on the other side of the street.

The 1970s would see me heavily involved in politics, thanks to the Young Turks. After our work with the Baruso campaign, candidates of both major political parties sought our input as well as our help. Most of us played important roles in campaign organizations. We became visible in almost every political campaign in Seattle and in King County as well as in statewide and national races.

In 1972, state attorney general Slade Gorton and Ralph Monroe, both close Republican allies of Governor Evans, came to our home to help the Young Turks plan the governor's reelection fundraiser. The next year, they approached Bob Santos about running for the state senate from Seattle's predominantly Democratic and ethnically diverse 37th District. They offered people and money resources. It was tempting. A year earlier, the Democratic Party had asked Bob to run for the legislature, but he declined because of the lack of campaign resources. Now, he was tempted to accept the Republican offers of assistance but wanted to make sure the Young Turks would manage his campaign. Although we were all strongly

Democratic in our political leanings, we supported Bob in his desire to run for the senate seat. Despite a well-run campaign, Bob lost the election. The large majority of Democratic voters in the district was too much for him to overcome.

Bob's campaign was noteworthy for the involvement of a person who would become the most infamous serial killer of the decade—Ted Bundy. The Republican Party loaned Bundy to help out with Bob's run for the senate, and he participated in campaign meetings, including several at our home. The Young Turks considered him somewhat aloof, with his clipped imitation-British accent, and he didn't participate in the social banter that usually accompanied our campaign meetings. Terri noticed, however, that he seemed to have a great interest in young girls with long straight hair, such as our *dalagas*. We still shudder when we remember that a monster like Bundy was in our home.

In 1975, I worked with the Young Turks as part of a pan-Asian effort to elect a more sympathetic candidate to the Seattle School Board. Residents of southeast Seattle had long sought to bring culturally relevant education to the large Asian population of the area. However, the conservative members of the school board refused to budge from their traditional policies. Consequently, the Chinese, Filipino, Japanese, Korean, and Samoan communities formed a coalition and began to seek a viable candidate, preferably Asian, to run for the seat. The coalition was well organized, attracted racially diverse community support, and developed a strong case for culturally relevant education for its schools. The group approached prominent members of the Asian community, including me, as potential candidates. All declined. Very few had a background in political campaigns and did not see themselves as political candidates.

At the end of June, with the primary election scheduled for September and the general election for November, time was running out. Twice before, I had turned down the coalition's request to run. However, when asked for a third time, I said yes. The coalition's cause was persuasive, and I thought it was time for a candidate who was culturally sensitive to Asian educational needs. As the father of children attending Seattle public schools, I could not turn the group down again.

Perhaps as persuasive, however, were the quality and ethnic diversity of the coalition's campaign organization. I knew I could count on the Young Turks to play essential roles in the campaign, and this time, capable, hardworking individuals from other ethnic groups joined us. I thought we had a good chance of winning, although the task was formidable. My strongest opponent, Suzanne Hittman, was a longtime educational activist, well known in the district as well as in the city's educational community. There were also two other candidates for the September primary. Despite our campaign's late start and the fact that I was a newcomer to school politics, I ran a close second to my better-known opponent, trailing by only 240 votes. The other two candidates were eliminated.

Considering that we had been campaigning for only two months, we looked at the primary results as a victory. Under election rules, the top two candidates would run against each other in the city-wide general election in November. We enthusiastically geared ourselves up to win the final election. It did not happen. In the end, Hittman's greater name familiarity in other city districts and my newness in educational circles resulted in a second-place finish. However, I did beat my opponent in our home district, testimony to the strong grassroots organization that supported my candidacy. I was understandably disappointed by the election result but pleased that the campaign marked the political beginning for a number of campaign workers. In subsequent years, Filipinos and other Asians, having cut their political teeth on the Jamero school board campaign, would become increasingly prominent in Seattle politics.

The school board election was my only experience as a candidate. While I was at ease with most aspects of campaigning, I was never comfortable about asking people for money. My reluctance turned out to be important when we ran short of funds in the critical last ten days of the campaign. The strongest reason for not campaigning as a candidate again, however, was the toll it took on family life. Almost everything had to take a backseat to winning the election. My heavy workload already took me away from home, and the campaign left me with no quality time whatsoever with my family. Consequently, the parental burden was on Terri's shoulders; she had to handle the daily responsibilities of bringing up our children, four of whom were teenagers.

The campaign also left no time for other community activities. After the election, I resumed my involvement in the community, speaking at or emceeing numerous Filipino, Asian, and mainstream events. I coined the catchy acronym FAPAGOW (Filipino American Political Action Group of Washington) for the new non-partisan political organization. I continued my long service as a board member of the Church Council of Greater Seattle. Tony Ogilvie, Bob Santos, and I took the thirty-minute ferry ride to Bainbridge Island and helped begin the empowerment process for IndoPino (Native American and Filipino) teens, who had historically faced discrimination in island schools. I resumed my active involvement in partisan politics. In recognition of my work with the Young Turks in Charles Royer's successful campaign for mayor of Seattle, I became a member of the mayor's Official Reception Committee. Whenever a nationally elected official or candidate flew into town, the committee provided the core of the official receiving line. As a member of the committee, I helped welcome President Gerald Ford, Democratic presidential candidate Jimmy Carter, and Vice Presidents Nelson Rockefeller and Walter Mondale to Seattle.

For Vice President Mondale's 1977 visit to Seattle, Terri and I stationed ourselves in front of the stage but became separated by the crush of Democratic supporters just before Mondale appeared onstage. As he spoke to the crowd, Mondale could not seem to take his eyes off Terri, strikingly attractive in a black cocktail dress. Following his remarks, he came down from the stage to shake hands with the audience. He shook hands with Terri and continued to hold her hand even while greeting other supporters. The unexpected attention from the vice president embarrassed her, but I found the whole sequence of events amusing. When we got home, I teasingly asked her, "Do you think the vice president will call you?"

Governor Evans chose not to run for another term in 1976. According to political tradition, all appointees of the outgoing governor were required to submit resignation letters to his successor, who had the option of tearing up the resignations or accepting them. The new governor was Dixie Lee Ray, the first woman to be elected governor of Washington. A Democrat, Ray had announced during her campaign that she intended to get rid of all of Governor Evans's appointees. I enjoyed my job and had already proved to be an effective director for the vocational rehabilitation program. Despite my long affiliation with the Democratic Party, however, I had to admit that the situation did not look promising. I decided to turn to my ace in the hole. In my four years as DVR director, I had developed a close personal and working relationship with John Bagnariol, chairman of the state's House Ways and Means Committee, who would shortly become Speaker of the House. He was a staunch supporter of my programs and was mostly responsible for DVR's strong backing in the legislature. Earlier, he had offered to speak to the new governor on my behalf, and shortly after Ray's victory, I took him up on his offer. Bagnariol, perhaps the most powerful Democrat in Olympia, went to Governor Ray with a letter requesting my retention, citing his "high regard" for my "contributions to the state." He persuaded Governor Ray to retain me as DVR director. The incoming governor kept only one other Evans appointee and accepted the rest of the resignation letters.

In 1978, Young Turks Dale and Jeannette Castillano Tiffany played key roles on Dolores Sibonga's successful Seattle City Council campaign committee, with the other Young Turks playing less visible supporting roles. Dale's organizational skills and attention to detail were excellent, and Jeannette had a well-deserved reputation for designing effective campaign literature. They proved to be able campaigners for Young Turk Dolores, the first Filipino American attorney to pass the Washington State bar and the first person of Filipino ancestry elected to the city council of a major American city.

During the same year, many of the Young Turks were active in

Mike Lowry's successful campaign for U.S. Congress. I had worked closely with Lowry in my efforts to obtain funding for the vocational rehabilitation program when he was staff director of the Washington State Senate Finance Committee. Lowry won the seat in the southeast Seattle district, where most of the Young Turks resided. Bob Santos and Terri were hired as staffers in the new congressman's Seattle district office. Bob was now a well-known figure in political circles, and Terri's behind-the-scenes work for the Young Turks and her community leadership as FYA board president would be assets for Lowry in his first term.

The Young Turks' activism was part of the Asian political movement that was beginning to bloom across the country, particularly on the West Coast. In the 1970s, Asians joined the struggle for civil rights. They were significant players in minority coalitions, swelled the ranks of campaign workers, and ran for elected office. Perhaps most important, Asian Americans began to look to their own community issues, such as programs for the aging and for youth and reparations for former Japanese American internees.

It was a heady time for Seattle Filipinos as well, now a force in community issues, thanks largely to the trailblazing work of the Young Turks. In addition, the group's activities extended to Asian politics at the national level. We lobbied for housing, mental health, aging, and youth programs for Asians. I was privileged to meet with Asian elected officials such as U.S. Senator Daniel Inouye of Hawaii and members of Congress such as Patsy Mink, also of Hawaii, and California's Norman Mineta. While I was chatting with Congressman Mineta, we discovered that our paths had crossed before. Unknown to both of us at the time, I took his place at the San Jose packinghouse summer job after he was drafted into the army in 1953.

These were also the years of an emerging Filipino political movement. Subsequent to the great success of the first Young Filipino People's Far West Convention in Seattle in 1971, other conventions followed annually in Stockton, San Jose, Los Angeles, Seattle again, and Berkeley. A growing network, with national implications, began to form among West Coast Filipino communities. However, the promise of empowerment for Filipino Americans soon disappeared because of divided loyalties growing out of the anti-Marcos movement.

The situation in Seattle reflected those in other Filipino communities. On the one hand, many young Filipino Americans joined the anti-Marcos organization Katipunan ng Demokratikong Pilipino (KDP). For them, working to overthrow the Marcos dictatorship in the Philippines was an opportunity to express Filipino pride and identity. Most of these young activists were new Americans, recent immigrants born in the Philippines, or, if they were American-born, their parents had come to America after immigration laws were liberalized in 1965. Their continuing interest in the mother country was understandable. The established Filipino community in Seattle, on the other hand, was strongly pro-Marcos. Composed largely of people from the Ilocano-speaking regions of the Philippines, the community stood firmly behind its provincial comrade.

Staking out yet another position were the Young Turks, Bridge Generation Filipino Americans, and those affiliated with Filipino Youth Activities. Our priorities centered on Filipinos in America. While we sympathized with Filipinos living under the Marcos regime, we considered their plight to be a complex problem affecting a country that was not our own. We also believed that involving ourselves in the affairs of the Philippines would severely strain our limited resources and energies. A deep schism developed within the ranks of Filipino Americans, aborting a promising movement that might have unified Filipinos across the country.

Most of the Young Turks stayed out of the fray on the Marcos issue. The only exceptions were the Cordovas and Bob Santos. Fred and Dorothy, who had strong kinship ties with the established Filipino community in Seattle, became embroiled in several confrontations with the anti-Marcos activists. Bob became a strong ally of anti-Marcos forces, since most of them had ties to his International District base. The deepening schism was not easy for me, as I was highly visible and active within the Filipino community.

Despite the constant pressure from pro- and anti-Marcos supporters, however, I managed to remain neutral. Happily, the differing
opinions on Marcos did not become a divisive issue among members of the Young Turks; our friendship was more valuable to us
than our views on the Philippines.

According to accounts in the *Philippine News* in 1973, the Marcos government had amassed a hit list of 150 enemies in the United
States. Most of the people on the list were Philippine-born anti-
Marcos exiles and Filipino American activists. Among the few
Bridge Generation Filipino Americans listed were Fred Cordova and
my sister Luna. While no one knew for certain how the names had
been selected, there was widespread speculation that leaders of the
Young Filipino Peoples Far West Conventions were primary targets. Fred had been the charismatic spokesman at the first convention in 1971, and Luna had chaired the 1973 Stockton convention.
Around the same time, my family and I went through a chilling
experience that seemed to be related to the hit list scare. While I
was on a business trip, Terri noticed a man in a parked car across
the street taking notes on who was coming and going at our house.
The surveillance continued for several evenings. The experience left
us shaken.

Karen was now attending the University of Washington, and our
other children had entered the critical years of deciding what to do
after high school. While they were growing up, Terri and I encouraged them to think about going to college. We also helped them
understand that as brown people, they needed additional attributes
so they could compete more effectively in American society. A college education would give them that extra edge. At the same time,
we told them we would be equally supportive if they decided to work
full-time after high school. It was their life choice. All Terri and I
asked was that they become productive adults. If their choice was
to pursue a college education, we could offer only minimal assistance. Providing for our large family precluded our saving enough
money to pay the entire cost of a college education. The kids would
have to come up with most of the financing through scholarships

or part-time work. As it turned out, they all opted to go to college, although they got there in different ways.

Peter enrolled at the University of Washington in 1975. To help pay for his education, Peter sought work in a salmon cannery in Kodiak, Alaska, in the summer of 1976. Beginning with the Manong Generation in the 1920s, Filipinos were the major source of labor for the Alaskan fish canneries. The International Longshoremen's and Warehousemen's Union (ILWU), Local 37, the predominantly Filipino union in Seattle, made all hiring decisions. Obtaining work at the Alaskan canneries usually required an in, an under-the-table "gift," or both. Thanks to the intercession of Bob Santos, whose uncle was a former union president, we had an in. Peter became an Alaskero, a Filipino cannery worker, along with Bob's son Danny. But Peter's summer job was short-lived. He injured his arm badly while washing out the "slimer," a machine used to clean salmon. The arm swelled to almost twice its normal size, but luckily for Peter, the injury turned out to be only a severe bruise.

An injured arm was not Peter's only legacy from Alaska. His work in the cannery also brought him face-to-face with the harsh realities of discrimination. He saw that only brown Filipinos worked in the most difficult and menial jobs such as scaling and cleaning fish and reported to all-white supervisors and managers. He saw Filipinos relegated to separate but unequal bunkhouses that lacked the amenities enjoyed by whites. Filipinos ate different (and cheaper) meals and rarely were served choice cuts of meat. The cannery's official explanation for the segregation and disparate treatment of Filipinos was "They like it that way." Peter may have come home injured, but he also came home much wiser to the ways of the real world.

The segregation and discriminatory practices Peter experienced in Alaska had been going on for decades. In an effort to remedy workplace inequities, the Alaska Cannery Workers Association filed a class action lawsuit in 1973 against the New England Fish Company, the largest cannery operator in Alaska. Four years later, the U.S. District Court in Seattle decided for the cannery workers. However, it would take years and many more court hearings before a financial settlement was reached. Peter was one of more than seven hundred plaintiffs who received cash settlements. The New England Fish Company, facing an additional multimillion-dollar judgment, filed for bankruptcy.

Karen graduated from the University of Washington in 1976 and for several years beginning in 1977, three of our children went to colleges in California. Cheryl worked and attended San Francisco State part-time, Peter obtained a modest financial package to help him transfer to the University of Santa Clara, and Julie received a grant to attend Menlo College, a private two-year institution just north of Stanford. The following school year, Cheryl decided to drop out of San Francisco State, but Jackie joined the ranks of our college-going children. She received a combination scholarship–work study grant to attend Whitman College, a small prestigious school in Walla Walla, in the southeastern corner of Washington State. Helping three kids through college took every penny we had or could borrow. However, Terri and I did not complain; our children had demonstrated that they also valued higher education. Just as important, they had shown that they were willing to work to achieve it.

In the spring of 1978, we received some unexpected news—Peter wanted to marry Jovanne Allianic. They were both FYA drill team members and had been going steady for a few years. We all liked Jovanne, and Terri and I knew the two were serious about each other. However, we were totally unprepared for their plans for marriage. Peter was only twenty-one, and Jovanne had just finished high school. Since neither had a steady job, marriage did not look like a good idea. But Peter was insistent. He argued that they were devoted to each other. They both planned to work, and they were emotionally ready. Finally, we reached a compromise agreement. Terri elicited a promise from Peter that he would continue his education by transferring back to the University of Washington and attending part-time. We would help by renting them the large downstairs room at a nominal cost.

Peter's and Jovanne's August wedding at the inner-city parish of Immaculate Conception Church set the standard for subsequent

Jamero family weddings. The large wedding party numbered twenty-four people. Jackie was one of two maids of honor, and Karen, Cheryl, Julie, Jeanine, and my niece Cindy served as bridesmaids. Peter's first cousin Patrick, my brother Herb's second son, was best man, and his cousins Michael, Chris, and Danny were groomsmen. Peter's Aunt Pula, his baptismal godmother, and his cousin Kathy served as godparents during the Filipino segment of the ceremony. In addition, Terri's sister Jane and brother-in-law Richard were godparents. There were so many individuals in the procession that we had to draft Luna as emcee. Young Turks member and lay minister Fred Cordova assisted the officiating priest, Father Manuel Ocana, with the Roman Catholic Mass. Father Ocana, originally from the Visayan island of Cebu and co-pastor at Immaculate Conception, added a nice touch to the proceedings with his whimsical, often humorous, references to Filipino life.

Supplementing the rites of the Roman Catholic Church, a beautiful Filipino ceremony bestowed symbolic blessings of love, joy, and prosperity. This tradition is composed of four interrelated rituals: lighting the candles, placing the veil, tying the cord, and sharing the coins. The candles, which are lit by the parents of both bride and groom, signify life, the very essence of a Filipino home, and love, the essence of holy matrimony. A set of godparents places the veil over the couple, symbolizing the groom taking responsibility for loving and caring for the bride and the bride accepting that commitment. When the cord is tied around the couple by a second set of godparents, it signifies the moment of union and the act of binding. The groom places the coins, given to him by a third pair of godparents, in the bride's hands, symbolizing the sharing of not only the wealth of their labor but also the treasures of the mind, heart, and spirit.

This was our first experience in putting on a wedding. I did not realize that hosting a wedding would be such a big production, yet Terri seemed to handle everything like an old pro. Except for the guest list and the composition of the wedding party, Peter and Jovanne left most of the rest to Terri. She oversaw much of the detail work with significant help from our girls. I remembered my own wedding, when Mama took major responsibility for making many of the arrangements. In that wedding as well as this one, there did not seem to be much of a role for me. I concluded that perhaps weddings were for females.

Despite a busy family and social life and a heavy schedule at work, I still found time to enjoy my passions of jazz and baseball. I upgraded my stereo system with a more powerful receiver, a turntable, and a cassette-tape deck. Over the years, my record collection increased dramatically and now numbered more than three hundred. Unfortunately, quality live jazz performances were scarce in Seattle. I had to be content to enjoy live jazz on my trips to California. There, I heard Bill Evans, the great pianist, and Filipino performers Flip Nunez and Corney Pasquil, both pianists, and my cousins, the singing brother-and-sister duo of Rudy Tenio and Josie Canion.

I had better luck with seeing my favorite baseball team, the New York Yankees. The Yankees visited Seattle twice a year to play the Mariners, the new American League team that came into being in 1977. That year, the Yankees were defending league champions and were on their way to a second straight championship with such players as home-run hitter Reggie Jackson and all-star catcher Thurman Munson. I made it a point to see as many Yankees games as possible.

At the Division of Vocational Rehabilitation, I became much more comfortable and relaxed after the crisis over the Educational Consultants contract was resolved. I poked fun at myself in front of employees with comments such as "English is my second language" whenever I used the wrong syntax or missed the point of a conversation. I also made jokes about my shortness. The looser atmosphere helped bring the staff together, which, in turn, resulted in DVR asserting itself as one of the more enlightened state programs in the country. As the program's director, I gained increased visibility and recognition. I was considered for a presidential appointment as commissioner of Social and Rehabilitation Services in Washington, D.C., and received an award from Chicago's Commission on Accreditation of Rehabilitation Facilities as the first state director of vocational rehabilitation in the nation to set minimum accreditation standards for sheltered workshops. The facility whose director had sought my ouster a few years earlier was among the workshops that benefited from my directive, and we developed an amicable working relationship. Terri remarked how strange it was that I got along with someone who obviously was not a friend. I responded, "It's only a business relationship that's good for both of us. I still don't trust him."

The award was followed in short order by my election to the executive committee of the Council of State Administrators of Vocational Rehabilitation (CSAVR). The organization exerted considerable force in influencing the federal government and Congress on rehabilitation policy and legislation. I was particularly proud of my election to the executive committee. Through the years, few people of color had ascended to leadership positions in the council, and I considered my election affirmation that I was accepted as an equal by an organization whose traditional leadership came from the Deep South. As it turned out, counterparts from southern states were among my strongest supporters, thanks to John Webb, the respected vocational rehabilitation program director for Mississippi. Webb was one of the first people I met at my first CSAVR national meeting. We learned, to our great surprise, that he had visited my hometown of Livingston many times to see his wife's cousins, my old schoolmates Joe, Bonnie, and Wilma Ulrich.

As a CSAVR executive committee member, I grew more visible in dealings with federal bureaucrats and members of Congress. At the time, the Washington State congressional delegation was one of the most powerful in the nation's capital, with Senators Warren Magnuson and Henry (Scoop) Jackson and Congressman Norm Dicks. I had already developed a good base of DVR support from the elected officials. Now that I had broader responsibilities, with CSAVR, their influence was as vital as ever. I found myself spending more and more time in Washington, D.C., and other cities across the country on CSAVR business.

The Washington State vocational rehabilitation program continued to be among the leading performers in the country. I was pleased with the program's accomplishments, proud of the staff's professionalism, and pleased with the personal recognition that came with being director. Under my leadership, the program's budget increased to an all-time high of $42 million. The Commission on Accreditation of Rehabilitation Facilities honored me with a Special Recognition Award on its tenth anniversary, this time for my leadership and commitment to accreditation. I also received several commendations from Governor Ray for my work on the Governor's Committee for Employment of the Handicapped.

I will never forget May 18, 1977. It was one of most physically taxing days of my life. In order to help dramatize National Handicapped Awareness Week, I had agreed to participate in an event called "My Day in a Wheelchair." I found that practically all the rooms in our house were inaccessible. I could not get into the bathroom because the doors were not wide enough. My Volkswagen Beetle posed another problem. I wasn't able to master the art of transferring myself from the wheelchair into the car. Moreover, after cheating my way into the space behind the driver's seat, I could not swing the folded wheelchair into the backseat. The toughest test came when I arrived at work and had to negotiate a long ramp to enter the office building. The ramp supposedly met accessibility standards, but you could not have proved it by me. Getting up the ramp took every muscle I had. "My Day in a Wheelchair" had the desired impact, and the event received wide coverage from the media. I was pleased with the publicity, but I sure was exhausted.

I have been proud of my efforts to support historically disadvantaged groups in their struggles to participate in mainstream America. My years as director of the Division of Vocational Rehabilitation coincided with a national movement for disabled rights. I was pleased to find that disabled people in the state of Washington were among the movement's leaders. From the beginning of my tenure, I included disabled people, along with others who were stakeholders in vocational rehabilitation, in developing the program's direction. The division's subsequent success would not have been possible without their valuable input. And the benefits were mutual. The state's foremost disabled advocacy organization, the Governor's Committee for Employment of the Handicapped, sought my input as well. I participated regularly in the group's deliberations and accepted a number of special assignments. Washington's disabled community continues to play an essential role in promoting disabled rights. I would like to believe that I made a small contribution to that effort.

I liked being DVR director, despite the occasional episodes of racism I experienced on the job. Once, while attending a national meeting of the Council of State Administrators for Vocational Rehabilitation in Nashville, Tennessee, the hotel clerk requested three pieces of identification before allowing me to register. I objected, asking, "Isn't this an unusual request?" He responded coldly, "This is routine procedure at this hotel." I thought that if the hotel clerk had been totally forthcoming, he would have admitted that he could not believe a brown person could be director of a state program. However, I refrained from telling him what I was really thinking. Later, I asked my white colleagues if they had been required to show personal identification. Of course, they had not. My colleagues were shocked that this type of discriminatory treatment still existed; I was not.

When I attended business meetings accompanied by a white staff member, people who had never met me before assumed that the white person was the state director. Again, these individuals took it for granted that a brown person like me could not possibly be the state director. These incidents confirmed my belief that whatever the position I might attain in my native land, racist individuals would judge me by the color of my skin. Most of the time, I shrugged it off as part of the reality that is America. However, there were times when I found it difficult to control my anger.

Despite these incidents, I continued to enjoy my job. However,

I began to feel that there was not much more for me to accomplish with the Division of Vocational Rehabilitation. By 1979, I began to consider other employment possibilities. I was now nearing eight years as director, the only program director remaining of the original DSHS secretariat. I had outlasted two Washington governors and three secretaries of the DSHS umbrella agency. Six months later, I, too, would be gone.

## 14  The Professor

I NEVER THOUGHT I WOULD WORK IN THE WORLD of academia. There was nothing in my background to suggest such a possibility. I did not have a PhD, and I had never taught. Nevertheless, in May 1979, I became a full-time faculty member of the prestigious medical school at the University of Washington (UW).

For about a year, Mike Clowers, associate professor at the Department of Rehabilitation Medicine, had been talking to me about possible employment at the university. Mike had built an impressive program of research and demonstrations, concentrating on the vocational aspects of rehabilitating disabled individuals. He was young, bright, ambitious, and likable. We developed a mutually beneficial working relationship and soon became friends and colleagues. According to Mike, his workload was getting unwieldy. He wanted to spin off some of the work to a person with administrative experience in employing and training disabled persons. At first, I dismissed the idea, pointing to my lack of academic qualifications and experience. I also mentioned that, even if I had the requisite experience, I doubted that the university would be able to come close to my salary. However, when Mike reported that Dr. Justus Lehmann, the chair of the Department of Rehabilitation Medicine, wanted to talk to me about a possible position, I decided to explore the situation further.

Dr. Lehmann, a brilliant physiatrist (a physician specializing in physical medicine and rehabilitation) with an international reputation, headed one of the foremost physical rehabilitation programs in the country. He had been a strong supporter throughout my years at the Division of Vocational Rehabilitation and was among the first to call on me to pay his respects when I was appointed director. He saw to it that I met important physicians in the field of physical rehabilitation. He stood by me during the dark days of the Educational Consultants contract controversy. Our relationship was reciprocal. As director of the Division of Vocational Rehabilitation, I wrote letters of endorsement for a number of grant proposals he submitted to the federal government. I also sought his counsel on controversial issues. A no-nonsense administrator, Dr. Lehmann had a reputation of being difficult to deal with. However, this was never the case with me. We worked well together.

Dr. Lehmann had given serious thought to the possibility of my joining the UW medical school's Department of Rehabilitation Medicine. It was not only because of Mike's heavy workload. Speaking with the accent of his native Germany, Dr. Lehmann said he wanted me on his staff because of my record of accomplishment in obtaining funding. He could see that the recent cuts in research funding enacted by the administration of President Ronald Reagan would eventually have an adverse effect on his programs. He knew about my effectiveness in working with federal, state, and local governments and believed that placing me on his staff might minimize future cutbacks in funding.

Regarding Mike's workload, Dr. Lehmann was confident that we could work out a logical division of labor. He was equally confident that my lack of teaching experience would not pose a problem. Dr. Lehmann planned that I would teach no more than one course a year and serve as guest lecturer in other classes. He felt that my work as state director could be transferred directly to teaching. As for my lack of a PhD, the only consequence was that it would limit my initial faculty appointment to the lowest level, that of instructor. But Dr. Lehmann was confident and optimistic. He believed I would encounter no difficulty in being promoted to assistant professor after serving the mandatory one year as an instructor. Finally, he said, "I would be willing to offer you a salary comparable to what you are making with DVR." I could not believe what I had just heard.

My DVR salary far exceeded the salaries of most other faculty members in the department. I was flattered. I was also inclined to accept his offer for other reasons. At this point in my career, I was confident of my abilities. I had already learned that my management skills were transferable within a variety of work settings, and a university setting should not be much different. After discussing Dr. Lehmann's offer with Terri, it did not take long for me to decide to accept it. Working at the University of Washington would mean the end of my sixty-mile commute to Olympia. The university's generous retirement package for its teaching staff was another incentive. Most important, I would have more time to spend at home with my family.

Before leaving state government, I attended going-away functions in almost every vocational rehabilitation district office across Washington, culminating in a large farewell dinner in Seattle. My tenure as state director was the longest I had ever worked at one job. I was leaving supporters and friends, not just coworkers, and I would miss the program and the staff. It had been a rewarding eight years, but I knew this was a good time for me to leave.

At the end of May 1979, I reported to my new job at the University of Washington. (According to Young Turk Fred Cordova, now employed in the Office of University Relations, my appointment to a full-time faculty position at the School of Medicine was another Filipino First.) Given that Dr. Lehmann's priority was to obtain additional funding, I immediately began to work on several proposals I had been considering. Mike suggested that I also orient myself to the various programs and projects for which he was responsible, so that we would have a better idea of how to divide the workload. Besides teaching, Mike supervised six counselors who were part of the rehabilitation clinical team at the University Hospital. He was also in charge of a number of special off-campus projects.

Because I lacked academic experience, I had expected that other faculty members might resent my appointment. However, thanks to Dr. Lehmann and Mike, my new colleagues welcomed me. I was still apprehensive about my inexperience, but as long as Dr. Lehmann did not have a problem with it, I figured I should not either. I began to feel more comfortable in my new work environment.

In July, I also became an adjunct faculty member of the UW School of Social Work. By a happy coincidence, the school was looking for a person to coordinate its newly approved Project on Physical Disabilities. Scott Briar, dean of the School of Social Work, whom I first met when he was teaching at the University of California, Berkeley, called me immediately upon learning of my appointment at the medical school. He assured me that the workload would be minimal. I would supervise one person and teach one class a year, and the School of Social Work would provide me with an office. It seemed to be a good fit. My training was in social work, and I knew several faculty members from the years I had served on Scott's Community Advisory Committee. The project grant included funds to pay part of my salary, which would ease the demand on Dr. Lehmann's departmental budget. Dr. Lehmann swiftly agreed to the shared arrangement.

Even though Mike and I had not yet completely decided how we were going to divide his tasks, I found myself assuming more and more of his workload. At first, it was because he went on an extended vacation. When he returned, he looked tired and appeared to have lost weight. He began to take an increasing amount of sick time. During our telephone calls, he said there was nothing to worry about, that he would be back in the office soon. One day, his wife Diane called and said that Mike wanted to see me. His appearance shocked me. He had lost even more weight and was only a shadow of the handsome and vital person I had known. His breathing seemed labored. I found out that the lining of his lungs had deteriorated from the long-term effects of asbestos; Mike had been exposed to asbestos when he worked at a medical laboratory at the University of Illinois. He had cancerous mesothelioma and was terminally ill.

Mike and Diane had known about his illness for some time. Mike was well prepared for his impending death and had already obtained a financial package that would provide for Diane and their two children. In a weakened voice, he asked me to continue the work that he had begun at the university. It suddenly occurred to me that this was why Mike had worked so long and hard to get me to join him on the faculty. He had a second request. He wanted me to look in on Diane and his kids from time to time. Finally, Mike asked me to keep the news of his illness to myself because he wanted to avoid the sympathetic calls and visits that were sure to follow if others knew about his condition. Dr. Lehmann was the only other person who knew. I was touched as I thought about how difficult it must have been for Mike to put all these plans in motion. I assented to his requests. Shortly after, Mike passed away. I helped Diane with Mike's funeral arrangements and delivered the eulogy.

Mike's exposure to asbestos led directly to mesothelioma and his death. A few months later, I testified on behalf of his family in a class action lawsuit brought against Johns Manville, the largest producer of asbestos in the country. The plaintiffs eventually won the lawsuit. Diane and her two young children were part of the huge settlement. However, all I could think of was that I had lost a colleague and a close friend whose bravery in his last days will never be forgotten.

I would soon lose another colleague and friend. John Bagnariol, the former Speaker of the Washington State House of Representatives, went to federal prison after his conviction for accepting bribes. The conduct of the investigation and the trial itself raised a number of ethical and legal questions. In a sting operation, investigators pretended to be representatives of a company that wanted to do business with the state of Washington. They resorted to entrapment and obtained tape-recorded evidence that led to Bagnariol's conviction. His damaging statements had been made on the advice of a close friend. I knew this friend well—Pat Gallagher, the same person who initiated the Educational Consultants contract when I was director of the state vocational rehabilitation program. Knowing Bagnariol, I was convinced that he had so trusted his friend that he did not question anything Gallagher asked him to say to the fake businessmen. I remain convinced that Bagnariol's political enemies used the unsuspecting Gallagher to set him up.

Democrat Bagnariol was the front-runner for the upcoming 1980 gubernatorial election, and the Young Turks were among his strongest supporters. Earlier, Bagnariol had asked me to be on his campaign committee. He met with the Young Turks at our home to discuss his political agenda. Bagnariol had done his homework. He knew our issues largely concerned civil rights and increased participation of the Filipino and Asian communities in state government. He addressed our concerns with well-thought-out initiatives of his own, including appointing me secretary of the Department of Social and Health Services. The Young Turks, most of whom had never met Bagnariol, were favorably impressed. They threw their support behind his campaign, which, sadly, never got off the ground.

In November 1979, we went to California to celebrate Mama's and Papa's fiftieth wedding anniversary. It was a grand occasion, attended by the ever expanding Jamero clan and scores of their friends. I was happy for my parents as they mingled with their guests. I also felt a tinge of sadness. It was like witnessing the passing of an era. The guests, like Papa and Mama, had come to America during the 1920s and 1930s, when Philippine nationals were highly sought after as a source of cheap labor. During the Great Depression, they became despised "brown monkeys" as previously shunned farm jobs suddenly became desirable to white Americans. In rapid-fire order, Filipinos found themselves categorized as aliens, transformed into "brave brown brothers" during World War II, and then returned to their status as unwelcome foreigners after the war. Through it all, they managed to raise families and pass their culture on to my generation, for which I will always be grateful. As I looked upon these aging members of the Manong Generation, I wondered if succeeding generations of Filipino Americans would truly appreciate their struggles in paving the way to a better life for us.

Papa died in his sleep on August 18, 1980, eight days before his eightieth birthday. There is no way one can really prepare for the passing of a loved one, even though we notice the passage of time and realize the inevitability of death. On our sad flight to California, I remembered the lessons I learned from Papa—his strong belief in family, his pride as a Filipino, and his skills in negotiating with farmers in a language he was still trying to learn. I also remembered how the years had changed him from an autocratic, disciplinarian father who seldom conversed with his children to a person who entertained us for hours with stories about his adventures in the Philippines, Hawaii, and America.

The services for Papa drew a large turnout of grieving friends and relatives. His lodge brothers and sisters of the Legionarios del Trabajo came in force from across the state. Farmers and fruit growers, who for decades had relied on Papa to provide laborers for their harvests, arrived to pay their respects. Members of the local Filipino community all seemed to be there. The Ivers and Alcorn funeral home and St. Jude's Catholic Church, where the last rites were read, were both filled to overflowing. It was a fitting tribute to Papa's life.

Mama asked me to deliver the eulogy. My biggest concern was not what I would be saying but whether I could maintain my composure. Papa had always stressed the importance of *walay ulaw*, or not bringing shame upon the family, especially in public. He would not have approved of my breaking down in front of his friends and relatives. I maintained my composure in public, not only during the eulogy but also for the remainder of our time in Livingston. In the privacy of our home in Seattle, however, I finally was able to grieve openly. I wept uncontrollably in Terri's arms. The Filipino cultural value of *ulaw* had a stronger influence on me than I had realized. I did not shame the Jamero family. Papa taught me well.

We had been in our perfect house on Holly Street for almost nine years. Although it accommodated our large family comfortably, Terri wanted to make it even more perfect. Her remodeling plan called for tearing down the wall between the kitchen and Peter's old bedroom and removing the small back porch, thus maximizing our view of Lake Washington and Mount Rainier. The back wall would be replaced with glass panels, and the large kitchen area would feature a huge island with a built-in stove, dishwasher, and sink. Terri's plans did not stop there. Since we were making major changes, she reasoned that we should also make the house more livable by installing a wraparound deck and double-pane windows.

At first, I thought her plans were unaffordable. "This is the time to remodel," she insisted, "and I know how to get it done." We had become friends with Larry Mortimer, an architect who had recently moved from California to southeast Seattle to start a neighborhood development business. After consulting with Larry, Terri showed me his cost estimate. It was much lower than I had anticipated. She also told me that the bank had assured her we should be able to get a loan at a reasonable interest rate since we no longer had three children in college at the same time. After reviewing the numbers, I was convinced. The remodeling began in January 1981. Three months later, it was finished, and shortly afterward, the remodeled house was put to the test. Terri and the children threw a surprise birthday party for me. It was wall-to-wall people inside, on the deck, and in the backyard. The house passed its first test successfully.

On December 15, 1979, our first grandchild, Lauren Michelle Jamero, was born to Peter and Jovanne. My feelings upon becoming a grandparent for the first time were so unlike the way I felt when I became a parent. When my own children were born, I thought about my responsibilities in raising them. With little Lauren, all I thought of was enjoying my first grandchild.

In June 1981, Peter received a bachelor of arts degree from the University of Washington. I also participated at the graduation exercises as a faculty member, wearing the green and gold colors of the Department of Rehabilitation Medicine. Terri was misty-eyed as she photographed the two favorite men in her life. Earning a degree was not easy for Peter, who had worked to support his family while also attending classes. Jovanne helped out financially through her job at the Boeing Company. However, the pressure was clearly on Peter to succeed at the university. He had grown up a lot in the last few years, much like his father under similar circumstances twenty-five years earlier. "How ironic," I thought. "Peter not only bore a strong resemblance to me, but the first few years of his marriage were also similar to my own at the same stage."

Our first grandson, Jeremy Peter Jamero, was born on October 25, 1982. Peter and Jovanne seemed much more at ease with Jeremy. No doubt Peter's college graduation and subsequent full-time job as an accountant at the Westin Hotel had much to do with the relaxed atmosphere. Terri doted on Jeremy as much as she ever did with Lauren. I must admit, so did I.

In 1982, Young Turk Roy Flores organized an all-Filipino slow-pitch softball team, appropriately named "Pinoy." The Pinoy played in the Seattle City League and were an instant success, winning the league championship in its first season. The team went on to dominate the league and postseason tournaments for the next three years. The Pinoy's third baseman was none other than our son Peter, the former Virginia Little League All-Star. He was in good company, as Roy did a masterful job in recruiting players who could hit as well as play defense. Roy was also skilled at integrating former high school and college stars with other players who had little experience in organized ball. The players were Filipino size, not physically imposing like most of the players on other teams. However, they were all good athletes and played well together. Terri and I were among the most loyal and loudest rooters, much as we had been when Peter played Little League baseball.

The Seattle Mariners were on the other end of the championship spectrum. They finished last in the league four out of their first five seasons. The only real excitement the Mariners generated in our lives was in May 1982, when Terri and I saw Gaylord Perry win the three hundredth game of his long career, a milestone only a few pitchers had reached. I continued to make sure I saw the Yankees play whenever they came to the Kingdome. Strangely, the last-place Mariners usually won their games against the Yankees, whose players were far superior.

Venues for live jazz in Seattle improved markedly with the opening of Jazz Alley in the University District and a Pioneer Square club owned by Seattleite Ernestine Anderson, the noted jazz singer. I saw and listened to artists such as trumpeters Chet Baker and Art Farmer, guitarist Kenny Burrell, and singer Mike Murphy.

We ushered in 1983 with a gala New Year's Eve party at our home, cohosted by Young Turk friends Roy and Angie Flores, Tony and Desiree Ogilvie, Sonny and Evelyn Tangalin, and Dale and Jeannette Tiffany. Formal dinner invitations went to fifty of our closest friends; no one sent regrets. We cleared the living room and dining area of furniture and rented tables and chairs to accommodate everyone. Guests wore their finest gowns and suits and enjoyed a never-to-be-forgotten New Year's Eve celebration with all the trimmings. After being greeted at the door by maitre d' Roy Flores, they were ushered to reserved tables, complete with the finest china, silver, and stemware provided by the five host couples. Candles lit the tables, and soft dinner music (jazz, of course) filled the room. Waitpersons Angie, Desiree, and Tony served cocktails, wine, and soft drinks without spilling a drop. The coup de grâce was the elegant prime rib dinner prepared by master chef Dale Tiffany and his kitchen staff—Jeannette, Sonny and Evelyn, Terri, and me. The party lasted well into the early hours of the morning.

Honors for my work in the community and in politics continued to come my way in the early 1980s. Filipino Youth Activities recognized Young Turks Roy Flores, Bob Santos, city councilwoman Dolores Sibonga, Sonny Tangalin, and me with a VIP (Very Important Pinoy) Award. The *International Examiner* named me an Outstanding Asian American in conjunction with Asian Pacific American Heritage Week. Terri and I hosted Joseph F. Kennedy II in our home at an Asian community fund-raising reception for his uncle, U.S. Senator Edward Kennedy, who was running for the Democratic presidential nomination. The young Joe Kennedy proved to be a popular draw as he exuded the famous Kennedy charm. Not surprisingly, many people, including Julie, Terri, and me, were photographed with him.

Meanwhile, I settled into my life in academia. After assuming most of Mike's responsibilities, I found myself with three offices—

one at the University Hospital, one at the School of Social Work, and another off-campus in the University District. Although I had a written schedule for each office, I did not always adhere to it, and Terri found it almost impossible to contact me by telephone. It seems that whenever she called, I was always "at my other office." However, my multi-office situation was also convenient. My brother George visited from California, and I was able to spend a lot of time with him. When he asked if I had to show up at one of my offices, I glibly replied, "No, I'm the boss. Besides, this is an exercise of academic freedom."

My work as an academician was going surprisingly well. I was already published in several journals and contributed a chapter to a textbook on employing the handicapped. Several grant proposals I wrote were approved for funding. My clinical staff seemed to find my supervision helpful in working with their hospital patients. I even looked forward to the weekly faculty meetings I once found intimidating and boring. If my response to George was glib, it was because I felt good about my work at the university. In recognition of the progress I had made, true to his predictions, Dr. Lehmann promoted me to assistant professor. Subsequently, several of my articles were published in scientific journals and received good reviews. In the February 1982 issue of the *Journal of Rehabilitation Administration*, reviewer John F. Newman wrote that my article on DVR's experiences within Washington State's umbrella agency "contributed significantly to the field of rehabilitation administration." I served two consecutive terms in the Faculty Senate, a body representing all faculty members in matters presented to university administration. Most important, especially for Dr. Lehmann, I brought in more than a million dollars in grants and contracts to the Department of Rehabilitation Medicine.

My only disappointment was the response I received from Dr. James Morishima, associate dean at the Department of Education. Things had gone so well for me that I was seriously considering a career in higher education. However, I knew that without a PhD, my career would soon plateau. A doctorate in education appeared to be my best alternative. Dr. Lehmann expressed strong support for the plan. He assured me that he would continue to keep me on as full-time faculty while providing enough release time for me to obtain a doctorate. All that remained was to obtain acceptance from the Department of Education. I decided to discuss the matter with Dr. Morishima.

I first met Dr. Morishima, a Japanese American, in 1973, when, as a newly appointed faculty member, he made a presentation on Asian communities before a group of state executives. The presentation completely ignored Filipinos, an omission I immediately called to his attention in a critical letter. He responded that he "wasn't an authority on the Filipino community." At the time, Fred and Dorothy Cordova described him as an ambitious new faculty member who "meant well." Since then, they said, Dr. Morishima had matured. Although my contact with him was limited, I was inclined to agree. He once told me that he had gained a better understanding of discriminatory practices aimed at Filipinos and would do everything he could to attract well-qualified Filipinos to his department.

Dr. Morishima expressed support for my plan to study and work at the same time. I then requested a waiver for the Graduate Record Examination (GRE). The purpose of the GRE is to determine one's likelihood of success in a graduate program. Most people who take the examination have just completed their undergraduate education and have little or no experience in a particular field. I pointed out that I had more than twenty years of high-level experience in health and human services. Furthermore, I was on the UW medical school faculty. I believed I had already proved myself as a doctoral candidate, but Dr. Morishima refused to grant the waiver. He would not even consider going to the chair of the department on my behalf. The more I argued my position, the more adamant he became. I went away thinking that he had not changed after all. It was especially galling that Morishima, a member of an ethnic minority, would probably continue to advocate for the fair treatment of minorities as long as it had nothing to do with his department.

I chose not to pursue the issue with Dr. Morishima as, again, fate intervened. A delegation of concerned citizens, most of them Asian, approached me about accepting an appointment as director of the newly established King County Department of Human Resources (DHR). Had this happened a few months earlier, I would probably have turned down the request. Recently, however, massive cuts in research monies proposed by the Reagan administration had jeopardized federal funding at the university. Despite my past success with grants and contracts, the future looked bleak. I decided I should seriously consider accepting the King County position.

## 15  King County

THE DELEGATION THAT SOUGHT ME AS THEIR
candidate for the Department of Human Resources appointment
had supported Randy Revelle's successful 1981 campaign for King
County Executive. Most were Asian Americans who cut their political teeth on my failed 1975 campaign for the Seattle School Board.
Included in the delegation were Young Turks Larry Flores, Tony
Ogilvie, and Sonny Tangalin. During the ensuing years, these young
Chinese, Filipino, Japanese, Korean, and Samoan Americans became
increasingly involved in virtually every political campaign in Seattle. By the time of Randy's 1981 run for county executive, Asian
Americans had emerged as a significant force in local politics. Their
support for Randy marked the first time the Asian community had
banded together as a whole to support a candidate in a countywide
election. In recognition of their hard work, Randy made a commitment to the community that he would appoint an Asian American to a high-level position.

I had also campaigned for Randy. He was from a prominent
Seattle family of French-English ancestry. He was sincere and
hardworking and had an impressive record of accomplishment in
supporting minority causes. During the campaign for county executive, I admired the way he handled questions about his chronic
mental health condition. Randy suffered from manic depression
(now known as bipolar disorder), but medication completely controlled the condition. He deflected inquiries into his mental health
by pointing to his stellar record of performance while serving several terms on the Seattle City Council. In the end, his opponents'

strategy of calling attention to Randy's mental health backfired, and he won the election handily.

I listened to the delegation's reasons for seeking me out. They believed that the job required a seasoned health and human services executive with a record of community involvement, qualities they felt I possessed in abundance. They also believed that Randy would follow through on his campaign commitment to appoint an Asian American to a high-level position. If I agreed to try for the job, the delegation had the people power and dollar resources to marshal support for me. However, I would have to campaign for the position, since Randy had decided to establish a public process. The delegation had inside information on possible candidates, and in their judgment, I was by far the strongest one. They had little doubt that I would ultimately emerge as Randy's choice.

Although it was an intriguing challenge, I was not sure I wanted to compete for the position. Sonny Tangalin pointed out several downsides if I accepted the delegation's offer. He reminded me that my previous jobs were won on my own merits and my own initiative, without the help of an old boys' club, political party, particular group, influential person, or affirmative action program. If I got the position because of the delegation, I might be beholden to a special interest group, much as a political candidate is beholden to a large contributor. In addition, the public might view my appointment as an affirmative action hire of an inferior minority candidate rather than a choice based on my being the best person for the job. There were other reasons for my hesitation. Job security would depend on Randy winning a second term as county executive. He was just beginning the second year of a four-year term. If he lost his reelection bid, I would have to look for another job in a few years. Moreover, King County was decidedly conservative, unlike Seattle. Perhaps it wasn't the best fit for me.

But after discussing the pros and cons with Terri, I concluded it was well worth the risks. I agreed with the delegation's assessment that I appeared to be the best-qualified candidate to direct the new department. I had faced similar challenges as director of the state's vocational rehabilitation program and was confident I could succeed on the job, should I emerge as Randy's choice. A salary exceeding $50,000 also factored into my decision. As to the possibility of being out of a job if Randy failed to win reelection, I was willing to take that chance since I had faced the issue before. And although King County was politically conservative, I had worked successfully with people from ultra-conservative eastern Washington when I was with the Division of Vocational Rehabilitation, so I felt I should be able to handle it. The only downside was the possibility that I might owe something to the delegation. Yet the delegation's priorities were mine as well, and its members did not appear to have any hidden agendas. The group was not likely to make any unfair demands on me.

The delegation came through on its commitment to mobilize wide community support for my candidacy. Every conceivable sector of the community sent support letters to Randy: ethnic groups, religious organizations, community clubs, health and human services organizations, education, business, labor, and the Democratic Party. The rigorous selection process consisted of interviews by a community review panel and Randy's executive cabinet members. Afterward, Randy asked me to come to his office. He did not hesitate to offer me the job; I did not hesitate to accept. We spent the rest of the time becoming better acquainted. I liked him and his ideas. He was personable and intense and had an ambitious vision for making King County livable for all its residents. That vision included a strong role for human services.

Randy was also thorough. Early in his administration, he was publicly embarrassed when it was discovered that one of his first appointments had used a falsified résumé. He resolved never to make the same mistake again. Subsequently, he used the most sophisticated sources, including the FBI, to check on his potential appointees. At the press conference announcing my appointment, one of the reporters asked about my background check, and Randy replied, "In all my years of public service, I have never seen anyone with such a squeaky-clean record as Peter. He's never even had a parking ticket."

I assumed my duties as department director in March 1983. The new Department of Human Resources consisted of two divisions and ten programs carved out from other parts of King County government. Six of the programs—Mental Health, Involuntary Treatment of Mentally Ill Persons, Developmental Disabilities, Aging, Youth Service Bureaus, and Youth Community Work and Training— were typical of human services. The four other programs were definitely atypical. The Women's Program was an advocacy program, and the Veterans' Program dealt with veterans' rights. The Cooperative Extension Program was concerned with gardening and agriculture, while the Public Defense Program provided legal services to people accused of crimes who could not afford counsel.

My job was to mold these ten diverse and independent programs into one cohesive department, a formidable task considering the apparent lack of commonality among them. Moreover, the programs in the new department had not had strong support from the county council over the years, with long-established popular programs like public safety and roads getting the lion's share of funding. The new department consisted of programs that were stepchildren insofar as county council priorities were concerned. Consequently, one of my first actions was to make courtesy calls on all nine members of the council. I was pleasantly surprised by the knowledge that Councilman Gary Grant, a Democrat representing south King County, appeared to have of my past work. I had met Grant when he served in the state legislature during my DVR days but did not know him well. Unknown to me, John Bagnariol had already briefed Grant about my abilities. During my tenure as director of the Department of Human Resources, Grant would be my strongest supporter with the King County Council, much as Bagnariol had been with the state legislature.

I developed a five-point strategy for setting the direction of the department. First, I planned to hammer out a mission statement that cut across all program areas. Second, I would work to gain support for the mission statement from staff and constituents. Third, I wanted to conduct a personnel audit in order to make staff functions and salaries more compatible. Fourth, I planned to get budget authorization to hire a special assistant. Fifth, I would colocate all the programs in one building.

My first year as director saw the successful implementation of all the strategic initiatives, except colocation, which was delayed until early 1985 because of unanticipated problems in finding a suitable site. I had inherited a department with a budget of $20 million and a staff of 150. I successfully pushed for a $30 million budget for my department, without increasing staff. I quickly organized the new department into a functional whole, but I did not accomplish it alone. The knowledgeable and politically astute staff was of great help, rallying around and meeting our collective need to organize into a functioning department. After years of being isolated in other departments that treated them as stepchildren, the programs were eager to help give human services a higher profile in King County.

I now turned my attention to other matters, initiating an aggressive affirmative action policy for all program units. Within a year, the Department of Human Resources was easily the leading department in the number of staff members who were women, ethnic minorities, or disabled persons. I was also pleased that the department included a significant number of staff members from the gay and lesbian community, several of whom held leadership positions. While the community was not technically a protected group under King County's affirmative action program, I considered it as part of my inclusiveness approach for the department. In the process, it was my good fortune to play a small part in yet another emerging civil rights movement. I hoped that my inclusive approach would make a similar difference for a group that well deserved full participation in American society.

For my own office, I hired a Japanese American, Joanne Asaba, as special assistant, and My-Dung Kurimura, a Vietnamese immigrant, as confidential secretary. Maureen McLaughlin, a fiscally knowledgeable career employee of Irish-Italian ancestry, became manager of the Community Services Division.

I retained Doug Stevenson, a respected mental health professional, as manager of the Human Services Division. One of my highest program priorities was to stabilize the mental health and involuntary treatment programs. Thanks to Doug's untiring efforts and my own contacts with state government, additional state funding and needed changes to legislation became realities. For all programs, I instituted effectiveness measures that showed the benefits the department provided and how much these services cost per person. I was back in the familiar milieu of directing human services.

Perhaps my most significant contribution to King County government was the creation of the Human Services Roundtable. The purpose of the roundtable was to develop a coordinated plan to minimize recent funding cuts in health and human services imposed by the Reagan administration. Its members included the King County executive and council president, the Seattle mayor and city council president, other heads of cities and towns within the county, and the president of the United Way. I convinced Randy that the Human Services Roundtable was perhaps the only realistic way for King County to avoid major reductions or elimination of local programs for vulnerable populations. He gave me the go-ahead to develop a plan. In spring 1985, the Human Services Roundtable was formally established. Together, local government leaders and elected representatives in Washington, D.C., helped head off major cuts in health and human service programs. For my efforts in organizing the Human Services Roundtable, I received another increase in salary from Randy. My work in combating the Reagan funding cuts also received national attention. On August 28, 1985, *USA Today* cited our experience in King County as strongly refuting Reagan administration claims that poverty was declining nationwide.

The position of director came with many benefits. I had access to Randy's luxury box at the Kingdome, where I hosted my Young Turks friends for Mariners baseball and Sonics basketball games. Through him, I was able to get four tickets at center court for the 1984 Final Four Basketball Tournament at the Kingdome, when the Georgetown Hoyas, led by their All-American center Patrick Ewing, emerged as national champions. My job as director also took me to conferences and meetings in places like Boston, Hawaii, Montreal, New York City, and Washington, D.C. Naturally, I combined these business trips with vacations in the welcome company of Terri.

My association with Randy enabled me to play a part in the 1984 conference of the National Association of Counties in Seattle, when King County was the official host for more than five thousand delegates. In addition to conference meetings, delegates enjoyed the many attractions of Seattle, including an unforgettable salmon dinner on a nearby island on Puget Sound. We took the ferry for the hour-and-a-half trip to the island, and along the way, I met two delegates with ties to my hometown of Livingston. I introduced myself to the person sitting next to me after noticing her name tag, which identified her as Ann Klinger, a county supervisor from Merced County. When I mentioned that I had grown up in Livingston, she asked if I knew John Lema. "Not only do I know John," I said excitedly, "we're classmates and old pals." It seems Ann was a schoolmate and old friend of John's wife, Eleanor. There was yet another surprise. Ann introduced me to the county supervisor from Contra Costa County, Sunne Wright McPeak, who also had graduated from Livingston High School and knew my brothers Silverio and Joe.

During my years at the Department of Human Resources, my family underwent a number of dramatic changes. In 1983, Cheryl married Philip Organo, a musician from San Francisco. Jeanine enrolled at the University of Oregon for the fall quarter of 1983, and, in 1984, Jackie received a bachelor of arts degree from the University of Washington after transferring from Whitman College. Three more grandchildren came into our lives—Jordan Ceferino Jamero and Janel Nicole Organo in 1984 and Marisa Gabrielle Organo in 1985.

The Young Turks, too, were experiencing profound changes. After the heady decade of the 1970s, when our group achieved success after success in sociopolitical activism, our passion had begun to diminish. Some members went on to pursue career opportunities, family obligations increased, and the high energy level that had sustained our efforts over the years waned as we approached our forties and fifties. Moreover, the Young Turks had grown disenchanted with Asian American coalitions. It was particularly galling that the Asian American movement we had helped launch was now reaping disproportionate rewards for other Asian groups, particularly at the state and national levels, at the expense of Filipinos. The Young Turks had made great strides in meeting the needs of their community in Seattle. There, Filipinos had an identity. Outside Seattle, however, the public thought of the Asian American community as made up of Chinese, Japanese, Koreans, and Vietnamese. Filipinos, particularly those with Spanish surnames, were more often than not lumped in with Hispanics.

The search for identity has long occupied the energies of all Filipinos, not just the Young Turks. As Malays—with Chinese, Japanese, Spanish, Caucasian, Arab, and African blood mixed through the centuries—our invisibility as an identifiable ethnic group was perhaps inevitable. On the one hand, it certainly had its positive aspects. For example, the lack of a clear identity helped Filipinos fit in comfortably with other groups, as when the Young Turks succeeded in coalescing Seattle's diverse community. On the other hand, it was disconcerting when Filipinos were often mistaken for Latinos or other Asians. And it was particularly disturbing that Filipinos were ignored when it came to receiving recognition, political appointments, or promotions in the workplace. At this time, Filipinos made up the largest Asian Pacific Islander population in the states of Washington and California. In the United States, the Filipino population of 1.4 million was second only to that of Chinese among Asian Pacific Islanders. Despite their greater numbers, however, Filipinos still found themselves struggling for their own identity.

The Young Turks began to drift apart during the 1980s. Political participation became more individual and sporadic, rather than group oriented. Some of us helped Dolores Sibonga, a Bridge Generation Filipina American, win two more terms on the Seattle City Council. In 1983, Terri and I hosted a community reception for Senator Alan Cranston in his bid for the presidency. We also helped

Randy in his successful campaign for county executive. However, these activities paled when compared to the political fervor of the 1970s. Social get-togethers, once regular events, were now only occasional occurrences for the Young Turks.

On the brighter side, the Filipino American National Historical Society became a reality in the early 1980s. The brainchild of Dorothy Cordova, the society's purpose was to provide a place for the historical documentation of the Filipino experience in America. Federal funding for the Demonstration Project for Asian Americans, where Dorothy served as executive director, was reaching an end, and the project had devoted much of its energy to researching Filipinos. Dorothy envisaged the historical society as a means of continuing the seminal effort. The effort was timely. The past decade had seen a great influx of immigration from the Philippines. Moreover, the Bridge Generation was making its own contributions to Filipino American history. Stories were waiting to be told; an exciting history needed to be documented.

In 1982, Terri and I were part of a small group called together by Dorothy Cordova to develop a national organization focusing on the Filipino experience in America. Most of the group had roots in Filipino Youth Activities of Seattle, which placed strong emphasis on Filipino American history. Other Asian ethnic groups had formed their own historical societies, and it was time for Filipinos to establish an organization to document their experiences in America. We unanimously endorsed the idea. Strategic calls to other parts of the country confirmed wide support for such an organization. Enthusiastic responses came from Barbara Posadas, a professor at Northern Illinois University; Marina Espina from New Orleans, who documented the historic San Malo settlement in the Louisiana Delta; Adele Urbiztondo of the San Francisco Mangos; Gil Pilapil, a Springfield, Illinois, physician; and Bienvenido Santos, the noted writer of short stories, who was then author in residence at a midwestern university. I first met Manong Santos in 1945, when I spent the summer with Uncle Silverio in Washington, D.C. At a 1983 organizing meeting for FANHS, we met again.

He was surprised to see me after almost forty years but remembered being introduced to me. He told me that shortly after I had left Washington to return home, he, too, stayed at Uncle Silverio's apartment for a few months.

Nationwide support for FANHS was no doubt spurred by the 1983 publication of Fred Cordova's landmark *Filipinos: Forgotten Asian Americans*, the first book to deal exclusively with the Filipino experience in America. On January 7, 1985, the state of Washington formally established the Filipino American National Historical Society as a chartered organization. Terri and I were further privileged to be founding members, having affixed our signatures to the FANHS articles of incorporation. Fred Cordova became the first national president, and I was the first vice president.

I experienced several other personal honors in those years. In 1985, I received the Filipino Youth Activities' Lifetime Achievement Award in Government. In addition, my position as department head with King County was noted as another Filipino First by that unofficial chronicler of Filipino American history, Fred Cordova.

My beloved New York Yankees no longer dominated baseball and had joined the ranks of the also-rans. Ever the loyal Yankees fan, I was usually in the Kingdome stands whenever they played Seattle. The Seattle Mariners were even worse. After the initial excitement of the first few years, attendance had dwindled to the extent that "crowds" of less than ten thousand were the norm in the cavernous Kingdome. One night, as I sat by myself in the nearly empty stadium, a reporter from the *St. Louis Post-Dispatch* interviewed me. He said he was traveling around the country to do a feature story on what drew fans like me to watch poorly performing major league baseball teams such as the Seattle Mariners. I simply told him, "I like baseball and have followed it faithfully since the World Series of 1941. A true baseball fan attends games regardless of how poorly the home team may be doing."

I fared much better in my other personal passion—jazz music. I purchased a compact disc player for my growing collection of CDs and bought a new receiver to power the upgraded stereo system. I also began to collect small percussion instruments—such as mara-cas, claves, bongos, tambourines, a *cabasa* (a hollow gourd covered with a net of threaded beads), and a cowbell—to go along with my collection of Latin jazz. Almost anyone could play the instruments, anyone with rhythm. The percussion instruments were always a big hit at Jamero house parties.

The Northwest experienced a resurgence in jazz, adding not only more clubs in Seattle but also an annual jazz festival in Port Townsend. In the summer of 1985, Terri and I attended the jazz fes-tival. We enjoyed established performers such as June Christy, Bob Cooper, Pete Jolly, Shorty Rogers, and Bud Shank—all veterans of the West Coast jazz popularized in Los Angeles during the 1950s. I had not seen them since then. During one of their breaks, we fondly reminisced about jazz venues in the Los Angeles of the 1950s, such as Tiffany's in Beverly Hills and the Lighthouse in Hermosa Beach. However, I could not help noticing how much the musicians had aged in thirty years, reminding me that I, too, had become a sen-ior citizen. Pete Jolly, the piano player, wore thick glasses. Bud Shank, the formerly boyish alto sax player, was lined and gray. June Christy, the vocalist who achieved fame with the Stan Kenton band, did not perform but was there with her husband, tenor saxophonist Bob Cooper. Always tiny, she now looked frail. Only Shorty Rogers, their leader and trumpeter, seemed the same. He was still short, approx-imately my height. Regardless of everyone's looks, the music was as marvelous as ever, a tribute to their enduring musical talents.

During my two years on the job, I found I liked working for Randy. A self-admitted workaholic, he surrounded himself with an executive cabinet composed of people who had similar work habits. They were also bright, visionary, and young. I was the old-est member of the cabinet, but I felt comfortable among these young achievers and even more comfortable around Randy. Randy was pleased with my work and also often sought my counsel on vari-ous community issues. I was not surprised when he asked me to be part of his reelection campaign committee. As a member of the com-mittee, I was visible during the campaign. Terri and I hosted a fund-raiser for him, and I was widely quoted extolling Randy's strengths. I was a partisan campaigner, an appropriate role for a political appointee. However, in November 1985, my comfortable world came crashing down. Randy lost by a microscopic .04 percent of the total vote. It was a disappointing end to a campaign we thought he had won. With Randy's defeat, I was out of a job, too. There was no way the new county executive would retain me. I was a liberal Democrat, and the winning candidate was a conservative Republican. However, I had no regrets, only disappointment over the defeat of a candidate in whom I strongly believed.

It is customary for political appointees of a defeated incumbent to submit letters of resignation to the winner. I submitted my resignation letter immediately after the final vote was verified. I was not surprised when the new county executive accepted my resignation with the curt statement that my "services were no longer required by King County after February 28, 1986." There was one small consolation. The new county executive followed my recommendation and appointed Maureen McLaughlin as my successor. As manager of the Community Services Division, she had been a major reason for my success as director. During the next few years, Maureen would finish the job that I had started, carrying my policies and program directions to fruition.

# 16 United Way

ON FEBRUARY 19, 1985, JUST NINE DAYS BEFORE
the end of my King County job, the United Way announced it was
seeking candidates for the position of Vice President of Planning
and Allocations. The job seemed tailor-made for a person with my
background. It called for experience as an executive in health and
human services, particularly in planning, distribution of funds, and
collaborative relationships with agencies affiliated with United
Way. The vice president was responsible for the distribution of $21
million, roughly the same amount as the budget I inherited when
I became director of the King County Department of Human
Resources in 1983.

United Way had recently expressed the desire to change its image
as a white-dominated, middle-class-oriented organization. It had
begun to improve its ethnic mix on the board of directors and had
also declared its intention to be more receptive to the service concerns of minorities. However, its executive and mid-management
staff remained all white, and policy and staff composition were
the same. Most of the changes were cosmetic. The few significant
changes came about only after community pressure. The large,
nationally affiliated agencies—such as the Boy Scouts, Campfire
Girls, Boys and Girls Clubs, YMCA, YWCA, and the Red Cross—
continued to receive the lion's share of United Way funds.

I also was not convinced that United Way was genuine in its
expressed desire to be more receptive to the minority community.
There seemingly was another, self-serving reason behind the
announced change in agency direction. The president and chief pro-

fessional officer, John Goessman, and Frank Melcher, the executive vice president, were from the United Way old boys' club of strongman national president William Aromony. Both came to their positions only after intensive pressure from Aromony. According to the grapevine, Goessman and Melcher considered Roger Thiebadeau, the longtime incumbent vice president of Planning and Allocations, to be a threat to their leadership and had forced him to retire earlier than he had planned. Thus, the recruitment effort may have been motivated by the need to remove an incumbent, not to improve services or broaden the ethnic mix of United Way.

Goessman's reputation as a tyrannical manager was another issue. Moreover, he was reputed to blame others if things went wrong and to take credit when things went well. But I had worked closely with him in committees and coalitions as well as on a one-to-one basis and had not experienced any of the reported behaviors. I was inclined to believe that my previous working relationship with him was a better measure of how we would work together than the horror stories I had heard about his management style. I decided to compete for the position. I felt confident of my ability to do the job, and the salary was comparable to what I earned with King County.

As I compared the qualities United Way sought to my own qualifications, I felt good about my chances but not overconfident. Under United Way's rules, Goessman could select anyone who placed among the top three. I was not certain that Goessman really wanted a person like me. In addition, if it were true that he had forced the incumbent's early retirement, it would be hard for me to trust him. Goessman seemed fully capable of passing me over. In light of these disturbing questions, I mobilized a community-wide endorsement effort similar to the one I used in competing for the King County position, hoping to improve my chances.

While awaiting word from United Way, I decided to take a vacation trip to Acapulco with Terri. We funded the trip with overtime pay I had accumulated during my years with King County. Acapulco was a welcome respite. I did not realize how much stress had built up over the course of Randy's campaign and the election loss. Acapulco was the perfect spot for getting away and relaxing. It was a world away. The exchange rate was favorable, enabling us to stay at the luxurious Acapulco Plaza Hotel and to dine at the best restaurants. There was only one problem. I had difficulty calculating the rate of exchange. On our first night in Acapulco, I mistakenly gave our waiter a 100 percent tip. I learned my lesson. From that moment on, Terri handled all of our cash transactions.

I learned yet another lesson, this one in Philippine history. Our cab driver seemed to know that we were of Filipino background. When I asked how he knew, he said, "There are many Mexicans of Filipino ancestry in the Acapulco area." He went on to explain that Filipinos came to Mexico during the eighteenth century at the height of the Spanish galleon trade. At the time, European nations were engaged in fierce competition over the lucrative spice trade, and Spain discovered that the fastest way back to Europe was by way of the Philippines and Acapulco. Spanish galleon crews were predominantly Filipino; officers were all Spanish. Because of the inhumane treatment they received from the Spanish officers, sailors jumped ship at their first opportunity. According to our knowledgeable cab driver, some Filipino sailors jumped ship in Acapulco, married local women, raised families, and became Mexican citizens. From Acapulco, the rest of the galleon crew went overland to Veracruz, on the Gulf of Mexico, where they caught ships bound for New Orleans before going on to Europe with their riches from Asia. Other Filipino sailors jumped ship in New Orleans and developed a successful shrimp and fish industry on the nearby island of San Malo in 1763, the first Filipino settlement in the continental United States.

By a happy coincidence, we met Filipina researcher Marina Estrella Espina, from the University of New Orleans, shortly after our return to Seattle. In 1979, Marina went to Mexico and conducted a six-month in-depth study of Filipinos and the Spanish galleon trade. She was in the midst of preparing the study for publication. She looked to share her research with Dorothy Cordova and a group,

Dr. Justus Lehmann, department chair, University of Washington Department of Rehabilitation Medicine. Jamero was invited to join the department in 1979.

Peter Jr. receives a BA degree in business economics from the University of Washington. Seattle, June 1981.

*Grandchildren and in-laws add to the Jamero family portrait. From left, seated: Jacqueline Jamero, Lauren Jamero, Peter Jamero, Terri Jamero, Cheryl Organo holding Marisa, and Jovanne Jamero holding Jordan. Standing: Julie Jamero, Philip Organo holding Janel, Jeanine Jamero, Karen Jamero, and Peter Jamero Jr. holding Jeremy. Seattle, 1985.*

*King County Executive Randy Revelle with Peter Jamero. Kitsap Peninsula, Washington, June 1985.*

*Peter Jamero, United Way vice president of Planning and Allocations, with Dr. Ernest Morris, United Way board of directors, on a fund-raising cruise on Puget Sound, August 1987.*

Peter Jamero, executive director of San Francisco's Human Rights Commission, in his office overlooking United Nations Plaza, with the city hall in the background. San Francisco, 1990.

Terri and and Peter Jamero, with San Francisco mayor Art Agnos at Candlestick Park, San Francisco, 1990.

*With the Young Turks. From left, standing: Larry Flores, Seattle City Councilwoman Dolores Sibonga, Jeannette Tiffany, Roy Flores, Dale Tiffany, and Tony Ogilvie. Seated: Sonny Tangalin. Seattle, June 1990.*

*Asian American activist Jim Miyano of Los Angeles and Bob Santos of Seattle, at Peter Jamero's retirement dinner in San Francisco, 1995.*

Jamero family picture. From left, first row: Zachary Armada, Alexander
Hada, Cecily Organo, Erika Hada, Matthew Silverio, and Michael Silverio
Jr. Second row: Lauren Jamero, Janel Organo, Jeremy Jamero, Peter Jamero,
Terri Jamero, Lindsey Hada, Jordan Jamero, and Marisa Organo. Third row:
Cheryl Organo, Philip Organo, Jacqueline Berganio, Richard Berganio,
Peter Jamero Jr., Ted Hada, Julie Jamero-Hada, Ron Armada, Karen
Armada, Michael Silverio, Jeanine Silverio, and Bonifacio Silverio.
San Francisco, 1999.

*Patrick and Lauren Hoolboom,*
*2002.*

*Peter and Caryn Swan Jamero,*
*2003.*

*Ceferino Silverio, 2004*

*Roslin Berganio, 2004.*

*Peter Jamero, returning to his roots in California's Central Valley and looking forward to many happy years of retirement. Atwater, California, 2003.*

including Terri and me, that was then working to establish an organization that would be known as the Filipino American National Historical Society. Marina's study confirmed what Terri and I had learned from our Acapulco cab driver. Galleon sailors from the Philippines indeed established the first Filipino settlement in America in 1763 after jumping ship in New Orleans, before there was even a United States of America. Other Filipino galleon sailors fought against the British alongside the pirate Jean Lafitte in the Battle of New Orleans in 1815. Marina's research provided important documentation of these history-making events. Unkind *puti* have said, "Go back where you came from." I could hardly wait for the chance to tell them, "*You* go back where you came from. We were in America before you."

We also learned from Marina that even before Magellan set foot in the Philippines in 1521, Filipinos had earned an enviable reputation as seafarers and were sailing under the flags of various European nations. In 1587, Filipinos were among the landing force that disembarked at what is now Morro Bay, California. The Philippines was also important to the galleon trade for its abundant forests, which supplied hardwood for building and repairing ships. By the eighteenth century, most Spanish galleons were built in the Manila-area seaport of Cavite. The Manila–Acapulco–Vera Cruz route to Europe was the preferred course for Spanish galleons from 1565 to 1815.

Upon our return to Seattle, I received the good news from United Way that I was scheduled to come before an interview panel, but not until April. My confidence began to wane. Why the delay? Did they really want me? How sincere were they in seeking a person of color as an executive? I was well aware of the administrative ploys that could be used to discourage minority candidates. However, I had little choice but to wait it out.

I forgot my worries, at least for a little while, on yet another vacation trip, this time to California. Along with Young Turk friends Sonny and Evelyn Tangalin, Terri and I went to San Francisco for the baptism of Cheryl's and Philip's second daughter, Marisa. We also visited Mama, as was my custom when I was in California. She was now in a residential care facility near Livingston because of the increasing difficulty of being cared for properly at home. She was no longer mobile and used a wheelchair to get around. Although she looked somewhat frail, Mama seemed well. She was happy to see us. She now spoke almost exclusively in her native Cebuano dialect. Mama seemed to be her usual cheerful, optimistic self. She told us that my old high school pal Joe Lema, whose aunt also was a facility resident, came by from time to time to say hello. Mama's physical health may not have been the best, but there was nothing wrong with her mental and emotional state. I was glad Terri and I had taken this opportunity to visit her.

Back in Seattle, the unanticipated length of United Way's selection process began to weigh on me more and more. To make matters worse, people I happened to run into seemed to be uncomfortable around me. A few avoided me. It was as if they did not know how to relate to me now that I was unemployed. At first, I felt hurt by their sudden change of attitude. Then I realized I was also uncomfortable among other people. This was the first time in thirty years that I did not have a job, and it reminded me of when I was in college and the *manongs* scolded me for not having a job. Being unemployed had not hurt us financially; we stayed afloat through Terri's job with the National Oceanographic and Atmospheric Administration, unemployment compensation, and the small amount of savings we had accumulated. Nevertheless, my sense of worth as a man and as the head of the family was threatened. I felt *ulaw*.

In late May, Frank Melcher, United Way's executive vice president, invited me to lunch. He offered me the position, adding that I was the unanimous top choice. I accepted without hesitation. In response to my question about the unexpected length of the selection process, he explained that the delay was due to the difficulty of reaching board members. According to Melcher, Goessman considered the position so important that he wanted to run my selection by key board members as a courtesy, a procedural step I had not known about.

Later, I learned that my backup strategy of asking for letters, telephone calls, and personal contacts supporting my candidacy apparently had the desired impact. After I emerged as number one in the selection process, the outpouring of community support, much of it from prominent citizens, made it virtually impossible for Goessman to pass me over. I did not know if he had been inclined to pass me over, but I was glad the strategy had worked. I reported to the United Way on June 1, a long three and a half months after hearing about the opening.

I was on the job for only a few days when I had to leave for California again. On June 3, I received the devastating news that Mama had passed away earlier that day. She was eighty years old. I had a difficult time fully accepting the reality of her passing. On our flight to California, I realized I needed time to grieve. I did not feel up to being the family representative and delivering the eulogy, as was expected of the eldest member of the family. I assumed these roles following Papa's death, in accordance with Filipino custom, and with my time tied up representing the family and preparing the eulogy, I was not able to grieve until I got back home. Fortunately, Herb offered to deliver the eulogy, and Junior volunteered to perform the duties of family spokesperson.

The whole Jamero family turned out for Mama's funeral, all eight of her children and their spouses, all twenty-six of her grandchildren, and all of her twelve great-grandchildren. Herb delivered a moving eulogy and composed a beautiful poem honoring her memory, and Junior handled the role of family representative without a hitch. Peter and six of his male first cousins served as pallbearers. However, unlike Papa's funeral six years earlier, there were only a few of Mama's friends of the Manong Generation in attendance. Sadly, death and failing health had taken their toll of her contemporaries. To me, it was also the end of an era—the era of the great immigration of Filipinos to America during the 1920s and 1930s.

Mama's death was not the only loss for the Jamero family in 1986. In October, cancer prematurely claimed the life of Herb's wife, Jeanne. She was just fifty-three.

Upon my return to work, both John Goessman and Frank Melcher expressed their desire to have United Way deal more effectively with the emerging social and health concerns of the community. They not only said they looked to me to help solve the problem but also assured me of their full support.

My top priority was to provide answers to United Way's most perplexing challenge. How should funds be allocated to small, mostly ethnic-minority agencies while maintaining support to large, established agencies, such as the Boy Scouts, YMCA, and Campfire Girls, that traditionally served mostly whites? The newer agencies were largely community-based organizations, such as Filipino Youth Activities, United Indians of All Tribes, Asian Counseling and Referral Services, and Consejo, an agency with a predominantly Hispanic clientele. These smaller agencies helped deal with contemporary social issues of gang violence, teen pregnancy, substance abuse, and cultural assimilation. Most offered bicultural and bilingual services, which they delivered with passion and a deep sense of commitment. In their view, the services offered by the more established agencies were not relevant to ethnic-minority clients. Consequently, these smaller agencies believed they were entitled to a larger piece of the funding pie. From a business and management perspective, however, their practices were often substandard. Most did not have an effective board of directors or sufficient financial reserves.

The larger agencies, however, were entrenched United Way affiliates and understandably were not eager to have their allocations reduced in order to support relatively unknown organizations. Most of them did not understand why the new agencies were necessary. They argued that they were already meeting many of the service needs of the emerging minority communities, and they had statistical documentation to back up their claims. These larger agencies were well run and met United Way's standards for management and administration. Their board members included some of the most prominent and powerful members of the community. To complicate things further, several of these agencies' former board members sat on the United Way board of directors, the organization's policy-making body.

It was an imposing challenge. Maintaining the support of 154 agencies with varying points of view on what level of funding should be provided to support what types of service was not going to be an easy task. My staff and I threw our energies into meeting the challenge. The first and most important task was to establish a rationale for making changes. We decided to develop a needs assessment study for the entire Seattle–King County area. Such an assessment would yield critically needed information on residents' current health and human service needs. More important, it would provide an objective foundation for prioritizing services and, ultimately, a rational basis for allocating dollars to sectors where services were most needed. I organized my twenty-two staff members and 250 community volunteers into teams that collected data, conducted interviews, and analyzed information. We promulgated the findings in the *Facts and Trends Report.* With the base information collected, the next step was to examine its implications for needed services. What did the data tell us about health and human service needs? Which needs were the most critical? As a way of addressing these issues, I convened a series of small-group forums composed of professionals and laypersons representative of the community's demographics. The forums analyzed, prioritized, and condensed service needs and published their conclusions in the *Implications of the Facts and Trends Report.*

The entire process took about a year to complete. The reports concluded that smaller agencies, which served a predominantly ethnic-minority clientele, should be receiving a larger share of allocated funds. I was pleased with the thoroughness and professionalism of the report, and United Way was pleased with the effort. The board of directors adopted the findings and directed staff to develop a process of allocating funds based on the service priorities identified by the report. While I was grateful for the outcome, it was not an easy process. The polarized views of the large, established agencies and the smaller, newer agencies were disruptive.

Some agencies tried to influence certain members of the board of directors; others complained directly to Goessman about the basic approach of the reports and/or my alleged biases in managing the process. In the end, however, United Way had an objective basis on which to allocate funds to its 154 affiliated agencies. While some agencies might have been unhappy about the prospect of decreased allocations, they found it difficult to argue with the objective findings that determined the amounts.

With the needs assessment effort well under way, I turned my attention to the administrative aspects of the job. I hired a Native American, Diane Williams, to serve as my secretary. I also hired three young people for the division, African American Dina Fergeson and Filipino Americans Elisa Del Rosario and Mike Flor, making Planning and Allocations the most ethnically diverse unit in United Way. And the underpaid employees were delighted by the approval of my budget request for an increase in staff salaries. My budget also included several new supervisory positions. I filled one of the slots with Bob Vaughn, a knowledgeable veteran of the nonprofit community, and he contributed significantly to the division's success. Bob and I shared a dubious distinction that was unrelated to work. We were both acquainted with Ted Bundy, before he was revealed as the infamous serial killer. Bob supervised Bundy at Seattle's Crisis Center, and, as recounted earlier, I worked with Bundy on several political campaigns in the 1970s.

Although I still worked in the familiar world of health and human services, United Way was very different from the public sector. It thought of itself as a large business corporation. The executive staff had titles such as president, vice president, chief operating officer, and chief financial officer. Moreover, as in the corporate sector, the generous salaries of United Way executives were way above the low pay of other employees. Executives enjoyed other corporate privileges. Each had a credit card and an expense account. A few executives, including me, were assigned an automobile for business-related travel. My company car was a late-model Buick Park Avenue. For security reasons, those with assigned cars had to take them home at night. This, of course, was still another benefit. In the beginning, I felt somewhat guilty about the great disparity in benefits and privileges of executives as compared to those of other employees. Before long, however, I conveniently bought into the agency's rationale: this was part of the corporate culture of United Way.

United Way was also different from my previous experiences in that I worked within a two-track reporting structure. In other words, I had two bosses. I reported to the volunteer chair of planning and distribution as well as to a paid executive. Dr. Ernest Morris, vice president of student affairs at the University of Washington, was my volunteer boss; he was responsible to the board of directors in the area of planning and allocations. On the line staff level, I reported to Frank Melcher, executive vice president. The two-track system may have resulted in additional paperwork and more time spent in meetings; however, it was manageable, thanks largely to the comfortable working relationship I was able to build with Dr. Morris. A thoughtful African American from a modest midwestern upbringing, he agreed that United Way's number one objective was to make meaningful changes in allocating funds to agencies serving a predominantly ethnic-minority clientele.

In the years following the two *Facts and Trends* reports, I directed the implementation of several other United Way reforms. I established an agency liaison function for volunteers serving on review panels, which resulted in a year-round volunteer program providing continuous relationships with agencies. I also established the Community Problem-Solving Initiatives Program, which set aside funding for small grants to help communities deal with problem areas. The board of directors offered strong support, thanks to Dr. Morris's leadership on planning and distribution operations. Shan Mullin, chairman of the board, was also invaluable. After I made a presentation to the board on July 21, 1988, I received a note of commendation from president and CEO John Goessman. The note reported that Mullin said my presentation "was the finest ever delivered to the board." Mary Gates, whose son Bill would become the billionaire founder of Microsoft Corporation, was yet another source of significant board support.

The Filipino Youth Activities drill team was at its peak during the 1970s, when its seventy-five to eighty kids won trophy after trophy for their superb performances. By the early 1980s, however, the team had fallen on hard times, with its ranks reduced by more than half. Reviving the drill team was one of Terri's highest organizational priorities when she took over as FYA board president in 1985. She asked Fred Cordova to come back and lead the team for one more year and dangled a tempting incentive—a trip to Washington, D.C., the next spring, for the Cherry Blossom Parade. Terri had successfully lobbied parade organizers and the Washington State congressional delegation to make the FYA drill team the first Filipino American marching group to perform at the famous parade. All she needed was a more representative group.

Fred did not disappoint. Because of his dynamic leadership and his ties to the Filipino American community, the team grew to one hundred eager young boys and girls, an all-time high. After six months of intensive practice, they were ready to make their appearance at the foremost parade of the nation's capital. Although the team did not win a coveted trophy, it performed well despite the humid and sticky conditions typical of Washington, D.C. The parade was the highlight of the trip, coming after several days of touring the many attractions of the historic city. Terri and I served as guides to the city that had been our home for three years. More than one hundred young people, their parents, and drill team staff were there.

If Washington, D.C., was the trip's highlight, then Virginia Beach was the most unforgettable. Located in southern Virginia, the city included a sizable Filipino American community consisting largely of U.S. Navy families. Most remarkable, however, were its young people. It was like traveling back in time. Interacting with these Filipino American young people was like reliving our Bridge Generation experiences during our growing-up years. Like us, they were second-generation Filipino Americans. And they expressed many of the same dreams, concerns, and frustrations that we had fifty or sixty years earlier. Moreover, their first-generation parents were remarkably similar to our parents in attitude and outlook. Those of us from the Bridge Generation looked at one another in disbelief. We spent our stay in Virginia Beach sharing our growing-up-brown experiences with Filipino American young people and their parents, all eager to soak up as much information they could. It was an unanticipated but most enjoyable finale to a great trip to the East Coast.

Our daughter Jeanine and Michael Silverio, the young man she had been going with for several years, were married in August 1987. As in earlier family weddings, the bride's entire family was included in the wedding party. This time, however, I had a greatly expanded role as the father of the bride. I not only gave Jeanine away but also assisted the officiating priest, Young Turk Harvey McIntyre, during the nuptial mass. Fulfilling these duties as well as my responsibilities during the Filipino segment of the ceremony had me going from one end of the altar to the other. After the ceremony, my sister Pula said, "Peter, I got dizzy just watching you move around."

A large contingent of our relatives traveled from California to attend the wedding. Of the more than two hundred guests, about half were relatives. Herb and Junior helped greatly with the food. They volunteered to buy the ingredients and contributed their considerable culinary skills to cook dinner for all our out-of-town relatives for two consecutive evenings. Their generosity as well as the help from other relatives who pitched in were, of course, much appreciated. The Filipino *bayanihan* tradition of our parents' generation was alive and well in America.

Jeanine and Michael's wedding was responsible for a new tradition—family entertainment at a Jamero wedding reception. Our girls presented a rousing lip-synch rendition of Aretha Franklin's "Respect," with Cheryl as lead singer. Peter and Jovanne followed, lip-synching several duets of Stevie Wonder tunes. For the finale, Terri and I, joined by Michael's parents Cris and Terry, sang "Sunrise, Sunset." When we sang the lyrics "I don't remember getting older, when did they?" my eyes suddenly became misty as I realized that our baby girl was now a married woman.

I continued to be involved in politics. I worked on Booth Gardner's successful 1986 campaign for governor and subsequently served as a transition team member, interviewing candidates seeking appointments in the new administration. In 1988, I campaigned for Terri's former boss, Mike Lowry, in his unsuccessful bid for U.S. Senate, was on the winning side as a member of the Asian Americans for Jim McDermott for Congress Committee, but was on the losing side with the Asian Americans for Dukakis for President campaign. In 1989, I helped found the Seattle Filipino American Democrats. One of the group's cofounders was a newly arrived immigrant from the Philippines and an anti-Marcos activist, Velma Veloria, who continues to serve as a representative in the state legislature.

The Filipino American National Historical Society held its Second Biennial National Conference in New Orleans in 1988, the 225th anniversary of the first Filipino settlement on American soil on the nearby island of San Malo. Historical documentation of the settlement was made available to delegates in the newly published book *Filipinos in Louisiana*, written by New Orleans University researcher Marina Espina, who was then president of the society. Delegates took a sentimental boat ride to the settlement site of San Malo, which had been destroyed by a hurricane in 1915. All that remained were a few pilings. Nevertheless, it was an emotionally charged experience for the delegates. After all, this is where our history in America started.

Descendants of these same Filipino pioneers—seventh- and eighth-generation Filipino Americans—were participants at the 1988 FANHS national conference. While the commingling of races and ethnic groups through the centuries had effectively erased almost all physical traces of their ancestors, these people, who looked white, followed traditional Filipino beliefs and customs. They ate steamed rice with their meals, cooked adobo, and told the same ghost stories we had learned from our elders. They continued to preserve their Filipino identity through folk dances, *pistas*, and social gatherings. Without a doubt, they were Filipino Americans. As they said in their unique mix of Cajun- and Southern-accented English, "We're Filipino and proud of it." Culturally, they were Filipino, but they were also Southern. Most still clung to the racial segregation of traditional Southern culture. For example, they did not socialize with those of Filipino-black parentage. "How ironic," I thought. "These ancestors of Filipinos from the Spanish galleons ostracize other Filipino Americans with the same historical background just because they happen to be part black."

After meeting these apparently white people who identified themselves as Filipinos, I suddenly thought about other "Heinz 57" Americans. Most simply considered themselves generalized Americans or Caucasians; they did not identify with any particular ethnic group. "How sad. They don't seem to have their own cultural traditions," I thought. "They don't know what they're missing."

Later that year, I attended a United Way meeting in Miami, marking the start of the longest journey I would ever take—my second trip to the Philippines. After the cross-country flight to San Francisco, I spent the night at Cheryl's home and then went to the airport to catch a plane bound for the Philippines. This time, I was accompanied by eleven other Jameros: Terri, Cheryl, Julie, and Jackie; my brothers Herb, George, and Joe; Herb's son Patrick and daughter-in-law Elena; and Joe's wife Lita and their daughter Angelita. It was the first trip to our ancestral land for George, Herb, and the younger Jameros. Terri and I visited the Philippines in 1971; Joe was stationed at the San Miguel Naval Communication Station when he was in the U.S. Navy; and Elena and Lita were both born there. We all looked forward to the trip with mounting excitement.

However, before we even boarded the plane, we narrowly avoided a swindle. The Filipino travel agent responsible for getting tickets for the entire party did not have Julie's round-trip ticket. She claimed we had not made the reservation and had not paid for a ticket for Julie. When we provided evidence to the contrary—a canceled check and confirmation of Julie's reservation at the airline's ticket window—she continued to stick to her story. It was not until Terri, Lita, and Elena threatened to call the police that the travel agent was willing to negotiate. Claiming she had misplaced her credit card, she suggested that we pay for the ticket with one of our credit cards, which, of course, was unacceptable to us. She then offered to give us travelers' checks if we charged the ticket. The offer did not make any sense, since it meant we would be paying for the ticket twice. When we asked her why she simply did not go to the airline and pay for the ticket with the travelers' checks, she came up with a convoluted explanation of why she could not do so. She further argued that we would not really be paying for the ticket because the travelers' checks would make up for the cost. By this time, we were dangerously close to boarding time. We suspected that the travel agent's plan was for us to board the plane with her uncashed travelers' checks, thus giving her a chance to claim they were stolen. However, Terri cleverly outfoxed the travel agent. She whispered to Elena to agree to charge the ticket to her credit card, go to an exchange counter around the corner, cash the agent's travelers' checks, and then use the cash to pay for the ticket.

Apparently, the travel agent had been conducting the scam for some time, fleecing large parties by holding back one or two tickets and then reselling them. Months later, she was convicted on multiple counts of fraud. One of the witnesses who testified against her was my brother Joe. The travel agent's clients were usually unsophisticated and easily intimidated Filipinos who were unwilling to report her to the authorities. What was particularly galling to me was that she took advantage of the trust of her fellow Filipinos.

The sixteen-hour flight to the Philippines was tiring, although nonstop movies made it somewhat more bearable. Finally, we arrived at Manila's Benigno Aquino International Airport, only to endure the long lines to go through customs. Traveling with such a large party certainly had its moments. It seemed like we were always waiting for someone's bag or looking for a member of our party who was lagging behind. We also were potential targets for unscrupulous cab drivers and overly aggressive young boys offering to carry our bags. Fortunately, we had Lita and Elena to look out for our interests. They advised us not to speak to one another so as not to call attention to our inability to speak Tagalog. When we arrived at the Cebu City airport, I felt somewhat more comfortable since people there spoke the familiar Cebuano dialect. The problem was that I was no longer fluent in the dialect. Furthermore, my Cebuano was in a time warp, limited to idioms and expressions used by my parents' generation during the 1930s and 1940s. I decided to leave the talking to Lita and Elena.

From Cebu, we could see the faint outline of Bohol, our ancestral island, fifteen miles away. We hopped a two-engine plane for the twenty-five-minute flight to the Tagbilaran City airport. Upon landing, excited relatives mobbed us. They remembered Terri and me from our 1971 trip and greeted us warmly. This was the first time they would meet other members of our group—with one exception, Uncle Canuto Galindez. Like Papa, Uncle Canuto was among the thousands of Filipino *sakadas* recruited to work in the sugarcane fields of Hawaii during the 1920s. He later followed Papa to California, where he was one of Papa's steady boys. Uncle Canuto returned to the Philippines after more than fifty years in America. He married a local woman in her thirties when he was in his early seventies and was the proud father of a teenage daughter. Now in his eighties, Uncle Canuto looked much younger. We hadn't seen him for almost two decades, and we were grateful for the opportunity to see our beloved uncle again.

Papa's and Mama's hometown of Garcia-Hernandez had not changed substantially in the seventeen years since Terri and I last visited. Electricity had been turned back on, but otherwise, the town and way of life seemed unchanged. There was stability to that sameness, so unlike America, where change was constant and often difficult to understand and adapt to. The most significant change was in our relatives. Uncle Pastor Jamero, nearing ninety years of age, had recently suffered a stroke that left him unable to speak clearly. However, he seemed to be fully aware of what was going on around him.

Uncle Pastor had a surprise for us, especially Terri. During our 1971 trip, Terri learned that Uncle Pastor was a rich source of Jamero family history. He could trace the family back to the 1700s, when it went by its tribal name, Bedjo. Unfortunately, though, nothing was in writing. It was only in his head, oral history passed down through generations. At the time, Uncle Pastor told Terri he would write it down and send her a copy, but the genealogical listing never came. Imagine her excitement as, seventeen years later, Uncle Pastor reached into the family Bible and pulled out a Jamero genealogical narrative, carefully documented in his own handwriting. According to the narrative, Bedjo had three sons—Beranjo, Juanidjo, and Tidjo. The name "Jamero" is descended from "Beranjo." It was my turn to get excited. Looking at the narrative, I saw that the very first Jamero was named "Pedro." I grew up believing I was named after my paternal grandfather, not knowing I was also the namesake of the first Jamero. Residents of Garcia-Hernandez have long believed that the name "Jamero" originated in their town. Many had anecdotal experiences of Jameros in other towns and islands who traced their lineage back to Garcia-Hernandez. Uncle Pastor's narrative provided written documentation of that long-held belief. Terri had a long interest in genealogy and had already developed a record of the Jamero family in America. From Uncle's narrative, she was now able to develop an impressive charting of the family that went back nine generations and 225 years. Her genealogical work—presented at FANHS national conferences in New Orleans, Chicago, and San Francisco—received high acclaim from conference delegates.

Manang Bebay Ochavillo, my first cousin and Mama's girlhood companion, was now an octogenarian. Cheryl, Julie, and Jackie immediately noticed the great similarity in looks and mannerisms between Manang Bebay and Mama. They were particularly moved when they heard Manang Bebay sing the same happy songs Mama often sang to them when they were little.

We stayed in the homes of various relatives, equally divided between the Jamero and Madelo families. The housing arrangements were shared for cultural reasons. I learned on my 1971 visit to Garcia-Hernandez with Papa and Mama that any appearance of playing favorites between the two families would be *walay ulaw* and was to be avoided at all costs. As the eldest member of our group, I made sure we met other cultural expectations. I spent several nights at Roman's as a sign of respect for the Madelo family. Gifts of canned food and clothing in the *balikbayan* (returning friends) boxes were distributed equally between the Jamero and Madelo families. I provided token cash gifts to the head of each Madelo and Jamero family just before our departure.

Particularly known for their warm brand of hospitality, our relatives did not disappoint. In the next few days, we enjoyed a *lechon* lunch at the local beach, were honored at a reception in the town hall bearing Papa's name, basked in the sun at the Playa Del Rey Resort, and feasted at a farewell picnic at the city park. Perhaps most memorable, however, were the intimate gatherings in our relatives' homes. There, we experienced the close family interrelationships, the respect family members had for their elders, and the important role that the Roman Catholic faith played in our relatives' day-to-day lives.

It was also during these smaller get-togethers that our relatives had a chance to know us better. My contemporaries in particular seemed especially interested in the racial climate in America. They knew there was discrimination against Filipinos and were curious about how we coped with it. My response reflected what I had learned through my activism in Seattle. First, know your Filipino culture; second, know your rights but pick your fights; and third, work with coalitions and other groups sympathetic to your cause. Our relatives also seemed to have more enlightened attitudes about Filipinos from other islands and regions. For example, my parents' generation considered Ilocanos overly frugal and prone to violence, but our relatives in Bohol did not express such provincial stereotypes. I was pleasantly surprised by their sophisticated level of understanding, so unlike the mentality typical of Papa's and Mama's generation.

Some of my relatives were political activists. My cousin Nenny Jamero Logarta was an anti-Marcos activist. She participated in the final days of demonstrations in Manila that toppled the longtime dictator and brought Cory Aquino to the presidency in 1986. Her brother Junior, who did not consider himself an activist, nevertheless was an intimate of anti-government guerrillas who hid in the dense mountain jungles of interior Bohol. Presumably, their well-read father and former town mayor, Uncle Pastor, influenced their progressive attitudes. I have long believed that Mama was the greatest influence in my involvement in politics and the community, with Papa running a close second. However, after learning more about the activism of Uncle Pastor, Nenny, and Junior, I now know I am continuing a family tradition. Consequently, it was not surprising to learn that their island province of Bohol has had a similar tradition. In 1744, Francisco Daguhoy led three thousand Boholanos in a revolt, freeing Bohol from Spanish rule for eighty years. He is still a folk hero to the people of Bohol.

As the time drew near for our departure, we were all grateful for the memorable experiences we'd had among family. It gave us all a chance to appreciate who we were and to know our culture much more intimately. I was also proud of Cheryl, Julie, and Jackie for their uncomplaining adjustment to life in a third world country. The humidity and lack of hot water and indoor plumbing did not seem to spoil their visit. They genuinely enjoyed being among relatives of their own age group. The stage was now set for the next generation of Jameros to continue the family tradition of periodically visiting our ancestral home.

Our next stop was a two-day layover in Cebu City, the country's second-largest city. Earlier, we had decided we would pamper ourselves and stay at the posh Cebu Plaza Hotel on our way back from Bohol. We did not make reservations at the time, since the hotel told us it was not necessary. When we arrived, we were hot, sweaty, and grimy. We were looking forward to a hot shower and real beds, niceties not available in the *barrios* of Garcia-Hernandez. Imagine our shock and disappointment when the front desk clerk said that there were no rooms available. Fortunately for us, however, the hotel manager told us that the Presidential Suite was the only space available that would accommodate our party. The suite was expensive by Philippine standards, but at the equivalent of $33 per person, it was certainly affordable for us. We had not planned on paying this much to stay at the Cebu Plaza, but given our circumstances, it did not take us long to unanimously agree to accept the offer.

The suite was literally presidential; it served as President Aquino's residence during her official visits to Cebu City. With three bedrooms, a living room, a kitchen, a formal dining room, a conference room, several bathrooms, and a study, the suite was easily roomy enough for our large party. I pulled family rank and took the largest bedroom for Terri and me. Cheryl and Julie occupied the second bedroom, while Patrick and Elena slept in the third bedroom. Herb and George requested rollaway beds and had the large conference room all to themselves. Jackie, the only one who did not have a bedroom, slept on a rollaway in the living room. (Joe and his family stayed with relatives in Cebu City.)

The suite came with the services of a butler, an unanticipated luxury. Our butler took orders for meals, served us in the spacious dining room, and made sure that all areas were clean and tidy. He also was a world of information regarding various attractions of the hotel complex. He called our attention to the casino, the nearby *sabong*, or cockfights, the nightly menus at restaurants, and various entertainment venues. The next morning, as we were served a Filipino breakfast featuring *tocino* (beef sausages), *longanisa* (pork sausages), eggs, and mangos, we lifted our glasses and toasted our good fortune. After roughing it in the *barrios*, we relished the opportunity to relax in the lap of luxury.

The next leg of our trip took us to the mountain city of Baguio, the summer capital of the Philippines, where government officials went to escape Manila's oppressive heat and humidity. Baguio had changed considerably in the seventeen years since I last visited; it had become a large city, with noisy buses and crowded streets. No longer did one see Igorot tribespeople, some clad only in G-strings, coming down from their isolated mountain homes to do their weekly shopping. Now, the only Igorots we saw were living in a government-subsidized village in Imelda Park, named after the extravagant wife of former president Ferdinand Marcos. Here, for a few pesos, Igorots posed for photographs for curious tourists. It was as if this once proud, indigenous minority group were in a zoo. I was shocked that the Philippines would demean its own people by displaying them in such an undignified manner. It reminded me of the 1904 World's Fair in Saint Louis, where an earlier generation of Igorots was exhibited before gawking Americans as "dog-eating savages." The exhibit was intended to justify America's recent colonization of a supposedly primitive country. Here in 1988 Baguio, I wondered what could possibly justify the exploitation of these modern-day Igorot tribespeople by their Filipino leaders.

Baguio's urban sprawl was disappointing, since I remembered it as such a beautifully laid-out city. The rain that fell all through our visit did nothing to lessen my disappointment. This was the monsoon season in the Philippines, and a torrential downpour accompanied us on our way back. The famous winding road of Baguio, normally a breathtaking and beautiful ride, was suddenly transformed into a dangerous thoroughfare of rain, rocks, and mud. Parts of the narrow road had been washed out, forcing our vehicle to come precipitously close to the edge of the cliff. After several anxiety-filled hours, we got back to Elena's hometown of Angeles City.

The rain subsided the next day. My brother Joe and I, along with our respective families, decided to travel ahead to the Manila Hilton Hotel, where we were to meet relatives. The rest of our travel party planned to meet us in Manila the next day. We should have waited, too. As we approached the outskirts of Manila, we found ourselves in another tropical downpour. Traffic slowed to a crawl. It took us several agonizing hours over flooded streets and detours to get downtown. We passed the infamous squatter city of Tondo, still the squalid home of thousands of poor Filipinos. All of a sudden, traffic came to a complete stop. We were only several blocks away from the hotel. Joe and I got out of the van and, sharing a flimsy umbrella, walked through the pouring rain to the hotel to make sure we hadn't lost our reservations as a result of our long delay.

Our reservations were still valid, but we were not happy with the accommodations. A musty smell, worsened by the recent rains, permeated our small rooms. After our stay at the Cebu Plaza, we were very disappointed with the Manila Hilton. When Rita Cruz, the daughter of Manang Bebay and the supervisor of housekeeping at the Manila Hotel, heard of our dissatisfaction with the Hilton, she said she would see what she could do. The next day, we checked into the elegant Manila Hotel. We not only got enough rooms for our whole group but had several suites assigned to us as well. The Manila Hotel, with its trademark bellhops and excellent service, was our comfortable base of operations for our last few days in the Philippines.

Also thanks to Rita, we were able to enjoy a special Sunday evening performance of the world famous Bayanihan Dance Troupe, which was based at the hotel. We were supposed to see the performance on Saturday evening, but because of a mix-up in our reservations, we were unable to attend. Embarrassed, the hotel arranged a Sunday performance especially for us. We were joined by about twenty relatives from the Manila area who had never seen the dance troupe perform. It was a perfect way to end our visit to the Philippines.

The next morning, we were on our way back home to America. We were travel weary but thankful for the chance to visit our ancestral land of the Philippines. After a few days of rest at home, I was ready to go back to work.

Despite my successes at work, I began to explore job possibilities in California. Terri had never fully adapted to Seattle's wet and overcast weather. She was able to endure the weather while the children were at home, but now that they had left the nest, she found Seattle to be increasingly depressing. She wanted to get back to family and friends in California. After nearly twenty years outside California, I was ready to return, too. The only drawback was that we would be leaving Karen, Jackie, Peter, and, of course, our three grand-children behind. Yet, in some ways, it would be a trade-off, since Cheryl, Julie, and Jeanine now called California home. In July, I interviewed for several department-head positions for the County of Los Angeles. I also went to several Filipino American functions in the Bay Area and Sacramento to let them know of my availability.

John Goessman's poor management style was a more important reason for leaving United Way. Often tyrannical and dictatorial in dealing with staff, he could be unpredictable and moody. John was short in stature and had a Napoleon complex. For example, he always insisted on sitting in the highest chair in his office so that others had to look up at him. Like other staff members, I was the target of his unpredictable behavior from time to time. However, after several recent high-profile controversies threatened to affect United Way contributions in 1988, his erratic behavior toward staff became more frequent and intense. And he increasingly singled me out as the target of his emotional outbursts.

I had been reporting to Executive Vice President Frank Melcher, the only vice president to do so, ostensibly because my division was the largest. The other vice presidents reported directly to Goessman. Early in 1988, Goessman suddenly announced that he would be supervising me directly because there was "no one more knowledgeable in the organization regarding planning and distribution." Ordinarily, I would have welcomed reporting to Goessman, as did the other vice presidents; however, he also instructed me to include other leadership staff from my division at our weekly conferences. These conferences were usually a one-to-one process, and at first I questioned his decision. But I decided to keep my doubts to myself in the hope that the unorthodox reporting arrangement would somehow work itself out. However, when Goessman arbitrarily filled the vacancy for my top assistant with no input from me, I could no longer keep my objections to myself. The appointee was known to be his confidante, and little in her background suggested she was even a good candidate for the position. Goessman ignored my objections. He had already made up his mind and would not discuss the matter. His motivation was obvious. He wanted an insider to report directly to him on division activities. He did not trust me, and I now had little reason to trust him either.

In the following months, Goessman increasingly subjected me to demeaning and demoralizing treatment. He often humiliated me in front of peers and subordinates. Once, he told me that I didn't know what I was doing. On another occasion, when I attempted to explain why the division might not be able to meet his proposed timeline, he yelled, "Don't give me that division mumbo jumbo!" He refused to take responsibility for his actions. Instead, he lied or blamed me for any of his decisions that did not turn out well. At an executive staff meeting, he strongly implied that I had forged his signature on a controversial letter to agency executive directors. He failed to support me in several situations involving poor staff performance. Morale among division staff rapidly declined as a result of his management style. We were all particularly concerned about his unilateral appointment of my chief assistant. Everything finally came to a head during a meeting on December 9, attended by other division staff, where we presented our recommendations for the 1989 division work plan. His face beet-red with anger, Goessman lectured me on the "inadequacy" of the plan, attributing it to my "lack of leadership." I chose not to react to his accusations but suggested that we discuss the matter privately. Goessman completely ignored the suggestion.

Until this latest tirade, I had made every attempt to handle myself in a professional and ethical manner, even when doing so put me in an unfavorable light. I had always prided myself on my ability to develop effective working relationships, something that now seemed highly improbable when it came to Goessman. I believed my professional reputation had been damaged, a reputation that had always been of consistently high caliber. Working under these stressful conditions had taken a toll on my physical and emotional health. My situation at United Way had become intolerable. There seemed little choice but to submit my resignation.

It took me several days to make a final decision. On the one hand,

I had no immediate job prospects, and resigning would place a heavy economic burden on the family. In addition, there were good reasons for sticking it out a little while longer. My record of performance was exemplary, and I enjoyed solid support from the board and staff. Moreover, Goessman had alienated the board and the community, and there were rumors that he might be leaving United Way soon. I could also opt to confront Goessman and fight him on the issues. Not only were his management practices questionable, but his disparate treatment of me could be construed as racially motivated and a violation of my civil rights. I had strong grounds for filing a discrimination complaint.

On the other hand, remaining with United Way might result in the further deterioration of my professional reputation and place my physical and emotional health at continued risk. And a public fight with Goessman would likely cause irreparable harm to the volunteers, staff, and board members of an organization that I still held in the highest regard. Yet another consideration: I was not a member of United Way's old boys' club, which made additional promotions unlikely.

After discussing the situation with Terri, I decided to resign without subjecting United Way or myself to the indignities of a public debate or taking my fight to the courts. Once more, the cultural value of *walay ulaw*, instilled in me by Papa, influenced my actions. On December 12, 1988, I submitted an official letter of resignation to Goessman and sent a copy to Dr. Morris. It was not the usual resignation statement. I did not pull any punches. The letter thoroughly detailed my grievances with Goessman's erratic behavior and his poor management style. I had kept a running diary documenting my difficulties with him and made sure my resignation letter included dates and quotes. My resignation was effective immediately.

Fifteen days later, on December 27, John Goessman resigned as president of United Way. I felt vindicated but not enough to ask to be rehired. It was much too late; psychologically, I had already left. Terri and I were fully committed to looking for a job and a home in California.

Leaving Seattle would be difficult. We had lived here for almost twenty years. We liked the city's progressive record, its commitment to diversity, and its multicultural population. Leaving the Filipino community also would not be easy. We had witnessed its emergence as a viable force in Seattle's sociopolitical life and felt that we were part of the community's social fabric. Leaving the Young Turks would be hardest of all. We not only were close socially but had been intimately involved with them in countless political campaigns and in many struggles on behalf of the Filipino American community.

Our thirty-fifth wedding anniversary celebration provided the opportune time for our last hurrah. The Young Turks attended en masse. Bernie Whitebear, the IndoPino leader of Seattle's Indians of All Nations, graced us with his presence. Other close friends and associates from work were there. Our children, their spouses, and our grandchildren all attended. My brother Herb flew up from California. The highlight of the evening was a beautiful rendition of "I Love You for Sentimental Reasons," sung in harmony by our girls, accompanied by Peter and our sons-in-law. Hearing her favorite song, presented by her loved ones, brought tears of happiness to Terri's eyes. We could not have asked for a better farewell party.

# 17  Whose Human Rights?

I FIRST LEARNED OF THE EXECUTIVE DIRECTOR vacancy on San Francisco's Human Rights Commission (HRC) during one of my exploratory trips to California in 1988. A number of acquaintances from the heady days of Filipino activism in the 1970s had been instrumental in electing Art Agnos as mayor of San Francisco. The group saw an opportunity to flex its political muscle by championing a Filipino candidate for the position of executive director. They also believed that the mayor was inclined to appoint a Filipino department head because Filipino employees had recently filed a discrimination complaint with the U.S. Equal Employment Opportunity Commission. The group actively sought me as its candidate.

Rodel Rodis, a young attorney, was leading the push for my appointment. Rodel's family fled the Marcos dictatorship in the early 1970s, and I had watched Rodel progress from a fiery, long-haired, young anti-Marcos street activist to a thoughtful professor of Filipino American history at San Francisco State University. He was now a politically active attorney with a growing practice in San Francisco. Alex Esclamado, the owner and publisher of the *Philippine News*, was also an early supporter. He used the power of his newspaper, which had perhaps the largest circulation of all Filipino community papers in the United States, to help elect Art Agnos and was now mounting support for my appointment through his paper. (We both were to learn that, in one of those strange twists of fate, Alex had worked as a farm laborer for Papa shortly after he came to America in the 1950s. His career as a farm laborer lasted one day.

According to Alex, "It was too hot, and the work was too hard." I could relate to that.)

I was flattered by the interest but reminded the group's members that I had no experience in administering a civil rights program. They felt that civil rights experience was not as important as the years of successful high-level executive experience I did possess. Neglected for years, HRC needed strong leadership, not technical expertise in civil rights matters. My employment background was precisely what they were seeking in a viable Filipino American candidate for the position. I told them I would submit a job application. Privately, however, I did not think it was the best fit for me. Because of my lukewarm interest in the job, I did not bother much with my application and submitted it just in time to make the deadline.

The selection process was a drawn-out series of canceled and rescheduled panel interviews, made more confusing by an unexplained decision to stop midway and start all over again. Consequently, I was surprised that I was still in the running, despite my hastily prepared application. I was looking at several other, more intriguing jobs, and my initial attitude toward the HRC position was that I would simply go through the motions. When the lengthy application process gave me time to explore the job more thoroughly, however, I began to consider it more seriously. I talked to contacts in Seattle's civil rights community, including the regional commissioner of the U.S. Civil Rights Commission, the director of the Seattle Department of Human Rights, and activists representing ethnic minorities and gays and lesbians. They generously provided me with invaluable insights on developments in the field of civil rights, including their assessment of the San Francisco position. By the time of my first panel interview on October 17, I was well prepared on the major issues.

My performance before the panel earned me an interview with Mayor Agnos on the same day. Up to this point, I still was not certain about the job despite favorable reports from Rodel and other supporters on the mayor's commitment to civil rights. Agnos, a

Greek American, had a strong record of responding to the needs of ethnic minorities in his many years as a state assemblyman from San Francisco. A Filipina American, Anita Sanchez, whom I met during the first Young Filipino Peoples Convention in 1971, was a longtime staff person. Nevertheless, I did not expect the strong and well-thought-out role Mayor Agnos described for HRC. With surprising passion, he expressed his vision of the commission as a critical component in bringing changes to city government's treatment of its diverse residents. I was impressed with the depth of his vision and his candor in admitting how tough he expected the job to be. Most of all, I was impressed with his sincerity about the need to achieve inclusiveness for San Francisco's ethnic and sexual minorities. I came away convinced that Art Agnos was a person I wanted to work for.

With that in mind, I went all out for the position. I got in touch with Rodel and other San Francisco supporters, who mobilized a community effort on my behalf. Ed Ilumin, another Filipino American activist with whom I worked during the 1970s, was particularly helpful. An affirmative action officer at the commission, Ed provided valuable insights on its inner workings. Asian American community leaders such as Dale Minami, a well-known attorney with a downtown law practice, and Yori Wada, the University of California regent and veteran civil rights leader, contributed their support. I was to learn later that I also had the help of street-smart Joe Lam, executive director of the Chinatown Youth Center. Joe's sister-in-law was none other than Evelyn Tangalin, the wife of close friend Sonny Tangalin.

On November 14, I received a most welcome letter from Mayor Agnos informing me that I was one of his top candidates and should be hearing about his final decision soon. The warm tone of his letter led me to feel optimistic about my possibilities. I looked forward to what I hoped would be an offer of employment. However, three months went by before I heard from San Francisco.

On February 24, 1989, I received an early morning telephone call from Tom Keane, a reporter for the *San Francisco Chronicle*.

He asked, "How do you feel about being appointed by Mayor Agnos as executive director of the Human Rights Commission?" Keene went on to say that the morning edition of the *Chronicle* was carrying his story that the mayor had appointed me to the position. The only problem was, I had not been officially notified about anything. There was no way I could comment on the story until I had personally heard from Agnos. A few minutes later, I got a call from the mayor, who confirmed that he indeed had decided to offer me the position. He had another piece of good news. My starting salary would be close to six figures as a result of a recent pay increase for all city employees. I immediately accepted the offer and agreed to report to work on March 1. After several months without a job, I was anxious to get back to the world of work.

While I knew my appointment would not be universally popular among San Francisco's diverse population groups, I did not anticipate the extent of the black community's opposition. On the very first day of work, I was greeted with the front-page headline "2 Black Leaders Assail Agnos' Hiring" in the morning *Chronicle*. The mayor's accusers were Lulann McGriff, president of the local chapter of the National Association for the Advancement of Colored People (NAACP), and Julianne Malveaux, president of the Black Leadership Forum, who would later work as a nationally syndicated columnist. The African American leaders accused Agnos of bypassing three black finalists and criticized him for his failure to appoint blacks to top-level positions in his administration. They further claimed that the job of HRC executive director had been a "black position" ever since the commission was created in 1964. The facts did not support their accusations. As to the first charge, the city's two deputy mayors were black, and two of the top three positions in the fire department were held by African Americans. Moreover, Agnos had appointed more blacks, among all minorities, to fill various city commission vacancies. And as for the HRC position being a historically black position, the first two executive directors were white.

The seemingly irrational reaction from the two African American leaders puzzled me. At first, I wondered if this was yet another case of brown being the wrong color. It was not. Rather, the issue was community political power, not racial prejudice. After learning that blacks had recently slipped from largest to third largest among ethnic minorities in San Francisco—behind Latinos and Asians—I had a better understanding of the leaders' attitude. Logically, black political influence could be expected to decrease with the decrease in numbers, but emotionally, African Americans found it difficult to let go of their hard-earned political power. Black community opposition would be a persistent irritant during my tenure as HRC executive director.

The black community was just one among many communities with whom I would have to develop working relationships. San Francisco prided itself on being the most ethnically diverse city in the country. The array of ethnic communities and their high level of empowerment were impressive. In Seattle, I worked effectively with Asians, blacks, Latinos, and Native Americans. San Francisco had the same ethnic groups. It also had significant subcommunities of Colombians, Guatemalans, Mexicans, and Nicaraguans within the Latino community and well-organized Cambodian, Laotian, and Vietnamese subgroups alongside the more established Chinese, Filipinos, Japanese, and Koreans in the Asian community. Moreover, I would need to work with politically sophisticated Arab Americans, East Indians, and the large gay and lesbian and Jewish communities, all of whom were empowered and influential in their own right. Unlike Seattle, however, where there was a long history of successful collaboration among ethnic-minority communities, in San Francisco, the various groups often had their own internal and interethnic disagreements.

According to the latest census, the population of Filipinos in the United States was 1.4 million, an 80 percent increase in a ten-year period. San Francisco boasted one of the largest Filipino populations in the country. The mayor kept his commitment to the Filipino community and appointed Rodel Rodis to the public utilities commission; Ernie Llorente to the commission on elections; Ron Quidichay to the municipal court as a judge; and Jim Arnold as captain in the police department. Filipina American Anita Sanchez, who had been on Agnos's personal staff when he was a member of the California State Assembly, continued to serve him as mayor in a similar staff capacity. My appointment as the first department head of Filipino ancestry for the City and County of San Francisco was another Filipino First for me. For the many Filipino American supporters of Art Agnos, however, my appointment was the crowning achievement in their community's struggle to gain political recognition.

The city charter required all department heads to live in San Francisco. The problem was that San Francisco happened to have the highest real estate prices in the country. In view of the prohibitive cost of housing and the uncertainty of political appointments, Terri and I opted to rent rather than purchase a home. We found a two-bedroom apartment at 1847 Nineteenth Street on Potrero Hill, with an unobstructed view of the Bay Bridge, Oakland, and the San Francisco skyline. It was ideally situated, a short ten-minute bus ride to work. Living and working in San Francisco was also an idyllic situation for the two of us. Terri and I had never forgotten our 1966 dream of residing in San Francisco. It took us thirty-three years to realize our dream. We could not wait to move into the apartment.

We were also delighted to be back in California with family and old friends. When Terri asked what I wanted for my birthday, I said, "I only want my kids and siblings to be here." It was the first time in more than thirty years that my five brothers and two sisters were together for my birthday. Our Potrero Hill apartment may have been crowded, but it was great to have those close to me help celebrate my fifty-ninth birthday. My brother Junior was at his entertaining best as he regaled us with his inimitable stories of unforgettable characters from our past. Particularly amusing were his anecdotes and impersonations of Papa and Uncle Opong, which had us laughing so hard it brought tears to our eyes.

After years of neglect, the Human Rights Commission was indeed a department in disarray. It suffered from a chronic backlog of discrimination complaints. In addition, the recent federal court decision striking down San Francisco's liberal contracting law effectively shut out minority contractors from lucrative city contracts. Already the object of heavy criticism from the black community, the commission was under pressure to find even more ways to open city contracts to minorities.

Internally, the commission had no standards of accountability. Highly paid supervisors did not adequately supervise the staff assigned to them. They rarely made hard decisions and routinely referred matters of substance to the executive director. Not only was there little in the way of program supervision, but line staff were permitted to operate independently without the benefit of program policies and procedures. The commission had no effective structure within which to operate. Communication protocols were virtually nonexistent. It was commonplace, for example, for staff to bypass their superiors and go directly to individual members of the commission or to the mayor's office to air their concerns. Moreover, there were serious imbalances in staff assignments. The commission had three major programs—investigation of discrimination complaints, administration of an affirmative action program in city contracts, and a women's advocacy program—yet 95 percent of staff were assigned to the contracting program. No wonder there was a backlog of discrimination complaints.

The years of neglect had left the commission without adequate staff, space, and equipment. The city created programs but failed to authorize sufficient staff to administer them. Employees worked in a crowded space located in one of the most dangerous blocks on Market Street. Insofar as equipment was concerned, the commission had yet to discover the world of modern technological devices. Workers still used rotary telephones and had no computers with which to maintain program and fiscal information. I immediately embarked on developing solutions to the problems at HRC. I instituted regular staff meetings, weekly conferences between staff members and their immediate supervisors, and reassignments aimed at eliminating the backlog in discrimination complaints. In addition, I initiated a work plan process that assisted in setting priorities, developed a policy/procedure bulletin to standardize work, and received authorization to hire a deputy director. Finally, I was able to convince the commission and the mayor's office to include funds for additional staff, safe and adequate space, and new telephones and computer equipment in the upcoming budget request.

The program remedies came at a good time. On June 27, HRC celebrated its twenty-fifth anniversary in the ornate City Hall rotunda. The event drew an audience of six hundred representing every segment of San Francisco's population. Sharing the podium with me were Mayor Art Agnos, Lieutenant Governor Leo McCarthy, and Willie Brown, Speaker of the California State Assembly. I took full advantage of appearing before a friendly audience with a distinguished group of speakers to talk about the accomplishments of my first hundred days and the future of the Human Rights Commission.

I wish I could say I received significant help from staff in developing remedial changes for the commission. I did not. Staff members had become accustomed to a great deal of independence over the years, so their reluctance to accept directions for increasing accountability and effectiveness did not surprise me. Nevertheless, I was pleased with my overall accomplishments thus far. I was also gratified by the warm welcome I received from city government and the community as a whole. Neither group exhibited the hostility I had encountered from the two black community leaders upon my arrival.

My feelings of well-being were short-lived. In July, after less than four months on the job, I began to have trouble with a few commissioners, members of the HRC's policy-making and oversight body. The mayor had appointed nine of the eleven commissioners to their unpaid positions just before he made my appointment. Representing every segment of the city's diverse population, the new commissioners were all recognized leaders in their own communities. Before long, I was caught up in long-standing community feuds and jealousies. When I put my energies behind a policy proposal for domestic partners, for example, an African American commissioner accused me of wanting to increase the influence of the gay and lesbian community at the expense of her community. It was virtually impossible to support the program priorities of one group without angering other groups.

Three African American staff members fed the festering resentments of the black community. The recalcitrant staffers were Frank Anderson, the most senior HRC supervisor, and two contract compliance officers, Kevin Williams and Zula Jones. Kevin, at the San Francisco International Airport, and Zula, at the Port of San Francisco, were the only outstationed staff members, which perhaps accounted for their attitudes. Frank was particularly disappointing, as he was of little help, despite his experience, and passively resisted my efforts to deal more effectively with the commission's many problems. I later learned that these three had secretly been going directly to several commissioners from the outset of my tenure, planting seeds of suspicion as they communicated their own interpretations of the direction in which I was taking the Human Rights Commission.

Everything came to a head at a public meeting of the commission late in 1989. The topic of discussion was the Minority and Women's Business Enterprise (M/WBE) contracting program. The cochairs of the M/WBE Committee wanted me to rescind my decision to reassign Kevin from the San Francisco International Airport to the massive Yerba Buena/Moscone Center site under construction in downtown San Francisco. While the move was motivated by Kevin's record of chronic confrontation with airport officials, I also believed he was the tough compliance officer I needed to oversee affirmative action contracting requirements at the site. To me, the transfer appeared to be a win-win situation. Kevin, however, believed otherwise. He felt that he had been reassigned as retaliation for his latest dispute with the airport, when he illegally tried to add a black subcontractor to an existing runway contract and then breached airport security. The two commissioners obviously did not understand that personnel matters were the exclusive responsibility of the executive director, not the commission. Attempting to be diplomatic, I replied that I would be willing to talk it over privately with them and that a public meeting was not the place for such a discussion. However, the two commissioners were adamant. They backed off only after the deputy city attorney confirmed that all matters relating to personnel were exclusively within the purview of my office.

Kevin further fanned the flames of suspicion regarding my leadership. He convinced the Black Contractors Association to demonstrate at city hall over the city's failure to provide more contracting opportunities. He filed a lawsuit charging that his transfer and my failure to support him in his dispute over the airport contract were discriminatory and retaliatory, although his case appeared to be without legal foundation. In the following weeks, he planted unsubstantiated stories in the *San Francisco Chronicle* and community newspapers. He even denounced my leadership at a March 1990 breakfast forum of Filipino community media. It was particularly disturbing that Kevin, a guest of Franco Consolacion, one of the forum's Filipino members, used outdated statistics as evidence in accusing me of being personally responsible for HRC's poor performance. That the statistics applied to a period before I was even part of HRC obviously was not important to Kevin and Consolacion. My old friend, attorney Rodel Rodis, a part-time columnist for the *Philippine News*, was livid as he rose to my defense. Rodel devoted his next column to the incident. Under the descriptive headline "Crabbing a Role Model," he bemoaned the tendency of Filipinos, such as Consolacion, to pull down other Filipinos, likening the behavior to crabs pulling down other crabs in a pot.

According to the city attorney, Kevin's reassignment was fully consistent with city ordinance and policy. I received a vote of confidence from the mayor. The commissioners, with the exception of the two M/WBE Committee cochairs, expressed their support. I received encouraging telephone calls from nearly every segment of the city's diverse communities. The increase in workplace effectiveness among HRC staff was also heartening. Nevertheless, I found myself in the midst of a public relations nightmare. Kevin seemed to be getting maximum mileage out of his publicity in the black community, while confidentiality requirements in matters concerning personnel and lawsuits prohibited me from speaking publicly. HRC's already poor public image steadily worsened, and my professional reputation was increasingly tarnished.

In an effort to stem the tide of public criticism, the commissioners and Filipino American city officials collaborated to organize a May 23 reception in my honor. The event exceeded all expectations. More than a hundred people crowded into the small hall at the office of the Philippine Consulate General to express support for the job I was doing. Among those in attendance were seven city department heads, three judges, a regent of the University of California, the sheriff, the fire chief, the chief of police, a college president, members of the board of education, and other city commissioners. Also attending were leaders of Filipino American organizations and representatives of virtually every ethnic, sexual minority, and religious organization. Leaders of the African American community were conspicuous by their absence. Although many black community organizations received invitations to the reception, only the president of the Urban League chose to attend.

After an emotional introduction by emcee Rodel Rodis, the reception evolved into a spirited rally on my behalf. President Karen Kai, one of my strongest supporters on the commission, recounted how I had thrown myself into understanding San Francisco's diverse communities and "a group of green commissioners" in order to resurrect an agency that had been neglected for years. She closed with the hope that everyone "will see a full picture of Peter Jamero, someone who has a broad-based commitment, someone who is working compassionately, and who really and truly deserves all the support that we can all give him."

Deputy Mayor Claude Everhart, representing Mayor Art Agnos, who was out of town, expressed the most powerful show of support. Everhart, an African American, noted that intolerance was "breaking out within communities and between communities" in San Francisco. In concluding, he said, "It is incumbent upon all of us to unite behind this commission, to unite behind this director so that the Human Rights Commission will have the resources and the people power that it needs to end intolerance in this city." Turning to me, he then said, "And Peter, you have my pledge to walk that road with you." The statement drew unrestrained cheers from the enthusiastic crowd.

The reception reaffirmed the community's faith in my ability to do the job and renewed my belief in myself as well. However, it failed to diminish the efforts of those who sought my ouster. The new contracting ordinance proved largely ineffective, which kept minority firms from equitable access to city contracts. Although I closely monitored Kevin's activities and issued several official reprimands, he continued to foment criticism of my leadership in the community. I was certain that he was behind the Black Contractors Association's efforts to pressure the commission and the mayor's office. I was also certain that he and other recalcitrant staff members surreptitiously provided commissioners with inaccurate information. Particularly troubling, the two commissioners who supported Kevin in his battle to stay at the airport became even more resistant to my leadership efforts.

However, the solid show of support at the May reception bolstered my confidence that problems at HRC would eventually be resolved. With the notable exception of the two cochairs of the M/WBE Committee, the other commissioners gave me reason to be optimistic. In the months following the reception, Karen Kai's support of my leadership grew even stronger. I also could count on the support of businessman Isadore Pivnick, of the Jewish community; Lucile Lockhart, a paraplegic activist; Leonard Graff, an attorney and representative of the gay and lesbian community; and Father Peter Sammon, pastor of St. Teresa's Roman Catholic Church on Potrero Hill. I was particularly thankful for Father Sammon's backing; as our parish priest, he tended to my spiritual and emotional needs as well.

In June, the five supportive commissioners were instrumental in developing an objective process for my performance evaluation.

First, we jointly identified eleven issues that served as evaluation criteria. I then prepared detailed responses to each criterion and submitted them for the commission's review. Finally, the commission scheduled an evaluation of my performance at a closed executive session on August 23. Unfortunately, everything that could go wrong went wrong. All but one of my supporters were absent: Karen Kai was on maternity leave, Isadore Pivnick had recently resigned because of business pressures, Father Sammon had been called out of town, and Lucile Lockhart was recuperating from surgery. One commissioner was brand-new, and another vacancy was still unfilled.

May Jaber, M/WBE cochair and my major antagonist on the commission, maneuvered her way into the position of acting president and promptly proceeded to ignore the evaluation criteria the commissioners had adopted in June. In the hour and a half of discussion, not once did they discuss the remedial actions I had taken. Instead, May permitted commissioners to vent their frustration over the city's record on the M/WBE program and HRC's poor image. She allowed some commissioners to make general statements, such as that HRC was not moving under my stewardship, without documenting their allegations. Completely ignored as precipitating factors were the federal court decision overturning the city's contracting ordinance, city government's past neglect of HRC, and the anti–affirmative action policies of the Reagan administration—all factors that were beyond my control. As far as the commissioners were concerned, I was solely responsible for HRC's problems. The executive session to evaluate my performance had turned into a witch hunt.

The commissioners' failure to follow their own rules, the acting president's failure to establish an orderly process, and the absence of supportive commissioners resulted in a flawed process conducted by a kangaroo court. Consequently, I was not surprised when the commissioners returned a no-confidence verdict on my performance. Obviously, I had been set up. Devastated by the decision, I listened numbly as May Jaber declared her intent to meet immediately with the mayor. She also made it abundantly clear that I was not to attend that meeting.

Her meeting with the mayor never occurred. Shortly after the August 23 debacle, I met with Mayor Agnos and Deputy Mayor Everhart and gave them my version of the events related to my evaluation. I was relieved when the mayor confirmed his support for my leadership. He agreed that the evaluation process was flawed. He also agreed that a biased presiding officer conducted the executive session unfairly and manipulated the no-confidence vote. Nevertheless, he was still faced with the awkward question of how to handle the votes of commissioners he had personally appointed. He decided to delay the meeting and wait for things to cool down and instructed the commissioners to sit on their decision. In the meantime, he suggested that I proceed with the direction I had set for HRC as if the August 23 vote had never happened.

Although I was buoyed by the mayor's vote of confidence, inaccurate stories on the problems at HRC persisted as did the inevitable rumors of my imminent departure. On a foggy October night, when I was again working late into the evening, Terri suddenly said, "Honey, I'm too young to be a widow." I turned around and listened as my misty-eyed wife of thirty-seven years told me of her increasing concern for my physical and mental health. "I've never seen you work so hard and bring work home every night. This job isn't worth it. You never get credit, only the blame—you ought to resign," she declared. Terri reminded me that we no longer had children to support. She expressed confidence that with my experience and professional reputation, it should not be difficult to find another job. Terri rarely volunteered her views on my work. When she did, she was usually right. In this instance, she was right on all counts.

As miserable as much of my HRC experience may have been, other aspects of my life went remarkably well. Terri and I became grandparents for the sixth time when Cecily Erin Organo was born to Cheryl and Philip on September 23, 1989. Karen married her longtime beau, Ron Armada, on June 30, 1990. The wedding ceremony was at St. Theresa Catholic Church in Seattle, the same church where I marched in a demonstration against a racist parish priest eighteen years before. On August 18, Jackie married Seattle native Richard Berganio, also in Seattle. Their wedding drew a large number of Jameros from California. My seven siblings and most of their children came, a strong testimonial to Jamero family solidarity. The two weddings were also a homecoming of sorts for Terri and me. We were able to get together again with old friends, particularly the Young Turks (now Old Turkeys) who had been so much a part of our lives in the years we resided in Seattle.

Our new sons-in-law were Filipino. When asked how it came to pass that all our kids had married Filipinos—a rarity considering the ethnic commingling of the times—I would jokingly reply, "Because I didn't permit them to go out with anyone else." Of course, this was pure fancy. We expressed no preferences, explicitly or implicitly, based on ethnic background. Nevertheless, Terri and I were pleased with our children's choices for mates. Our involvement and pride in our Filipino identity seemed to have rubbed off on our children.

As far as my love for jazz was concerned, I was in music heaven. San Francisco featured much more in the way of straight-ahead jazz. I became a regular at such venues as Pearl's of North Beach and The Ramp, located off the bay in China Basin. I had the opportunity to listen again to an old friend, pianist Flip Nunez, a fixture at a number of clubs throughout the Bay Area, as well as my piano-playing cousin Rudy Tenio, who performed at The Cannery's Quiet Storm. San Francisco was also home to KJAZ, a great radio station whose DJs played jazz twenty-four hours a day. Their selections enabled me to keep up with the latest recordings, which resulted in my buying more compact discs, which, in turn, inspired me to update my stereo equipment

I never missed the chance to see my beloved New York Yankees when they played the Oakland A's across the bay, an easy ride away via BART (Bay Area Rapid Transit). The A's, not the Yankees, were the dominant team in baseball and featured such stars as slugging outfielder Jose Canseco, all-time greatest base stealer Ricky Henderson, home-run-hitting Mark McGwire, and pitching ace Dave Stewart. They ran away with the 1989 American League pennant and in October were poised to meet the San Francisco Giants in the World Series.

The first game of the Series was on October 17. I left the office early and caught a bus for home, where I intended to watch the game on television. Suddenly, the bus began to lurch crazily, and I at first thought it had suffered several blowouts. I looked outside and saw that the pavement appeared to be moving like small waves. It was 5:04 P.M. The largest earthquake since 1906, measuring 7.5 on the Richter scale, was hitting San Francisco. A number of panicked passengers jumped out of the bus. I had been through several quakes and chose to remain inside until the earthquake subsided. I walked the five blocks uphill to our Potrero Hill apartment only to find that we had no electricity or telephone service. Terri was also out; she had gone shopping in Daly City. I could see smoke rising from Oakland, the Bay Bridge, and what seemed to be the Marina District in San Francisco and felt frustrated and helpless because I couldn't find out what was going on elsewhere. An hour later, I remembered our small, battery-powered black-and-white television stored away in the hall closet. From the only TV station still operating, I learned the true extent of the massive earthquake. Damage was far greater than what I could see from the apartment. According to the TV news reports, we lived in one of the safest areas in the city. Potrero Hill was made of the hardest granite in the Bay Area, capable of withstanding quakes much stronger than the 7.5 registered earlier in the day.

I grew increasingly concerned about Terri. Traffic clogged the main thoroughfares, and because of power outages, traffic lights were not operating. In addition, she was new to the streets of San Francisco. But she arrived home around eight o'clock, safe and sound after a harrowing three hours of wending her way through unfamiliar streets and getting lost. I should have known that somehow she would make it. On other occasions, she had demonstrated an uncanny ability to know the precise direction in which she was traveling. I thanked God for giving her that ability.

On October 23, 1990, I submitted a letter of resignation to Mayor Agnos. I negotiated a generous severance arrangement with the mayor, who later issued a press release praising my leadership and accomplishments with HRC. As part of my negotiations, I also insisted that acting commission president May Jaber issue a conciliatory memorandum to HRC staff. In her November 5 memorandum, my major antagonist on the commission wrote: "Peter came to us during a difficult time. He has displayed a firm commitment to human rights, the disadvantaged, and the citizens of our city. We have made progress in responding to hate violence, in eliminating a backlog of discrimination cases, in protecting the rights of the disabled, and in providing a new data system to monitor compliance with the City's M/WBE program." Although it lacked sufficient detail, her memo satisfied my basic desire for a conciliatory tone and accurate content. My last day of work as executive director of the Human Rights Commission was December 31, 1990.

Despite the resistance and disappointments I'd encountered, I felt proud of my accomplishments. My involvement with minority communities opened funding opportunities for other ethnic groups. The Samoan community was a prime example of a group that was finally able to obtain critically needed funding. The gay and lesbian community received additional resources. One of my proudest moments as HRC executive director was when I rode in an official car as part of the Gay Pride Parade, the largest of its kind in the country. I received ripples of applause from the crowd, appreciative of the commission's support for their community, all along the parade route. Under my leadership, the city's chronic neglect of HRC came to an end. Staff moved to a more spacious workspace with updated office equipment and computers. New working agreements, designed to increase opportunities for minority contractors, were in place for the airport, the Department of Public Works, and the Port of San Francisco. I eliminated the large backlog of discrimination complaint cases. Finally, the development of a new automated reporting system for the M/WBE program enabled HRC to generate reliable city-wide data for the very first time.

A year after my resignation, the M/WBE reporting system provided a record of my performance at the commission. During the time I served as executive director, city contracts for minority- and woman-owned businesses increased by more than $20 million between 1989–90 and 1990–91.

Ed Ilumin, HRC affirmative action representative and undoubtedly my strongest supporter on the staff, was thoughtful enough to send me the report. He also wrote, "Finally the report is out which I believe totally vindicates you of the irresponsible charges leveled at you by your detractors. You should be credited for this and for bringing HRC into the computerized world because without this, HRC would still be floundering." Thanks to the report and Ed, I felt increased pride in my accomplishments at the commission.

## 18  Community Based

LATE IN 1989, WE PURCHASED A MODEST TWO-
story home in a large residential development in Daly City, eight
miles from San Francisco. At the time of its construction, after World
War II, the housing development was ahead of its time. Now, it simply looked like an unending series of similar boxy homes. We chose
Daly City because the price of houses in San Francisco, the highest in the country, was beyond our reach. We thought of the house
as an investment, with Cheryl and Philip and their girls renting from
us. It was a win-win situation for all of us. Terri and I also considered
the house a hedge against the job uncertainties of political appointments. Perhaps it was prophetic. Following the announcement of my
resignation from the Human Resources Commission, we already had
a home to move into.

The house, at 49 Pinehaven Street, was located only a few blocks
from Daly City's huge Westlake Shopping Center. The backyard
abutted on a greenbelt, which meant we did not have neighbors
behind us. But although the newly renovated house was large
enough to accommodate all of us, the rooms were on the small side.
In addition, the large backyard was overgrown with weeds, with no
sign of a lawn. That didn't seem like a major problem, however, considering our love of gardening.

Daly City was also home to a large Filipino community. With
35 percent of the population, Filipinos constituted its largest ethnic minority. It was fitting that my next job should be with an organization that served a large number of Filipinos. Asian American
Recovery Services (AARS) was a community-based nonprofit

agency in San Francisco providing substance-abuse services. AARS targeted Cambodians, Chinese, Japanese, Koreans, Laotians, and Vietnamese in addition to Filipinos. Its staff reflected the pan-Asian composition of the community. The agency had initiated a nation-wide search for an executive director in the summer of 1990. Several members of the Asian community contacted me to determine my possible interest. In light of the problems I was experiencing in San Francisco at the time, the job was somewhat attractive. However, the announced salary level for the work was much too low. I declined to become a candidate. After the nationwide search failed to attract suitable applicants, AARS issued a new announcement. This time, the salary was more appropriate to the position and better matched my personal expectations. On October 30, 1990, seven days after I submitted my letter of resignation to the Human Rights Commission, I applied for the position of executive director at Asian American Recovery Services.

The agency was relatively new, having been organized in 1985. It was much smaller than the multimillion-dollar programs I had previously directed, with a budget of around $2 million and a staff of sixty-five. It also had undergone several changes in executive directors, both clinical psychologists, in the five years of its existence. The board of directors had dwindled to the bare minimum, which was of concern to me. At the same time, I was intrigued by the possibility of working in a community-based nonprofit with a record of serving Filipinos. Except for United Way, all my employment experiences had been with public agencies.

As I prepared for my job interview on December 11, I was not sure what to expect. I wondered about the degree of professionalism at AARS, particularly in view of its newness and the relatively small size of its budget and staff. I need not have been concerned. The three-person interview panel, under the leadership of board president Nelson Holl, followed a professional and structured format based on the agency's priorities. Nelson, in particular, was knowledgeable about the operation of a nonprofit organization, having served as the interim executive director for most of the year.

During the job interview, I had the distinct impression that Nelson, a recovering addict who had helped found AARS, wanted to make sure that the organization hired an executive director who would succeed in continuing his work.

From the outset, it was clear that panel members were seeking a person with a record of accomplishment in top-level administration. Specifically, they wanted someone well versed in the prudent management of financial resources, knowledgeable about obtaining grants and contracts, capable of collaborating with other agencies and representing the organization before funding sources, and prepared to provide leadership within the Asian community. These were all qualities I possessed and, as it turned out, was able to convey to the panel. In January, I received a job offer, and I readily accepted. While the beginning salary still represented a reduction compared to my earnings at the Human Rights Commission, the panel assured me that an increase would be forthcoming at the end of a successful six-month probationary period. The job offer included a generous benefits package, paid parking, and an expense account. I reported to work as the new executive director on February 1, 1991.

The agency sponsored a reception in April to introduce me to the community. The function drew VIPs from local government and the substance-abuse community as well as people from pan-Asian communities, all curious to find out about the individual who had been selected to head Asian American Recovery Services. It was an ideal opportunity for me to begin the process of developing working relationships, and I was grateful for the chance to meet them all. The most enjoyable aspect of the reception was the great turnout of old Filipino friends, supporters, and family. Terri and Julie plus Cheryl and Philip and their girls were all there for the festivities. Particularly gratifying was the presence of many who had been there for me during my dark days at the Human Rights Commission.

At the time I was hired, the board of directors and I agreed on an ambitious set of eight priority work projects with which to begin my tenure at the agency. While the work projects would not be easy, I believed they were doable. When my six-month performance evaluation came around, I had either met or exceeded the completion timetable for all the projects. Perhaps my most important accomplishment was retiring the budget deficit I had inherited. The board was pleased with my performance, particularly the elimination of the deficit, and authorized the promised increase in salary.

I was happy about the good start, but I could not have done it without quality help from the staff. The agency's employees were eager for direction. Some had untapped talents and skills that seemed tailor-made for my plans. I assigned Peng N'gin, a hardworking immigrant from Malaysia, to the task of establishing policies and procedures and asked Hawaii native Bart Aoki, an analytical clinical psychologist, to develop a brand-new research program. In addition, I hired Vicky Berry, an accountant from Tennessee, as fiscal manager, to focus on retiring the deficit.

The board of directors was serious about wanting me to be visible and accessible with funding sources. In the spring of 1991, after only a few months on the job, I traveled to Honolulu for a substance-abuse prevention conference convened by federal officials. My presence and participation helped ensure continued funding of the Asian Youth Substance Abuse Project (AYSAP), our agency's largest program. It was the first of many such trips I would be making for AARS. The Hawaii trip was memorable because Jackie was also at the conference. She had preceded me into the substance-abuse field by a few years, working as the prevention specialist for King County, Washington. I learned a lot about the field from Jackie. In the next few years, Jackie and I would be fellow delegates at events in Barbados; San Francisco; San Juan, Puerto Rico; Seattle; and Washington, D.C. I was proud to see her professional development and to be her colleague. We had always had a close bond, perhaps because I took care of her as an infant when Terri had to take a part-time job. Moreover, Jackie shared my love for politics and community involvement. Now we had yet another reason to strengthen that bond.

Toward the end of 1991, the board of directors went on a planning retreat at a quiet setting in the Marin County foothills. The session was facilitated by a professional trainer and was the first planning session conducted away from San Francisco. I had lobbied the board for such a retreat, believing it would provide the opportunity to develop critically needed program and funding direction for the agency. The retreat was a success. The board came up with a three-year strategic plan that provided the basic blueprint for the agency's operations for the remainder of my tenure. The retreat also enabled us to strengthen our working relationships. The remoteness of the retreat setting forced us to know one another more intimately and develop the trust so important for a functional organization.

In 1992, I turned my attention to the priorities generated by the strategic planning retreat. I also paid increasing attention to the Asian Youth Substance Abuse Project. AYSAP was overseen by a consortium of executive directors from six participating agencies: AARS (which also acted as lead agency and fiscal agent), the China-town Youth Center, the Japanese Community Youth Council, the Korean Community Service Center, the Vietnamese Youth Development Center, and the West Bay Pilipino Multi-service Corporation. The relationship between some members of AYSAP and AARS was marred by suspicion and hostility. There were rumblings that the project should withdraw from its arrangement with AARS, act as its own fiscal agent, and assume the responsibilities of lead agency within the consortium. Admittedly, this would not have been in the best interests of AARS, but I also knew that no other consortium member could meet the federal requirements for performing such functions.

I decided on a two-prong strategy to try to remedy the situation. First, the members of the consortium needed to be educated on the nuances of being a fiscal agent. AARS fiscal manager Vicky Berry thoroughly understood federal requirements. However, she was unable to communicate them clearly to consortium members who had come up through the ranks and were unfamiliar with the technical aspects of fiscal accounting. Fortunately, my previous experiences had taught me the basic requirements of a fiscal agent. I took the lead in trying to help consortium members with the complicated requirements. Gradually, consortium attitudes toward AARS began to change. However, it was Ben Tan, an accountant from a well-to-do family in the Philippines, who had the most success with the consortium. Ben was hired as fiscal manager after Vicky Berry left to continue her education, and his relaxed manner and openness in dealing with financial issues significantly reduced the consortium's opposition.

Second, I began to do some fence-mending with consortium members, particularly Jeff Mori, the feisty executive director of the Japanese Community Youth Council and the consortium's spiritual leader. Jeff had long expressed suspicions that the agency's hidden agenda was to completely control the AYSAP program and eliminate the consortium. Over time, I convinced Jeff that the agency's major interest was to ensure that federal requirements were met so as not to jeopardize continued funding. Furthermore, I assured him that AARS had no desire to take over the consortium's role in providing program direction. It helped that Jeff liked to conduct business in various eating and drinking establishments, a pleasant practice to which I had long been accustomed. It also helped that I had behind-the-scenes support from Joe Lam, Chinatown Youth Center executive director and brother-in-law of Young Turk Sonny Tangalin.

If there were doubts about my leadership, Nelson Holl's decision to retire from the board of directors completely dispelled them. He would not have left if he did not have confidence in me. Nelson had been the driving force behind the agency since its inception. He served in the dual capacity of board president and interim executive director before I came on board. The Asian community thought of him as "Mr. AARS." Because of Nelson's close identification with the agency, some doubted that he and I could coexist as board president and executive director. They were wrong. Nelson may have had his own ideas of how to run the agency, but he also respected my views. We had no serious disagreements. Shortly after his retirement, I received a note that included the following comment: "I want you to know that I feel I'm leaving AARS in good hands . . . you've done a great job." The entire board of directors agreed with Nelson. In commenting on my 1992 performance evaluation, the board wrote: "Mr. Jamero has exceeded his duties as Executive Director. His effectiveness as an administrative and fiscal manager, his leadership in multiple environments, and his attention to organizational goals are a few of his outstanding qualities practiced in his relatively short tenure with the organization."

Another of my principal responsibilities as executive director was to be actively involved in professional associations concerned with the treatment of drug abuse. Now called "therapeutic communities," these associations, consisting largely of former addicts, began in the drug culture days of the 1960s with Synanon, the well-known southern California movement and program. The movement evolved into a commune and then a quasi-religious cult, before it disintegrated in the late 1980s. The movement's revival as an association of therapeutic communities brought it into mainstream America and respectability. The Therapeutic Community Association of America (TCA) carried considerable weight in Washington, D.C., resulting in awards of millions of dollars to its various affiliates, including AARS. If AARS was to continue receiving federal money for its treatment program, I had to be visible at association functions. I soon found myself an active participant at national conferences with the Therapeutic Community Association, at state meetings with the California Therapeutic Communities, where I served as secretary, and at international functions as a delegate with the World Conference of Therapeutic Communities. Again, business travel became a major part of my work schedule.

In April 1992, a Therapeutic Community Association meeting in Washington, D.C., expanded into a mini-vacation in New York City for Terri and me. We saw *Miss Saigon* on Broadway and listened to great jazz in Greenwich Village. For me, the highlight on that trip was going to the Baseball Hall of Fame at Cooperstown, in upstate New York. I spent the whole day excitedly taking in the displays of old baseball stars, especially those heroes of my favorite team, the New York Yankees. There was a special commemorative display of Joe DiMaggio in the main foyer; busts and photographs of Yogi Berra, Bill Dickey, Whitey Ford, Lou Gehrig, Tony Lazzeri, Mickey Mantle, and Babe Ruth; and pictures of past Yankees championship teams. I was in baseball heaven.

I have been a rabid baseball fan for more than sixty years and often wondered about my strong attraction to the sport. In many ways, my love for baseball and the Yankees is a reflection of my life. Traditionally known as "America's pastime," baseball came into my life when I was a boy trying to assimilate as an American. What better way to be American than to be a baseball fan? I also drew inspiration from the fact that so many baseball players at the time came from immigrant families and had become respected members of their communities. As to the perennially competitive and successful New York Yankees, I believe their success reflects my lifelong drive to make it in American society. The Yankees have achieved a proud record of an unprecedented number of championships. While my achievements have been much more modest, I feel the same pride in the many Filipino Firsts I achieved during my career.

My only disappointment with the Yankees was their reluctance to hire black players for so many years. Jackie Robinson broke the major league color line with the Brooklyn Dodgers in 1947, ending the "whites only" chapter of baseball. While other teams swiftly added black players to their rosters, the Yankees confined the few black players the team did sign to the minor leagues. The Yankees did not have a black player on their roster until 1955, when Elston Howard joined them, but only after they shifted him from outfielder to catcher, perhaps the most difficult position to master. Despite these barriers, Howard became a star player, beloved by all Yankees fans. In refusing to open their team to black players, the Yankees chose to perpetuate the racist tradition of their sport. As a Filipino American, I knew about the pain of exclusion, and although I continued to be loyal to the Yankees at the time, it was difficult to watch my favorite team carry out its racist policy. The Yankees have since seen the error of their ways.

In October 1992, I traveled to the World Conference of Therapeutic Communities in Venice—a trip Terri was not about to miss. However, her work schedule did not permit her to leave until a day later, which seemed a minor problem at the time. What I did not realize, however, was that Venice had no airport. Visitors landed at an airport and then took an hour-long water-taxi ride to Venice. Since Terri would be arriving after the conference started, special boats for conference goers would probably not be available. I became panicked at the thought of Terri arriving at the airport, unaware of her situation, not knowing the language, and not knowing where to go. I went to our travel representative repeatedly to make sure someone would be there to meet her and then to the pier to await her arrival. I need not have worried. Terri arrived in Venice on schedule, without experiencing a single problem.

The World Conference was unlike anything I had ever experienced. At every session, sophisticated electronic devices interpreted the English-language proceedings into Chinese, French, German, Italian, Japanese, and Spanish. It reminded me of a United Nations General Assembly session. However, interpreting was a slow process, and the listening devices did not always operate effectively, thus interrupting the flow of discussion. I found the conference boring. The informal conversations with delegates from other countries were much more interesting and instructive.

This was our first trip to Italy, and Terri had always dreamed of seeing its attractions, particularly the artwork and ancient ruins. We took in all the sights, mostly on foot, since there were no cars, buses, or streetcars, only small boats, water taxis, and ferries that traveled on the network of canals and waterways. Fortunately, many of the attractions were near San Marco Square, crowded with pigeons and people, which was only a few blocks from our hotel. The total absence of automobiles made for a welcome change from the clamor of other cities. However, we were not prepared for the high prices, especially for food. Consequently, we limited ourselves mostly to *panini* (sandwiches) for lunch and rolls for breakfast at the numerous stand-up food bars. One night, we went to a restaurant for a spaghetti dinner plus wine that cost more than a hundred American dollars.

When we first arrived in Venice, Terri and I avoided the famed gondolas because of their exorbitant cost. But on our last day there, we concluded we could not leave without riding the romantic boat. The boatman first asked for the equivalent of $100, but after a few minutes of negotiation, he agreed to take us for about $40. Terri and I thoroughly enjoyed the leisurely cruise through the intricate network of canals that crisscrossed the city. The knowledgeable boatman pointed out such attractions as Marco Polo's home and various palaces and museums. At the end of our tour, I paid him and included a generous tip. He hurried off. That evening, as Terri was reconciling the day's accounts, she noticed a shortfall of 100,000 lira. We realized then that I had misread the bills and given the boatman 100,000, rather than 10,000, lira for a tip. No wonder he hurried off.

At the end of the conference, we caught a train to Florence. The city was a center of fine art, from the paintings at the renowned Uffizi Gallery to the breathtaking Michelangelo sculpture of David. All the outdoor piazzas featured beautiful statues and fountains. Everywhere we went, we saw replicas of well-known art in souvenir shops and at vending stands. The city was also known for its gigantic steaks. Terri and I went to a steak restaurant off the usual tourist trail to savor Florentine culture and the famous steaks. We were not disappointed. The steaks were truly enormous and delicious, and the service, despite our inability to speak Italian, was impeccable. The steaks were so large that Terri requested a "take-out." With a smile and a nod, the waiter took away the steak, and that was the last time we saw it. After an interminable wait, we concluded that our otherwise efficient waiter had interpreted Terri's waving of arms to mean he should take the steak away.

Rome was easily the highlight of our trip, with its ancient ruins, beautiful cathedrals, and historic sites. We saw the Colosseum, the

Roman Forum, the Pantheon, and the Spanish Steps. We also caught a quick glimpse of the Trevi Fountain on a tour bus. A surprisingly efficient subway system made touring a breeze.

We were surprised to see a significant number of Filipinos on the crowded streets of Rome. We learned from a Filipina street vendor that most came to Italy as domestics. The excesses of the Marcos dictatorship had sunk the Philippine economy to such depths that 10 percent of the Philippine workforce was estimated to be employed in foreign countries. Overseas employment was often the only way for Filipinos, many of whom were trained professionals, to provide for their families. Filipinos were in high demand in Europe because of their industrious work habits, and they preferred working in Italy, as they felt more comfortable in the predominantly Roman Catholic country. The street vendor also said that Filipinos were treated far better in Europe, compared to Saudi Arabia or Hong Kong, where they were often subjected to shabby and discriminatory treatment.

We spent most of our time touring the Vatican. The original painting on the ceiling of the Sistine Chapel and Michelangelo's pietà in the Basilica of Saint Peter took our breath away. Outside the basilica, we spied a sign pointing to an elevator that took visitors to the dome. We did not realize that the elevator would take us only to a second-story landing, with the dome another 320 steps away. The steps not only were steep but also narrowed considerably as we climbed higher. When we neared the top, there was barely enough room for us to squeeze through. There were no signs posted to alert visitors to this potential problem. For those who were too large to fit, there seemed no other alternative than to turn back. Once we reached the top of the dome, we were rewarded with a 360-degree view of Rome. We remained at the top for a long time, admiring the view—and catching our breath.

The following year, the World Conference of Therapeutic Communities was in Kuala Lumpur, Malaysia, the first stop of a two-week combination business-vacation trip that would take us to four countries. After a brief overnight stay in Singapore, Terri and I flew into the modern airport on the outskirts of Kuala Lumpur. We were surprised and impressed by the level of development in the country. Freeways ringed the city. Right outside our suite at the Hilton, construction had begun on what would become, in 1998, the two highest skyscrapers in the world, the Petronas Twin Towers, towering 1,483 feet above sea level. Everywhere we looked, we saw evidence of Malaysia's economic progress. Late-model automobiles filled the streets, and new homes dotted the landscape. Sidewalks were clean, with no homeless people in sight.

We were amazed by the remarkable physical resemblance between Malaysians and Filipinos. Malaysians likewise noticed the resemblance when they first saw Terri and me but immediately knew we were foreigners from the way we dressed and carried ourselves. Some thought we were from the Philippines. We noted other similarities as well. For example, Malaysians often used the same words as Filipinos, such as *sundang* (sword). They also had the same passion for cockfighting. Some of their foods were similar to Filipino foods, except they did not eat pork, which is forbidden by their Islamic religion. One morning, while getting breakfast at the hotel's self-service cafeteria, Terri asked in frustration, "Do you know where I can find the bacon or sausages? All I see are turkey bacon and turkey sausage." She had forgotten about the religious ban on pork.

The Kuala Lumpur conference proceeded at a much faster pace compared to the Venice conference, mostly because there was less interpretation of languages. Malaysia is a former British colony, and Malaysians are familiar with the English language, as were most of the other delegates, who came largely from Australia, Canada, China, Indonesia, India, Japan, New Zealand, the Philippines, Singapore, and the United States. I spent much of the conference in the company of Malaysian delegates. I was fascinated by the cultural diversity of their group, which included Chinese and East Indian ethnic groups as well as different religions such as Buddhism, Hinduism, and Islam. According to these delegates, Malaysia had none of the ethnic and racial disharmony of the United States. When I asked how Malaysians were able to achieve intergroup harmony, they attributed it to the lessons they had learned in working together to achieve independence from the British. They also believed that their longer history as a country, which had given them more time to live together, was a significant factor. Although their idealistic responses were not entirely convincing, their easy manner of relating to one another left me with a positive impression of Malaysian interrelationships.

Immediately after the end of the World Conference, Terri and I flew to Manila. An aide to Paul Aquino, prominent attorney and brother of Benigno Aquino, the assassinated Philippine hero, met us at the airport. Benigno Aquino's wife, Cory, became president of the Philippines after Ferdinand Marcos was ousted. We received red-carpet treatment, completely bypassed customs, and, within minutes, were ushered into an air-conditioned van. Terri and I gazed incredulously at each other. Normally, checking in through Manila's Benigno Aquino International Airport took hours.

We got our special treatment courtesy of Lupita Aquino Kashi-wahara, the sister of Benigno and Paul. A longtime resident of the San Francisco Bay Area, Lupita had worked closely with me on several community functions. Upon learning we were going to the Philippines, she called Paul and made sure he would take good care of us. We paid a courtesy visit to Paul in his comfortable office in a Makati high-rise. He was a take-charge individual with a rapid-fire way of speaking, much like his sister. Apparently, Lupita had briefed him well, and he seemed to know about my political and community activities. I was thankful we did not talk about Philippine politics, since I was not up-to-date on the ever changing political conditions of his country. He noted that the *barong tagalog*, the traditional Filipino shirt, I had purchased on my last visit to the Philippines in 1988 was no longer fashionable. At first, I was taken aback by what seemed like a rude remark, but then I remembered that Filipinos often express themselves in ways that Americans consider tactless.

I also had some AARS business to conduct in the Manila area. I had an appointment to meet with Charito Planas, the vice mayor of Quezon City. She had contacted me a few months earlier to request help in developing a drug and alcohol treatment center patterned after the residential treatment program at AARS. As it turned out, Vice Mayor Planas did not need much in the way of consultation; the center was already up and running smoothly.

The short layover in Manila gave us a chance to visit our old friends the Castro family and my niece Rita Cruz and her family. Thanks to Paul Aquino's aide and the air-conditioned van, we also took the opportunity to play tourist. We visited Taal, the site of one of the world's smallest and most active volcanoes, a two-hour drive from Manila. The volcano is in the middle of a lake. The lake, originally a crater, was created by the same type of eruption that resulted in what is now Crater Lake, in Oregon. On our way back from Taal, we passed through Cavite, site of the former U.S. naval base. The U.S. Navy abandoned Cavite during the late 1960s, when it transferred operations to larger facilities at Olangapo in Subic Bay. Rundown houses and strip malls surrounded the old base. The navy left Olangapo in 1994, when the U.S. Congress failed to reach agreement with the Philippine government on renewing its lease. I wondered if a deteriorating city would be Olangapo's fate as well.

The next stop of our whirlwind trip was Garcia-Hernandez, Bohol—Mama's and Papa's hometown and home to countless relatives. This was our third visit, but it was the first time we were traveling without an entourage of relatives from the United States. Once more, Terri and I brought the obligatory gifts and divided them between the Jamero and Madelo families. Again, out of respect for both families, I stayed in the home of the head of each family. It was good to have a more leisurely visit with our relatives, who were now dear to both of us.

My cousin Nenny updated us on the Philippine political scene. She expressed optimism about the country, primarily because of the strong leadership demonstrated by President Fidel Ramos, who had succeeded Cory Aquino. Nenny believed that the economy was turning around after more than twenty years under the Marcos dictatorship and the chaos that followed the countless attempted coups against President Aquino. The old oligarchic system that had historically controlled the country was still in existence. However, according to Nenny, it was devoid of the corruption and police-state tactics of the Marcos years.

I also had business to attend to in Garcia-Hernandez, family business. Although Mama's property remained in her name, it had not been under her legal control or that of her heirs as she had hoped. Shortly before I left, the family provided me with power of attorney in order to clarify the situation. My cousin Roman Madelo had been diligently caring for the land since Mama left the Philippines, using the tillable properties to support his family. While we wanted to exercise legal control, we still intended that the property be available to Roman and his family. My Madelo relatives took me on a tour of Mama's property. It consisted of six parcels: three in the mountainous countryside surrounding Garcia-Hernandez and three in the flatlands of the town. Trope Ochavillo, Manang Bebay's son, was particularly helpful in searching for the pertinent documents at the town hall. However, transferring control of Mama's Philippine property to her heirs in the United States was a more complicated legal process than we had foreseen. We left the arrangement unchanged.

Our next stop was Hong Kong. We were not prepared for the frightening flight path that took us between tall buildings before we landed in the middle of the city. It reminded me of landings at Juneau, where planes had to maneuver through a narrow passageway between tall mountains. Hong Kong was the nearest thing to New York City we had ever experienced. It was vibrant with activity; we could almost feel the throbbing of the city and the trading of millions of dollars in its many banks and busy shops. The streets were jammed with people, cars, and double-decker buses. Like New York City, Hong Kong also had great food and, a pleasant surprise, straight-ahead jazz. One evening, as we were enjoying cocktails and listening to a jazz trio, I thought the music sounded strangely familiar. The pianist was Allen Youngblood, from Seattle. We last saw him during the 1980s, when he entertained at a wedding. He was almost as excited as we were to visit with familiar people from home, especially in far-off Hong Kong.

We had a wonderful time in Hong Kong, except when we observed the second-class treatment of Filipinos by ethnic Chinese. As in Italy, Filipinos were in great demand as domestics, and a large number of Filipino domestics lived in the greater Hong Kong metropolitan area. Unlike in Italy, however, Filipinos were not treated well. At the airport, customs agents rudely detained all Filipino passengers, including a man with nothing but a small carry-on bag, to look for contraband. Terri and I were spared an intrusive search, presumably because we carried American passports. At Hong Kong restaurants, we also noticed that ethnic Chinese consistently received service before we did, even if we arrived first. We walked out of one restaurant but did not complain, as we would have in America. We were angry but felt we had to accept the customs and practices of another country.

On our last evening in Hong Kong, three of my Madelo cousins surprised us with a visit. We had never met, but they were eager to make our acquaintance after their families in Garcia-Hernandez had told them we would be in Hong Kong. Two of my cousins had gone to college, but because of the poor economic conditions in the Philippines, they were working as domestics. Their pay was better than any salary they could earn in the Philippines, and they were able to send money home regularly to their families. They were treated well by their longtime white American and European employers, unlike some of their compatriots, who endured abuse and exploitation. They agreed that Filipinos were treated shabbily by ethnic Chinese in Hong Kong but said they had to learn to tolerate discrimination. Otherwise, they would have to return to the Philippines, where they were unlikely to find comparable employment. They found some solace on their Sundays off, when Filipinos from across the Hong Kong metropolitan area gathered in the central city to visit with other domestics from their hometowns. Sadly, I could not help thinking that this Sunday get-together of domestic workers was strikingly similar to that of the lonely and home-sick *manong* farmworkers of the 1930s and 1940s. In my mind, I still see the *manongs* congregated on Stockton's El Dorado Street, desperately seeking a familiar face.

The hectic pace of our activities continued when we arrived home. Our involvement in the Filipino American National Historical Society took most of our time, especially Terri's. She was elected to a two-year term as national president at the 1990 conference and was reelected in 1992. One of her top priorities was to develop additional chapters for the society. By the end of her tenure as president, the society had doubled the number of affiliates, with new chapters in California for the Central Coast (Santa Maria), Central Valley (Livingston), Fresno, Los Angeles, Monterey, Stockton, and Vallejo; for the Midwest (Springfield, Illinois); and for New England (Boston).

Terri's second major priority was to hold a 1994 national conference in San Francisco. The conference, for which I served as program chair, was a huge success, with a record attendance of more than five hundred people. Holding the conference in the San Francisco Bay Area, with its large population of Filipinos, undoubtedly contributed to the number of participants. Another factor was the conference theme "Honoring the Bridge Generation." Within a hundred-mile radius of San Francisco, there were more members of the Bridge Generation than in any other part of the country. We also had another reason to celebrate. One of our own, Ben Cayetano, had been elected governor of Hawaii, the first Bridge Generation Filipino American to attain that lofty position.

The Saturday night banquet was the highlight of the conference emceed by Lloyd Lacuesta, Filipino American newscaster from Bay Area TV station KTTV. Fred Cordova delivered a rousing speech on the Bridge Generation's contribution to America. Equally emotional was the presentation of VIP (Very Important Pinoy/Pinay) commemorative plaques for lifetime achievement to Bridge Generation men and women. Among those earning VIP Gold Awards were Colonel Antonio "Dixon" Campos, World War II veteran of the Philippine liberation; Vicky Manalo Draves, the 1948 Olympic diving champion who won two gold medals; Jose De Vega, who costarred in the original Broadway production of *West Side Story*; Dolores Sibonga, the two-term Seattle City Councilwoman; Joe San Felipe, the first Filipino to pass the California State Bar; Barbara Posadas, professor at Northern Illinois University; Fred Basconcillo, former president of the Iron Workers Union in San Francisco; Deanna Balantac, professor at Sacramento State University, who made her contributions in the field of health sciences; and Domingo Los Banos, former superintendent of the Leeward School District in Hawaii. I was also honored with a VIP Gold Award for achieving a number of Filipino Firsts as a government executive.

The record attendance at the national conference of the Filipino American National Historical Society was not surprising, considering the prior experience of its conference leadership. Three years earlier, Terri and Dixon Campos cochaired the Grand Reunion of Filipino American Athletic Youth Clubs, which attracted a turn-away crowd of more than seven hundred people. Most of the participants were Bridge Generation Filipino Americans. I served as chair of the program committee. The event was an emotional get-together for the former members of youth clubs that flourished in northern California from the late 1940s through the 1960s. The camaraderie and ease we used to feel with one another in those long ago days seemed to be unchanged.

It was also a time for serious reflection. We remembered how the clubs developed at the end of World War II, in response to the exclusion of Filipino youth from mainstream activities and, in cities like Stockton and San Francisco, to segregation. Young Filipinos turned to one another mostly because they had to fend for themselves. It was natural for us was to form youth clubs focused on sports and social interaction. Sports were part of American mainstream culture, and social interaction gave us the opportunity to know one another as Filipinos. We organized and funded our own activities, and, in doing so, we learned the importance of self-sufficiency, support systems, a strong work ethic, and getting along with one another. This last quality had its roots in the Filipino value of *paki-kisama* (maintaining harmonious relationships). Everything we learned became essential to us in our adult lives.

The Bridge Generation has had a lasting impact on FANHS. Today, the membership of ten of the eleven California FANHS chapters is predominantly composed of Bridge Generation Filipino Americans. At the same time, the large number of aging Bridge Generation members poses a potential problem for the organization. The society will need to recruit younger Filipinos if it hopes to remain viable.

I played an even more visible role as banquet speaker at the next Grand Reunion of Filipino American Athletic Youth Clubs, held in Santa Maria, California. I had made countless presentations and speeches and had learned to be comfortable appearing before groups, but this was different. The audience of more than four hundred was made up of many people who had known me for most of my life. My speech had to be on the mark. Suddenly, I broke out in a cold sweat. Despite my apprehension, my remarks seemed to strike the right chord with the audience, and at the conclusion of the speech, I received a standing ovation.

I coined the term "Bridge Generation" for the 1994 FANHS conference to call attention to my generation's unrecognized contributions to America. It was certainly understandable for non-Filipinos to be unaware of the Bridge Generation; however, some Filipinos, particularly those who had come to America since immigration was liberalized in 1965, had no sense of our history in America. For example, a newly arrived Filipino young man said to me, "You are not Filipino because you talk like an American. You don't have an accent." He went on to tell me that I could not possibly be Filipino because Filipinos had not immigrated to the United States until after 1965. For a second example, an article appeared in the October 1994 issue of *Filipinas* magazine, with a readership that is largely Philippines-oriented, reporting that first-wave Filipino immigrants of the 1920s and 1930s did not produce families. Thus, according to the article, there were no new Filipinos in America until

1965, when immigration restrictions were relaxed. I wrote a letter to the editor of the magazine, stating that I could personally attest to the existence of thousands of Bridge Generation Filipino Americans in northern California alone. Moreover, my own family could proudly count five generations that have lived in America. When the magazine chose to respond only with lip service, I canceled my subscription.

While it was disconcerting to realize that recent Filipino immigrants were blind to the existence of the Bridge Generation, I wondered if they were similarly in the dark about the lessons our generation had painfully learned in America. For example, did they have a realistic view of the role that their color brown played in this country, particularly in the workplace, in school, and in housing? Or did they buy into the myth of the melting pot? What about the old boys' club? Or did they believe that succeeding on the job is wholly dependent on hard work and keeping one's nose clean? Did they truly appreciate their own Filipino culture and values here in America? Or did they adopt the values of our materialistic society so that they could be "American"? From whom will they seek advice when their color brown becomes an issue? I only hope that a Bridge Generation Filipino American will be nearby to help.

I continued to participate in politics, particularly as it involved the Filipino community. I supported longtime friend and colleague Rodel Rodis in his run for the Bay Area Rapid Transit board of directors, which he lost by a razor-thin margin, and his winning campaign in 1994 for board member of San Francisco Community College. I actively opposed California State Proposition 187, which would have denied basic public services, such as education, to families of immigrants who were thought to be undocumented. I worked on a Filipino fund-raiser for Kathleen Brown in her unsuccessful run for governor.

My most gratifying campaign experience was Mike Guingona's 1993 victory as a candidate for Daly City council member. I had worked closely with Mike, a Filipino American, in his two terms as AARS board president. When he asked me to join his campaign committee, I immediately accepted, believing the personable attorney had an excellent chance to win. No Filipino had ever been elected to the city council, although Filipinos composed 35 percent of the population. Through the years, other Filipinos had run, but all failed, largely because they limited their campaign efforts to their own ethnic group. Mike ran an energetic campaign that appealed to all groups, not just Filipinos. He was the right candidate at the right time.

I also made time for the wider community. I was a board member of the YMCA Embarcadero, the same YMCA where I spent my first night after joining the navy in 1948. In addition, I served several terms on the board of directors of the Bay Area United Way.

Despite my heavy travel schedule, AARS continued to flourish. The agency received several additional government grants, bringing its budget to an all-time high. My good fortune in being able to recruit quality staff undoubtedly was a big factor in the agency's success. Ben Tan, director of finance and administration, and Faye DeGuzman, the highly efficient executive assistant, were particularly helpful. Ben and Faye, both of Filipino ancestry, gave the agency's upper management a decidedly brown hue. At first, I was concerned that this might cause friction among the pan-Asian staff, but non-Filipino employees quickly assured me there should be no problem; I learned that earlier administrations had been top-heavy with Japanese or Chinese administrators without affecting morale. What was more important was to make sure that AARS maintained the appropriate focus on pan-Asian substance-abuse issues.

The board was also pleased with my vigorous advocacy for greater Asian representation in national conferences. For years, the federal government had been underwriting the costs of an annual conference, Counseling and Treating People of Colour, but had never invited Asians. After I brought the oversight to their attention, embarrassed conference organizers invited me to participate at the 1993 conference. I was able to gather a small but impressive delegation of Asians to attend the conference in Honolulu, and we were warmly received by the largely black and Latino delegates. It was a modest but positive beginning for Asians.

At the end of the conference, Terri and I toured the newly opened Plantation Village Museum at Waipahu, Oahu. The museum consisted of restored camps of Chinese, Filipino, Japanese, Korean, Portuguese, and Puerto Rican plantation workers who had harvested the pineapple and sugarcane fields that once dotted the island's rolling hills. The Filipino camp reminded me of the Jamero camp, with its simple cots, walls decorated with reminders of the Philippines, and pictures of movie stars like Betty Grable, Rita Hayworth, and Dorothy Lamour. Waipahu also provided me with another memory. Papa worked at this very site before coming to California. I remembered his vivid description of the mill that still dominates the landscape. I also remembered that Papa was reluctant to talk about the treatment of Filipino plantation workers. Seeing the more comfortable Portuguese quarters, I wondered whether the stories I often heard from the *manongs* about the cruelty of their Portuguese *lunas*, or field supervisors, were true.

Terri and I met the hardworking director of the Plantation Village Museum, Domingo Los Banos. As we talked, it dawned on us that we had met. Domingo was a World War II army buddy of Frank Padin, who founded the Filipino American Youth Club in Livingston. After the war, Domingo spent a summer with Frank, and we played softball together on the youth club team. What a small world! Terri took advantage of our meeting to recruit Domingo for FANHS, and he not only remained a member but later sat on the board of trustees.

The following year, I was asked to serve as one of three permanent conference sponsors in order to ensure that future conferences addressed the substance-abuse service needs of the Asian community. In the next few years, my involvement with the conferences would take me, and Terri, to such exotic venues as Barbados, Hawaii, and Puerto Rico.

San Juan, Puerto Rico, hosted the 1994 People of Colour conference. We went by way of New York City, so that we could again take in the attractions of the Big Apple, where Terri and I celebrated our forty-first wedding anniversary. We saw the lavish production of *Showboat*, in its second week on Broadway, and singer Mel Torme at Michael's Pub, the jazz hangout of Woody Allen. Called the "Velvet Fog" in his youth, Torme was still in fine voice as he entertained the audience, made up largely of senior citizens. After his performance, I had the opportunity to meet him and was surprised that he was so short—only a hair taller than I was.

Jackie, a recognized professional in the substance-abuse field, was a delegate to the conference and joined us in San Juan. Puerto Rico has been a commonwealth of the United States since the Spanish-American War of 1898, the same war that led to the American colonization of the Philippines. It is a bilingual country, so we had no language concerns as we toured the many attractions of Old San Juan, including Moro Fort, which once protected the city from marauding pirates.

The 1995 People of Colour conference was held on the Caribbean island of Barbados. Again, Jackie was a delegate, and this time, her husband Dickie accompanied her. The four of us traveled to the conference via New York City. Jackie and Dickie were first-time visitors, so Terri and I showed off our familiarity with the Big Apple and took them to all our favorite places—Greenwich Village, the twin towers of the World Trade Center, the Empire State Building, and Rockefeller Center. Our most memorable experience was being in Macy's department store on the day after Thanksgiving. The sheer size of the elbow-to-elbow crowds, eager to find bargains in the most famous store in America on the busiest shopping day of the year, was unbelievable. It was a wonder we did not become separated from one another.

Barbados, toward the end of a long string of islands that make up the Lesser Antilles, is located just off the coast of South America. The conference site was Sam Lord's Castle, the home of a nineteenth-century English pirate, which had been transformed into a comfortable resort. As on most Caribbean islands, descendants of former African slaves form the largest segment of the population of Barbados. The original inhabitants, Caribe Indians, are extinct, wiped out years ago by European diseases. Despite their large numbers and free status, however, blacks appeared to be at the bottom of the three-tier employment hierarchy in Barbados, below whites and East Indians.

In addition to my work schedule, our family continued to keep me busy. Karen and Ron welcomed Zachary Matthew Armada into our lives on May 4, 1991, our seventh grandchild. The Jamero family held its first ever reunion on the last weekend of June 1991 at South Lake Tahoe, California. The whole clan came, including our Seattle contingent. Everyone got a powder blue T-shirt imprinted with the head of a *tamaraw*, a fierce buffalo native to the Philippines, proudly emblazoned with the words "Jamero Family Reunion, 1916–1991." Each family brought a display board replete with photographs and descriptive captions of all family members. During the evening program, the head of each family narrated the displays. As I was in the midst of narrating Papa's and Mama's display board and sharing some of my fondest memories, my voice broke with emotion. Wiping my suddenly moist eyes, I looked up to find other family members similarly dabbing at their own tears.

Julie's wedding to Ted Hada on August 29, 1992, was literally the wedding to end all Jamero weddings —she was the last of our children to marry. The ceremony took place at Holy Angels Catholic Church in Colma, California. A large number of relatives and friends were in attendance, the wedding party included all members of the bride's immediate family and their children, and the ceremony had a Filipino segment. Both Terri and I walked Julie down the aisle, a nice departure from tradition. Ted, of Japanese ancestry, is the only non-Filipino to marry into our family. Out of respect for his culture, Julie wore a traditional Japanese kimono when greeting guests at the reception, where guests enjoyed several family musical numbers, a tradition at Jamero weddings. The grand finale was a rendition of "One," from the Broadway hit *A Chorus Line*, complete with top hats, lip-synching, and our own choreography..

Our eighth grandchild, Michael Anthonie Silverio Jr., was born on December 11, 1992, to Jeanine and Michael. And Julie and Ted, in their early thirties, wasted no time in starting their family. Erika Teresa Hada was born on June 18, 1993, our ninth grandchild. Father Peter Sammon, our former parish priest in San Francisco, baptized both babies into the Roman Catholic faith in July 1993. In 1994, we were blessed with two more grandsons—Alexander Jamero Hada, born on June 3, and Matthew Jamero Silverio, born on July 26. The following year, Lindsey Christine Hada joined the family on September 7.

On my sixty-fifth birthday, in August, I had not yet decided when I would be retiring. I believed I would know when the time came, and by October, I knew it was fast approaching. While AARS continued to prosper under my leadership, the world of work was not as enjoyable. A number of laws written to protect the individual rights of employees had been enacted in recent years. Unfortunately, some provisions placed undue burdens on employers. As executive director, I was increasingly involved with frivolous employee grievances and lawsuits, which gave me less time to devote to client services. Moreover, I could no longer be as spontaneous in my relationships with staff in light of having to maintain a politically correct atmosphere in the workplace. Perhaps most important, I was beginning to realize that all my coworkers were at least twenty years younger than I was. My contemporaries had long since retired.

It was a perfect time for me to retire. The agency was functioning well. It had increased its budget by 64 percent, adopted a new mission statement and strategic plan, expanded into San Mateo and Santa Clara Counties, implemented an innovative research program, and attained local, state, national, and international visibility. Most important, I had brought organizational stability to AARS. Terri agreed that the time was right. We decided to retire in Livingston, where we would be close to relatives and which had an affordable cost of living. On November 15, 1995, I submitted a formal letter of retirement to the board of directors, effective December 31, 1995.

AARS honored me for my contributions at its annual dinner at the Grand Hyatt Hotel with testimonials and a commemorative plaque. A number of people from my distant past were among the out-of-town guests: Filipino American activist Royal Morales, whom I first met while I was a UCLA graduate student; San Jose State University professor Simon Dominguez, a member of my 1961 staff in Sacramento County; Jim Miyano of Los Angeles, a key player in the West Coast Asian movement of the 1970s; and Bob Santos, my Young Turk pal from Seattle.

The last retirement celebration was a beautifully staged affair at the International House at the University of California, Berkeley. Terri and our children made all the arrangements for two hundred guests. It was a typical Jamero family celebration, with skits and musical numbers. Hilarious stories were told by an entertaining group of roasters-toasters that included Bob Santos, who again flew down from Seattle; Ray Paular, my roommate from college days; my sister Luna; and my daughter Cheryl. Former boss Randy Revelle and former San Francisco mayor Art Agnos, former Washington governor Mike Lowry, and President Bill Clinton sent congratulatory letters.

I could not have asked for a better send-off, surrounded by family and close friends. I looked forward to the next chapter of my life—retirement.

# Epilogue

SINCE MY RETIREMENT AT THE END OF 1995, TERRI and I have been blessed with several wonderful additions to our family. Our fourteenth grandchild, Ceferino Jamero Silverio, was born on March 3, 2002; Lauren married Patrick Hoolboom on October 23, 2002; Caryn Swan was welcomed into the clan following her marriage to our son Peter on August 10, 2003; and Roslin Jamero Berganio, our fifteenth grandchild, came into our lives on April 20, 2004, when she was adopted by Jackie and Richard.

Terri and I are comfortably settled in Atwater, six miles from my hometown of Livingston. I have kept physically and mentally active—listening to my collection of straight-ahead jazz, following the New York Yankees, gardening in the yard, serving as chairman of my fiftieth high-school reunion, participating in the Filipino American National Historical Society, being the patriarch of the one-hundred-strong Jamero clan, and, of course, working on my memoirs. Most important, I am enjoying the company of our children and grandchildren, who gave us a beautiful fiftieth golden wedding anniversary party in October 2003, when our extended families and closest friends gathered to help us celebrate the occasion.

If writing my memoirs has pointed out anything to me, it is that I am indeed thankful for what I have experienced in life. In the words of my boyhood hero of the New York Yankees, Lou Gehrig, "I consider myself to be the luckiest man on the face of the earth." My story could happen only in America: the eldest son of immigrant parents learns about life growing up in a farm-labor camp, goes on to experience the world, and achieves success in his work and personal life.

Terri and I must have done something right with our children. They all went to college, have done well in the workplace, are secure in their Filipino identity, and are married and raising their own children with the same values we instilled in them. In short, our children have made us very proud. They have always been our first priority, whether it was deciding where we lived, the job I sought, or the house we bought.

My primary purpose in writing these memoirs was to provide my children and grandchildren with a resource from which they could gain a more complete understanding of my experiences growing up brown in America. To that end, I hope I have succeeded.

It was also my hope that my story could begin to address the lack of documentation on the experiences of Bridge Generation Filipino Americans, ignored by historians and often unknown to recent arrivals from the Philippines. I hope I have also succeeded in that.

I knew the process of developing my memoirs would likely be long and often tedious. It was. What I did not anticipate was that writing my life story would also be uplifting, even cathartic. For this reason, I am glad I decided to tell the story. In this undertaking, I received help from many other people. I am particularly grateful to my daughter Jackie, for the editing and valuable advice; to my daughter Julie, for her technical help; and to Ron Chew, for his unwavering belief in my manuscript. My thanks also go to Fred and Dorothy Cordova, for their inspiration, and to Peter Bacho, for sharing his experiences as a writer of Filipino literature with me.

Finally, I would like to express my deep appreciation for emotional and technical support from the love of my life, Terri, without whose help these memoirs would not have been possible. To the person who has been my partner in life for fifty years, I am eternally grateful.

PETER JAMERO
*January 2004*

# *Afterword*

THEY SAY YOU CAN TAKE THE BOY OUT OF THE country, but you can't take the country out of the boy. It must be so with one Peter Madelo Jamero, who was born and raised in a rural California town called Livingston. But the navy snatched Pete from the byways of Highway 99 and made a man out of him before academia took over to mold him, degreed and certificated as a social worker, via San Jose State, UCLA, and Stanford.

Transformed into a top-level government executive—by way of federal, state, and county bureaucracies—the country boy, now referred to as "Mr. Jamero," did his darnedest to help change a turbulent world for the better. His career progressed at a dizzying pace, as he traveled to metropolises like Sacramento, Washington, D.C., Seattle, and San Francisco, where he directed a variety of health and human services programs and became a university faculty member.

Not bad for a country boy from Livingston. A Filipino boy at that! A brown boy whose growing-up values centered around family, agricultural farm life, friends, and a tightly knit Filipino American community. Has he changed throughout his career? Not to many people's knowledge. Of course, Terri, his loving wife, makes him stay on the straight and narrow.

In his own words, Pete has said, "I have never forgotten my roots."

He is still called "Pete," the name everyone has used since his boyhood. He is still entrenched in the same values, believing in family, farm life, friends, and community, particularly his Filipino American community across the nation, which has developed into an emerging force within American society.

Pete's story has a literary tilt because the country is still in the boy, who is now a man of achievement. His fine reputation not only centers around the countryside in central California but is known throughout the whole U.S.A.

In his "retirement," Pete has returned to the Livingston environs in the byways of Highway 99. Nope, you can't take the country out of the boy.

DR. FRED CORDOVA
*Filipino American National Historical Society*
*January 2005*

# Index

Library of Congress Cataloging-in-Publication Data

Jamero, Peter M.
Growing up Brown in America : memoirs of a Filipino American / Peter Jamero.
p.   cm. — (Scott and Laurie Oki series in Asian American studies)
Includes index.
ISBN 0-295-98642-5 (pbk. : alk. paper)
1. Jamero, Peter—Childhood and youth.   2. Jamero, Peter—Family.   3. Filipino
Americans—California—Livingston—Biography.   4. Livingston (Calif.)—Biography.
5. Livingston (Calif.)—Social life and customs—20th century.   6. Filipino Americans—
Ethnic identity.   7. Jamero family.   I. Title.   II. Series.
F869.L65J36   2006
305.89'921079458—dc22          2006013057
[B]